Contents

Introduction

Joy, incredulity, fear, panic, delight, relief, euphoria, apprehension, dread. There are possibly only two times in a woman's life when she might feel so many emotions in the space of a few seconds – one is watching a thin blue line appear on a plastic stick; the other when the midwife lies that tiny, bloody newborn baby on her chest.

Pregnancy and childbirth are without doubt the biggest emotional roller-coaster rides of a lifetime, particularly for the first timer. For those women facing it alone there are a few extra triple loops to contend with.

While in 'real life' you might run a successful business single-handedly, and think nothing of taking a holiday by yourself, going through pregnancy alone can leave you feeling pretty much out in the cold in this warm, fuzzy world of ecstatic parents-to-be. In fact it can often seem as if you've slipped into some kind of weird parallel universe populated entirely by couples called 'mummy and daddy' (for example, 'Mummy, you must make sure Daddy feels part of the whole birthing experience'). Doctors, midwives, healthcare workers and even complete strangers often don't help, with most automatically assuming that there is a husband or at least a partner on the scene.

Pregnancy magazines and books are full of photos of couples gazing lovingly into each other's eyes at antenatal classes, and information on 'keeping your sex life alive during pregnancy'. Unfortunately, life isn't always that neat or predictable.

Whether it was an unplanned pregnancy or a conscious choice, you've probably still spent the last few weeks agonising over whether you've made the right decision – choosing to have a baby on your own. I spent my own pregnancy feeling like a combination of mother earth/superwoman, and the most stupidly irresponsible person on the planet. My mind kept telling me I was 'too young', 'not ready yet' (at 32!) and that there was 'so much more I had to do in life'. How would I cope financially and physically? I worried about having twins (a strong possibility in my family). Sometimes I felt like a pioneer and at other times a social pariah.

I read articles on single mothers and how they 'drained government coffers', feeling shame that I was to be one of them and anger at one-eyed, biased reporting. I raged at my baby's father for not wanting to be involved and secretly dreaded one day he'd turn up and try to claim his child. I sometimes felt lonely, and, rather like travelling alone, was sad at being unable to share my experiences with a partner. I felt guilty that my child would grow up without a father. I dreaded running into people I knew, with my big belly and at the same time was dying with pride, wanting to show it off to the world.

I would feel sick to my stomach with fear at the thought of actual childbirth. I remembered with trepidation my 32nd birthday binge, when unknowingly pregnant, I knocked back endless tequila slammers and puffed away on my yearly pack of cigarettes. I thought about the painkillers I'd taken when I'd put my back out and worried I'd give birth to a child with ADD (Attention Deficit Disorder) who'd grow up and steal cars. I despaired of how I'd manage, being self-employed with an erratic cash flow. I cried at advertisements on TV, on public transport when no one gave up their seat for me, and when I saw a couple with a baby. I grieved at the loss of a lifestyle I loved and the possibility of ever meeting Mr Right. (Who'd want to go out with a woman with a young baby?)

I also marvelled as I felt my baby having his own private footy game in my womb. I was amazed seeing him on screen for the first time and couldn't wait to meet him. I sang to him and had conversations in my head. I basked in the warmth of strangers' indulgent smiles. For the first time in my life, I really loved my own body and what it was capable of. I felt wonderful when friends told me how much they admired me, how strong they thought I was, how they wished they had the courage to do the same thing. I felt high, womanly, powerful and very strong. Some days I felt all of the above in a couple of hours!

The point is that being pregnant and giving birth can often bring with it problems as well as joy. Being a single mother just brings with it a different set of problems. They are, however, manageable ones and with the help and support of family and friends, your pregnancy and the birth of your child will be the most wonderful experience of your life.

Natascha Mirosch

The Thin Blue Line

CHAPTER ONE

WEEKS 4–7

Positively Pregnant

Some women say they 'just know', intuitively recognising they are pregnant straight away. Others can get as far advanced as 5 months without clicking. The majority of women suspect something is up when their period is a week or so late. They do their sums, and in one horrible heart-stopping moment things start to fall into place and they rush off, panicking and sweaty-palmed to the chemist for a pregnancy test.

While peeing on a plastic stick may seem undignified, the trade-off is that modern pregnancy tests give almost instant results and are practically idiot-proof. They work by detecting the levels of the pregnancy hormone hCG (human Chorionic Gonadotropic) present in the urine and are up to 99.9% accurate, even when a period is only a few days late.

Within a month of conception, many of us have had a few not so gentle hints from our bodies anyway. Apart from the obvious lack of a period, as your hormones kick in you might experience tender breasts, morning sickness, a need to go to the toilet more often, and you may feel particularly tired.

If you've returned a positive pregnancy test but feel you want it confirmed and validated by a professional, visit your doctor who will repeat the urine test, or perhaps do a blood test or internal examination.

Circumstances such as the ending of a relationship, a birth control failure, or even the death of a partner can leave some women to face one of the most important and emotional times of their lives on their own.

I met my daughter's father through work. We'd always gotten along extremely well and I had always found him attractive but had never acted on it. But this time, my biological imperative was being, well, rather imperative, and I found myself doing something I never thought I would. So why was I no longer content to wait for Mr Right? Well, the truth is that as I've gotten older, I've also gotten fussier and fussier. I have standards, and being a thinking, independent woman of the world, I recognise the fact that I would be far happier on my own than being with a man who isn't right for me. I think also, that given my feminist leanings, I have found very few men over the years who would make good 'partners' in every sense of the word. And in fact, the ones I have found were already snapped up by very discerning women! But, although I'm confident and self-sufficient enough to know how to be happy on my own, there is no doubt that it can be a very lonely existence. I used to wake up and squirm at the thought of being 40, 50, etc, and being all on my own with no significant other. So, there I was at the grand old age of 31, with no man in sight, and, indeed, the hope of one fading fast, and a daring thought occurred to me.

When I was young, I used to joke with my friends that if I reached 30 and still wasn't married, I would 'go out and find a suitable sire and have myself serviced'! And well, this was the thought – why not go out and do it? I was desperate for somebody to lavish love on, and I know that sounds somehow weak and pathological, but it's basic human nature.

The man I chose for this endeavour was perfect for the task – good looking, tall and well built, and with a complete disinterest in fathering a child with me! It was extremely important to me that he not want children – it seemed to me that I was unlikely to be able to find the perfect 'detachable' father who would not only be happy to father a child for me, but be exactly the kind of separate entity that I was hoping for. I certainly didn't want to choose the wrong man and end up hurting him very badly. Having a child to a caring man, and then denying him access is unnecessarily cruel. So this man fitted all the requirements to be a successful sperm donor. Of course, he wasn't terribly bright, but they say now that intelligence is not just a matter of genes but of 'environment' as well. So, I 'seduced' him, and our affair began. Strangely enough, he never even questioned contraception, but seemed happy to assume that I was 'taking care of it'. I did, in fact, borrow a box of the 'Pill' from a friend to leave conspicuously on my chest of drawers – just in case! Did I have any doubts about what I was doing? You bet – all the time! In fact, until I actually fell pregnant, I'm not sure that I was really committed to going through with it. It just seemed to me like I was playing with the concept, and I guess, because waiting to fall pregnant is so passive (in a way!), that I didn't feel like I was consciously pursuing my objective. I had taken a very active role in paving the way for the 'event', but after that it was in the lap of the gods. But I remember thinking all the time about whether I had a right to do what I was doing. It would involve so many lies and deceit, and I knew that most people would never understand why I had done it. But the big things which bothered me were things like: How will you cope financially? Is it fair to bring a child into the world without a father? Do you have a right to have a child when so many people doing it the 'right' way can't? And most damningly, 'What will people think?' The more I thought about it though, the more I felt that most of the things I questioned were societal constructs anyway. The only truth in this world relates to our most basic nature – it's the most loving and natural thing in the world for a woman to want to have a child. Our 'affair', such as it was, lasted for around 5–6 months, or when I found out I was pregnant. After making it clear that he would be more than happy for me to have an abortion, the conversation ended, and I have never heard from him since. Lucy

My pregnancy was unplanned and unexpected but never unwanted. I was on the Pill at the time, as I had been for the 5 years previous to that. In late November 1996 my period was late. I did a home pregnancy test and found out I was pregnant. I was very stunned as I had been told by doctors that it would be difficult for me to conceive due to the endometriosis I had between the ages of 15 and 18. I knew straight away that I wanted to keep the baby. I had the test confirmed by my doctor who tried to convince me to have the pregnancy terminated because of my situation. I knew I would not be doing that. My baby's father and I had only been together for a short time although we had been good friends for over 6 years. He made it quite clear that he was not interested in being a father and that he was leaving the area as he had previously planned. Nadene

The issue of motherhood was something I never questioned, but always assumed would be a reality, with probably two children. As part of this scenario, I also assumed that I would have a caring and supportive partner.

When neither partner nor children had eventuated by my late 30s, I realised that unless I took pro-active steps, my opportunity to be a mother would be gone. By this stage, my desire to have a child had become all consuming and intense, as did my bitterness at my single state and limited opportunities. I felt betrayed and like a social reject. If I hadn't been successful in my attempt to have a child, I am not sure how I would have dealt with the resultant depression.

After researching my options as a single woman, I discovered that I was eligible for IVF treatment using donor sperm. I considered this option carefully, but preferring not to have an unknown father for my child, I approached an old friend and lover and asked if he would father a child for me. As we lived on opposite sides of the country, conventional methods of conception were a little difficult, although we did try initially. Finally, he came to visit and left a sperm donation at a local clinic, which was frozen for my later use.

I never made an issue of being a single woman at the clinic. Because I fronted up with my own sperm, the assumption was there that I was part of a 'couple'. Not wanting to raise any unwanted ripples in the process, I glossed over my private life, and no one really asked the intimate details. I simply said that my partner was working away, and was not readily available. No further questions were asked. I tried two treatments without success. The third treatment was successful, and the result is now my son, Oliver James Rupert. Dorothy

I remember being 5 years old and sitting at the breakfast table feeding my doll, Penelope, Weetabix™ wishing so badly that she were a real baby, a baby to play games with and who could have tea parties with me. How simple life seems through the eyes of a 5-year-old.

As I grew, the realities of having children became clearer. The mother with four fighting children standing in the queue at the supermarket with that glazed look as though dreaming of a faraway place. The 3-year-old fighting with his mother after being told for the umpteenth time that he doesn't need washing powder, as pretty as the box may seem and the screaming newborn wanting to be fed now! I also remember thinking, 'my children will never be like that'. So I went on admiring the mothers of the world. Always loving babies and children, but also happy it wasn't me who had to deal with the screaming, the tantrums, the poo and, God forbid, giving up my Friday and Saturday nights.

I moved from London to a lovely, remote part of the country, a place where I could spend all day relaxing, walking and just taking it easy. That's when I met my ex-boyfriend. He was the most laid back person I'd ever met. I think that's what attracted me to him, although at first I never would have thought.

We were just hanging out as friends, partying and having fun together. Nothing serious. Then I was telling him how I wanted to spend some time travelling, but that I first had to go to London to earn some money. He told me that was what he wanted to do and that he would like to do it with me. Maybe, I thought, things were more serious than I had originally thought.

Anyway, 3 months later we came to London. It was a big shock, even to me, to be back. Back to the hustle and bustle. No more early-morning strolls to refresh you and ready you for the day, just a hot shower and a strong coffee. I can't even imagine how scary it must have been for my boyfriend, to leave all his friends, his family, and the peaceful surroundings of the country.

We both found jobs pretty quickly. I worked days and he worked nights. I loved the days that we got to spend together. I was falling in love, he was so gorgeous. I thought he felt the same, but love does make you blind. I was blind to his unhappiness, his loneliness.

I never knew how bad it was, until he left. In true male style he just packed up and left. That morning we had kissed each other goodbye and he wished me a good day. I remember thinking how beautiful he looked. I left for work so happy. After work I went to see some friends but made sure I was home in time to welcome him home. Something seemed off, but I was too preoccupied to notice what it was. He kept his stuff in a different room. I had dressed and poured the wine and put the radio on when my mum came down and said, 'He's gone, there's a message on the machine to say he's gone, thanks anyway'. A knife stabbed me right through my heart. I didn't know what to do so I ran. I ran and ran and ran in the freezing cold, wearing next to nothing. I didn't care, I was numb already for I felt as though I had died. I wanted to. It still brings tears and pain to my heart to think of that night. How could he do it? Not even a word. Nothing. Anything would have been better than nothing. I felt terrible.

The next couple of weeks I felt as though I had a ball and chain around my ankles. I was forgetful at work and clumsy. I felt sick to the core. I went out to clubs with friends to try and bury my pain beneath loud music. It only made it worse. I felt like shit and looked even worse. Then, I threw up... Ngaire

● ● ● ● My relationship with John was fairly casual; although we'd been seeing each other for nearly a year, it was quite uncommitted and sort of 'yeah, ok then, I'll call you soon'. Truthfully I guess it was more about companionship and sex than any great love. It had almost run its course and I think we were both about ready to move on when IT happened. How IT happened I'll never know, as I was on a contraceptive injection at the time. Anyway I told John and he went mad! He became someone I had never seen, raving about my motives, questioning his paternity and even whether I was pregnant. He walked out slamming the door and screaming at me to have an abortion. I heard nothing from him for 2 weeks; he wouldn't return my calls or emails. Then one night, he turned up at about 3.00 a.m. He'd been drinking and when he walked in he just looked at me sadly and we both just fell into each other's arms. We both cried and he apologised for his behaviour and told me how very scared he was, how he didn't feel ready to be a dad, and that he wasn't in love with me. I reassured him that I didn't love him either, well not in THAT way, and I would not consider an abortion, but between us, we would work this out. From that moment, once he realised that I was not expecting him to marry me or anything, John changed. He became totally supportive of my pregnancy and what was happening to my body. Our relationship improved too; we moved it to a platonic level and it seemed to make us both relax and we started to really like and appreciate each other as we never had as lovers. Luckily, being self-employed, his time was flexible and he came to all my antenatal classes and midwife's appointments. It was a really steep learning curve for him and considering he had never been around pregnant women before, he was very tolerant of my moods and whims and the occasional bout of anger at him. That's not to say it was all roses; he still annoyed me as much as he had when we were lovers, with all his irritating habits, but I guess knowing he was my baby's father and we now had a life-long connection made me tolerate him more. John came to the birth, and from Josh's arrival fell totally in love with him. We are doing well, both as co-parents and good friends and while our situation is unusual, for me it's about as close to perfect as it gets. Francesca

Going It Alone

Emotions during pregnancy are unstable and fickle due to the high levels of oestrogen and progesterone pumping through your body. While some negative feelings may be hormonally magnified, others are real and you may need to talk to someone about them. Friends can lend a sympathetic ear, but it's great to talk to women in the same situation when you're feeling a bit wobbly – there's strength and comfort in numbers. A good place to start is to check out your antenatal clinic's noticeboard. Often you'll find information about groups and informal coffee mornings for mums-to-be and sometimes even contact details for some kind of single mother's support group who may be able to give you help and advice. Midwives are also an invaluable source of information, usually knowing what's available in the local community.

If it is difficult for you to get out and meet other women but you're connected to the Internet, there are some useful information and chat sites where you can 'talk' to other like-minded women (see Useful Contacts on page 209). However, if your worries and uncertainties about being pregnant are really becoming overwhelming, it may be a good idea to get some professional counselling. To be able to express your fears and doubts to someone who can give unbiased support and advice is worthwhile. Your doctor may be able to refer you to a counsellor, or check under Useful Contacts on page 208–209 for more contacts.

● ● ● ● I had felt like death and looked even worse for 2 weeks. Then, I threw up. Hmmm? Could it have been that funky drink? Two days of no sleep? How long since I last ate? That's why my period's late isn't it? Then I threw up again. Hmmm...maybe a trip to the chemist would be a good idea. Positive. Maybe another trip to the chemist? Two lines...shit. I didn't know whether to laugh, cry or scream, so I did all three. I was going to have a baby. I was so happy, but also scared. Ngaire

● ● ● ● Shock! But also underlying joy and calm at this massive 'surprise'. I had finally reached a point in my life where I was old enough, mature enough, and strong enough to cope with motherhood and parenthood alone if it so be. There was no question of termination, only determination. Finding out I was pregnant:

1. Solved the mystery of why I had been feeling 'odd'.
2. Gave definite and positive direction and focus in my life instantly.
3. Opened up a well of emotions with regard to 'the father'. Jane

● ● ● ● Absolute panic! To tell you the truth, my first thought was that I would have to have an abortion. Jonathan and I had only been out a couple of times and he was a bit of a wild boy, partying every night and going to all the latest openings and 'in' clubs. I knew he'd never give up that lifestyle and would be mad as hell and expect me to have an abortion pronto! So I had a bit of a cry and went to bed vowing to make an appointment the next day. I don't know what happened that night, but I woke up, feeling totally different and knew I could never go through with it. Angie

● ● ● ● Surprise, fear and delight in that order. I have polycystic ovaries and was told since I was a teenager I probably couldn't have kids. Anna

● ● ● ● Sick...literally. When the little blue line appeared in the square, I felt faint, then I had to rush off to the toilet and throw up. Julie

● ● ● ● My mind started going at a million miles an hour. How was I going to tell the father? How would I tell my family? God, what would my grandmother say for Christ's sake! What if there was something wrong with the baby? How would I cope with the pain of childbirth when I faint even when I have to get a needle! Michelle

● ● ● ● I remember going to the doctor's so sick that I was convinced I was dying, and yet still somehow it hadn't occurred to me that I was pregnant, possibly because I was so sick

I hadn't noticed that I was 2 weeks late! The doctor informed me that I was pregnant, and I was completely unprepared for this incredible joy I felt. I just felt so damn happy about the whole thing that I just knew it was meant to be! Kathryn

●●●● I became completely depressed knowing that I didn't have a very high paying job and the demands of raising a child are so hard. I knew that going through pregnancy without a partner was going to be really difficult, especially that, despite it taking two to develop a life, some men feel free to walk out and not accept responsibility. We are just as scared as they are. Brenda

●●●● Uncontrollable laughter followed by tears of joy. When my husband and I were together, we tried for 4 years to get pregnant. Then we split up and in desperation I asked a wonderful male friend if he'd help me. The first (and only) time we had sex I got pregnant. I found out on my 38th birthday. Rebecca

A Hormonal Hurricane

On film and in the charmed lives of supermodels, the pregnant woman floats around in little Collette Dinnigan dresses, glowing and gorgeous. Down here on planet Earth, we mere mortals are more likely to be suffering at least a little during this hormonal hurricane that is the first month of pregnancy. In all likelihood, you may be experiencing some or all of the following:

Morning Sickness

Despite its name, morning sickness can last the entire day and affects approximately half of all pregnant women, from conception to birth. Usually it occurs during the first trimester and is just a vague, awful memory by week 12 to 14. No one is really sure what causes it and why some women have it more severely than others; however, women carrying multiple fetuses tend to have it more often, suggesting that it may be due to the levels of hCG, the pregnancy hormone, in the blood.

Morning sickness feels like a combination of a killer hangover (minus the headache) and seasickness, and ranges from mild nausea to being unable to keep any food down. (Make sure if you are experiencing constant vomiting you keep your fluids up.)

The worst part is that there is little in the way of prescription drugs to gain relief, which is why resourceful women worldwide have worked out their own systems to deal with it. Some suggestions include:

- Homeopathic remedies. These can be safely taken throughout pregnancy, but visit a qualified homeopath to make sure you're getting the most effective treatment.
- A dry piece of toast before getting out of bed. Pretty useless unless you have someone to bring you breakfast in bed! Keeping a few rice cakes on your bedside table will do the trick just as well.
- Ginger. Put a few drops of ginger essential oil on a hanky and inhale when you feel queasy, or chew on a piece if you like the taste. Drinking dry ginger ale is also good for settling the stomach. (Read the ingredients to make sure it really has some ginger in it and is not just a caramel-coloured artificial ginger flavoured drink!)
- Supplements of vitamin B, zinc and magnesium.
- Avoid eating fried food.
- Eat a protein snack just before going to bed to help lower blood sugar levels in the morning.
- Drink anise, peppermint or raspberry tea.
- Drink a teaspoon of cider vinegar in a cup of warm water.
- Increase iron rich foods in your diet.
- Aromatherapy oils. Try a massage with lavender, rose or geranium or a combination in an aromatherapy burner. (See Other Cautions on page 21 for which oils should be avoided.)
- Eat little and often.
- Sea bands. These acupressure bands worn on the wrists are usually used for seasickness, but can also be useful in quelling nausea.
- Acupuncture. Some women swear by acupuncture for a whole range of pregnancy-related symptoms, including alleviating morning sickness.

Painful Breasts

Almost immediately after conception, you'll notice changes in your breasts. Seemingly, they may appear to get bigger overnight and more tender (although at this early stage you're unlikely to wake up looking like Pamela Anderson). Usually a woman can expect to go up one size during her pregnancy. The areola (the nipple area) will become darker and larger. Your breasts may feel tingly, full, heavy, hot and painfully sensitive, and as pregnancy progresses, you may also start to see the blue veins carrying the extra blood supply around. As for morning sickness, breast tenderness usually settles down after the first three months but a way of both protecting your breasts against sagging and reducing the discomfort is to invest in a good quality bra (bye for now Wonderbra!) While it's probably not worth getting a heavy-duty maternity bra yet (that is a pleasure yet to come!) you do need a good supportive comfortable bra now.

The best bras are ones that are 100% cotton with wide straps and no underwires. They should have a number of fasteners at the back to expand as you do. Alternatively, try a good sports bra. Many pregnant women wear their bras at night to help against sagging, as well as making it less painful to sleep on your side.

Fatigue

I couldn't believe how quickly exhaustion hit me, particularly in the first month. I'd fight my way home from work on public transport on a dark cold winter evening, just about manage to eat a salad and a tub of yoghurt, or anything else I didn't have to cook and fall into bed at 7.00 p.m., at times not even being able to make it out of my work clothes. Mornings were okay, but by 3.00 p.m., exhaustion would knock me sideways again. Letita

There's not a lot you can do about fatigue; the only consolation is that it usually doesn't last past the first few months.

Coping with Fatigue

- Eat healthily.
- Cut down on social activities and long hours at work if possible.
- Take long warm baths with some stimulating essential oils such as geranium and lemon.
- Have naps in the afternoon if possible.
- Try to get a little gentle exercise and some fresh air. If you're working, instead of spending your lunch hour at your desk or rushing around shopping or doing errands, find a quiet place to relax, perhaps in a local park, eat your lunch and put your feet up.

Phew! Smell Sensitivity

During pregnancy your sense of smell might be heightened and certain odours may make you feel queasy. Unfortunately, there's not a lot you can do about it, apart from avoiding those things that make you feel sick. Smell sensitivity usually doesn't last too long into pregnancy.

Pregnancy and your Health

The best bit about being pregnant? This is the once in a lifetime opportunity for a no holds barred, indulge yourself-fest. Me, Me, Me. That's all you should think about for the next 40 weeks, so be extra kind to yourself and allow others to spoil you. If you're in the best possible health, both mentally and physically, your baby will benefit too. Take long warm candlelit baths, curl up with a good book, eat well, sleep as often as possible and surround yourself with calm. Try to relax and enjoy the changes your body is going through.

The first trimester of your pregnancy is the most important time for the formation of the baby and there are some basic rules you need to follow to ensure optimum health for you and your baby. You should avoid the following:

Alcohol

Drinking more than two units of alcohol a day whilst pregnant is not encouraged by the medical profession, as alcohol crosses into the fetal bloodstream. A glass of wine with dinner or the occasional social drink probably won't hurt, but binge drinking can cause Fetal Alcohol Syndrome (FAS), which can result in birth defects such as deformities of the head, limbs, heart and central nervous system. It also increases the likelihood of miscarriage, having an undersized baby, and delivery complications. Babies born with FAS can also develop learning, behavioural and social difficulties in later life. About ⅕ of babies with FAS will die within the first few weeks. The good news is that many pregnant women can't even face the thought of having a drink without gagging. It's Nature's way of protecting the unborn child.

Caffeine

It's known that caffeine crosses the placenta and enters the bloodstream but little is known about its effects on the developing baby, although it has been linked to miscarriage. Caffeine acts as a diuretic which, apart from adding to the endless times you have to go to the toilet, can interfere with the absorption of iron. You don't have to give up your morning coffee, but try to limit it and be aware of drinks such as cola, and some energy drinks, which also contain caffeine.

Over-the-counter and Prescription Medication

Aspirin and codeine can prolong pregnancy and labour, while codeine may also cause constipation. Paracetamol is the recommended form of pain relief, as it's safe for pregnant women. With all prescribed medications, check with your doctor that it is okay to take them.

Vaccinations

Ideally you should avoid vaccinations during pregnancy. Live vaccinations are particularly risky, as the antibodies in the virus can harm the embryo. If you are travelling, you may need to revise your plans as some vaccines, such a yellow fever, carry a high risk of complications for pregnant women. Discuss all potential vaccinations with your doctor.

Tobacco and Marijuana

While drug use before conception is not known to have any long-term effects, using any form of drugs during pregnancy, including nicotine, can have a detrimental effect on your baby's development. Almost ⅓ of undersized babies in the United Kingdom are believed to be a result of cigarette smoking.

Babies whose mothers smoke are also more likely to suffer apnoea (pauses in breathing while sleeping) and are twice as likely to die from SIDS (Sudden Infant Death Syndrome). As nutrition and oxygen passes through placental blood vessels, narrowing these through smoking may restrict the baby's growth and development, as well as increasing the risk of miscarriage or premature labour. Dangers are posed by passive smoking too, so if you live or work with a smoker, beg or bribe them to give up.

While there is no conclusive evidence that smoking marijuana can cause deformities, it has been suggested that it may interfere with the production of the placenta, cause rapid labour, and result in a low birth-weight baby. Mothers who smoke marijuana during their pregnancy are more likely to have an inadequate weight gain.

Illicit Drugs

Many illicit drugs have been linked to causing birth defects in babies. Amphetamines have been associated with early labour and miscarriage, as well as the possible cause of increasing the heart rate of mother and baby. The baby consequently receives less oxygen, which increases the likelihood of it being smaller at birth.

Cocaine can cause damage to the placenta, retarding fetal growth. It can also result in premature labour, breathing difficulties and behavioural problems in later life. The use of heroin and methadone can result in low birth-weight babies, increase the possibility of infections, cause breathing problems and result in withdrawal symptoms.

Herbal Products

Check with a trained herbalist or doctor before taking any herbal medicines – some herbs have been known to harm the embryo.

HERBS TO AVOID DURING PREGNANCY		
Aloe vera (internally)	Dong quai	Parsley seed
Angelica	False unicorn root	Pennyroyal
Autumn crocus	Feverfew	Peruvian bark
Barberry	Golden seal	Poke root
Basil oil	Greater celandine	Pseudoginseng
Black cohosh	Horehound	Pulsatilla
Blue cohosh (especially during first and second trimester)	Horseradish (fresh)	Rue
Cascara sagrada	Hyssop	Sage
Celery seed	Juniper	Sassafras
Chamomile (Roman)	Juniper oil	Senna
Chaste tree	Kava	Southernwood
Cinnamon	Lady's mantle	Stinging nettle
Clove oil	Licorice	St John's wort
Comfrey	Male fern	Tansy
Devil's claw	Mandrake	Thuja
	Mistletoe	Wormwood
	Mugwort	Yarrow

Other Cautions

- X-rays should be avoided during the first 12 weeks due to the possible effects of radiation on the embryo.
- Excess vitamin A can cause heart, lip and head deformities (see table on page 25).
- Some aromatherapy oils should be avoided. They include aniseed, basil, camphor, cedarwood, chamomile, cinnamon, citronella, clary sage, cypress, clove, fennel, hyssop, juniper, marjoram, myrrh, nutmeg, oregano, parsley, peppermint, rosemary, sage and thyme.
- Massage. You don't have to give up your massage, but make sure you tell your masseuse you are pregnant, so a modified massage specifically tailored for pregnant women can be given.
- Overheating. Beware of saunas and spas, which should be avoided during pregnancy.
- Cat litter and cat faeces can carry Toxoplasmosis, which can cause birth defects or miscarriage.
- Chemicals used for perms and hair colours (although this is debated).
- Electric blankets which can raise body heat excessively.
- Dental work. There is some debate about the use of local anaesthetics and the

possible adverse effects they can have on the fetus. The second trimester is the safest period for dental treatment. Check with your dentist before having any work done.

- Some prescription drugs may have to be changed – talk to your doctor.
- Pesticides and herbicides.
- Paint fumes, solvents and bleach.

Try to substitute some of your normal cleaning products with chemical-free ones, for example, use vinegar with a few drops of lavender essential oil to clean wooden or tiled floors.

What to Eat

Ah ha! I thought, at last I can eat whatever I want, pregnancy providing the perfect excuse for my natural gluttony. Unfortunately eating for two is a fallacy. The extra calories needed during pregnancy add up to a measly 150, about two teeny mouthfuls of a chocolate mud cake. You need to consume those extra calories with healthy stuff like milk, wholemeal bread or fruit to ensure you and your baby are getting all the necessary nutritional requirements.

A balanced and varied diet with foods chosen from all five food groups is important. Eating the right foods from conception will not only improve your own health and help to stave off anaemia, fatigue, nausea, indigestion, constipation, cramping, and mood swings, but it will also have a positive effect on the developing fetus. Stillborn, low birth-weight, premature babies, and babies with some form of defect are more frequently born to mothers who've had an inadequate diet throughout their pregnancy. It is also vital to avoid certain foods during your pregnancy. Infections caused by bugs found in particular foods can not only make you feel very ill, but can also adversely affect the fetus. For more information on the right food to eat during pregnancy consult your GP and see the Reading Recommendations on page 205.

Listeriosis

There are some foods pregnant women should avoid, due to the risk of listeriosis. Listeriosis is a flu-like illness caused by the bug *Listeria monocytogenes* which can cause miscarriage and stillbirth. The bug can be found in certain foods (as listed below). A good rule is to only eat foods which have been prepared in the last 12 hours and avoid the following:

- Soft unpasteurised cheeses, such as brie and camembert.
- Chilled, ready-made meals.
- Takeaway cooked diced chicken, such as in sandwiches.
- Raw seafood, such as sashimi and oysters.
- Meats preserved with nitrates, such as salami and smoked meat or fish.
- Raw eggs (including mayonnaise).
- Liver and pâté.
- Soft ice-creams from a machine.
- Pre-prepared salads like those in restaurant salad bars.

Toxoplasmosis

This is an infection caused by the bug *Toxoplasma gondi*, which can affect the unborn child (one in 10,000 babies is born with severe congenital Toxoplasmosis). The bug is mainly found in cat faeces, but also in raw meat such as lamb. It can also be found in contaminated soil. The best way to prevent being infected with Toxoplasmosis from a cat is not to deal with cat faeces while you are pregnant. If you do own a cat, have it tested for the infection. Make sure it doesn't have kittens while you are pregnant, and don't let it eat raw meat. Try not to handle the litter tray yourself, but ask someone else to do it and change it every day. Wear gloves when gardening and wash your hands properly after handling animals. To avoid Toxoplasmosis from meat, make sure it is always properly cooked and hot. Scrub all preparation surfaces such as chopping boards after use.

Folic Acid

Neural tube defects such as spina bifida (abnormal development of the spinal cord), anencephaly (absence of most of the brain), and encephalocele (when the brain forms outside the skull) are the major causes of birth disabilities. Research has shown that a diet rich in folates can reduce this number by up to two-thirds. The Food Standards Agency provides advice on taking folic acid and other aspects of diet during pregnancy (see Useful Contacts, page 209). Folic acid protects the neural tube allowing it to close properly, leading to normal brain and spinal cord development. There is also research showing that folates may reduce the incidence of miscarriage, pre-term delivery and low birth-weight. It is recommended that women trying to conceive take folate supplements, but taking them as soon as you suspect you're pregnant is sufficient. The recommended dose is 400mcg per day. Sources of folate include fortified or wholegrain breads and cereals, dried peas and beans, leafy vegetables, fruit and yeast.

Added Extras

As well as eating more calories, and additional vitamins and minerals, supplement your diet with omega oils, such as those found in tuna, which are very important for brain development, and drink a minimum of 8 glasses of water a day. Drinking water not only keeps you well hydrated but also reduces the risk of dizziness or fainting through dehydration, and also decreases the likelihood of urinary tract infections by flushing out toxins from your bladder and discouraging constipation. You also need to moderate salt intake, as large amounts can increase the likelihood of fluid retention and high blood pressure. Although pregnant women need extra vitamin A, an excess can be toxic, which is why nutritionists recommend that pregnant women avoid liver, or vitamin and mineral supplements containing vitamin A. Instead, try to get it in the harmless form of beta-carotene which is found in yellow and orange fruit and vegetables, such as carrots and pumpkin.

Recommended Daily Allowances

The following table compares the recommended daily allowances of various vitamins and minerals for women at various stages of their lives. It provides a guide to how much more nutrition is required for your developing baby.

NUTRIENT	19–54 YEAR OLD FEMALE	54+ YEAR OLD FEMALE	PREGNANT FEMALE	LACTATING FEMALE
Vitamin A	750mg	750mg	+0mg	+450mg
Thiamin	0.8mg	0.7mg	+0.2mg	+0.4mg
Riboflavin	1.2mg	1.0mg	+0.3mg	+0.5mg
Niacin	13mg	11mg	+2mg	+5mg
Vitamin B_6	0.9–1.4mg	0.8–1.1mg	+0.1mg	+0.7–0.8mg
Total folate	200mg	200mg	+200mg	+150mg
Vitamin B_{12}	2.0mg	2.0mg	+1.0mg	+0.5mg
Vitamin C	30mg	30mg	+30mg	+45mg

NUTRIENT	19–54 YEAR OLD FEMALE	54+ YEAR OLD FEMALE	PREGNANT FEMALE	LACTATING FEMALE
Vitamin E	7.0mg	7.0mg	+0mg	+2.5mg
Zinc	12mg	12mg	+4mg	+6mg
Iron	12–16mg	5–7mg	+10–20mg	+0mg
Iodine	120mg	120mg	+30mg	+50mg
Magnesium	270mg	270mg	+30mg	+70mg
Calcium	800mg	1000mg	+300mg	+400mg
Phosphorus	1000mg	1000mg	+200mg	+200mg
Selenium	70mg	70mg	+10mg	+15mg
Sodium	40–100mg	40–100mg	+0mg	+0mg
Potassium	1950–5460mg	1950–5460mg	+0mg	+0mg
Protein	45g	45g	+6g	+16g

TABLE INFORMATION COURTESY OF NATIONAL HEALTH AND MEDICAL RESEARCH COUNCIL.

All the nutrients listed in the table above are based upon estimates of the requirements with a generous 'safety factor' added. Recommendations for vitamin D are not considered necessary unless people are housebound, as the vitamin D intake is determined by their exposure to UV light from the sun. The recommended intake presented for thiamin, riboflavin, niacin and vitamin B_6 are based on the average energy requirements in existence. The figures for iron are expressed as a range to allow for differences in bioavailability of iron from different types of foods. The recommended iron intake shown for pregnant women is for the second and third trimesters.

Best Sources of Nutrients

Eating a balanced diet from the five food groups will enable you to obtain all the vitamins, minerals and supplements required for yourself and your developing baby. Listed in the table below are the best food sources for the multitude of nutrients you require when pregnant.

NUTRIENT	BEST FOOD SOURCES
Vitamin A	Red peppers, spinach, carrots, broccoli, pumpkin, endive, mango, pineapple, pawpaw, yellow peaches, apricots, egg yolk, margarine, butter and whole milk
Thiamin	Bread and cereals, wheatgerm, lean meat, nuts and seeds
Riboflavin	Milk, yoghurt, cereal, yeast products such as Vegemite
Niacin	Bread, cereals, lean meat, milk and eggs
Vitamin B_6	Found in plant and animal foods, mainly bananas, lean meat, nuts and avocado
Total folate	Kidney, spinach, broccoli, endive, green vegetables, wheatgerm, avocado, oranges, nuts and yeast products such as Vegemite
Vitamin B_{12}	Meat, eggs, milk, yoghurt, cheese
Vitamin C	Green and red peppers, pawpaw, pineapple, mango, strawberries, oranges, grapefruit, mandarins, kiwi fruit, broccoli, cabbage, cauliflower, tomatoes
Vitamin E	Nuts and seeds, wheatgerm and green leafy vegetables
Zinc	Kidney, lean red meat, nuts and wholegrain flours
Iron	Lean red meat, chicken, legumes, bread and cereals
Iodine	Vegetables
Magnesium	Wholegrain bread and cereals, wheatgerm, figs, legumes and nuts

NUTRIENT	BEST FOOD SOURCES
Calcium	Milk and milk products such as yoghurt, cheese and buttermilk, and seeds
Phosphorus	Liver, wheatgerm, yeast, cheese, eggs, wholegrains, legumes and nuts
Selenium	Kidney, liver, nuts, wholegrain cereals, butter and garlic
Sodium	Chicken, green vegetables, carrots, bran, salt, water, lentils and peas
Potassium	Lentils, dried beans, potatoes, spinach, avocado, kelp, nuts and seeds

Eating the Right Amount

It is important to eat the right nutrients from all the food groups during pregnancy. The minimum number of serves for each food group required by pregnant women is:

FOOD	MINIMUM NUMBER OF SERVES PER DAY	EXAMPLE OF A SERVE
Vegetables	4–5 serves	1 cup cooked vegetables or 1 cup salad vegetables
Fruit	2 serves	1 piece of fruit or 1 cup fruit juice or 1 cup diced fruit
Bread and cereals	5 serves	1 slice bread, or 1 roll, or 2 cracker biscuits, or 1 cup cooked rice or pasta, or 1 bowl breakfast cereal or 2 Weetabix™ type biscuits
Dairy foods	3 serves	200ml (¾ cup) milk or 40g (1 slice) cheese or 200g (1 small tub) of yoghurt

FOOD	MINIMUM NUMBER OF SERVES PER DAY	EXAMPLE OF A SERVE
Meat and alternatives (including beans and legumes)	2 serves	1 small slice of lean meat or chicken 1 medium fillet of fish or a small can of tinned fish 1–2 tbsp peanut butter 1 cup of nuts 1 cup of cooked beans or lentils
Fats and oils	1 serve	1 tbsp oil or margarine

Sample Meal Plans

The following sample menus are only a guide, and can help you to understand what to eat during pregnancy to ensure you are getting the right nutrients and amount of calories for your developing baby. Be sure to also drink at least 6–8 glasses of fluid per day. Preferably drink water but weak tea, some herbal teas, juice and milk are fine too.

EXAMPLE MENU	
BREAKFAST	Orange juice 2 Weetabix™ with milk 1 slice of wholemeal toast with butter and honey
MORNING TEA	2 cracker biscuits with sliced tomato
LUNCH	2 slices wholemeal bread with salmon, lettuce and avocado 1 apple
AFTERNOON TEA	1 slice of fruit bun
DINNER	Pasta with a tomato, lamb and eggplant ratatouille Side salad 1 tub of fruit yoghurt 2 slices of melon or piece of fruit, such as a pear, or other fruit in season
SUPPER	Cup of hot chocolate made with low fat milk

The Vegetarian Mother-to-be

The vegetarian mother-to-be should suffer no problems through not eating meat, although strict vegan diets are not recommended for pregnant or breastfeeding women. However, it is important that the vegetarian mother monitors her diet carefully, to make sure she is getting the correct amount of essential vitamins, minerals and nutrients.

Calcium can be a particular problem for non-dairy eating vegetarians, so it's important to eat tofu and soy milk fortified with calcium. Some orange juices have also been fortified with calcium. Vitamin B_{12}, found primarily in animal products such as meat, dairy and eggs should be taken as a supplement, along with iron and folic acid. If you are vegetarian and have any concerns about your diet, it may be a good idea to visit a dietitian or nutritionist who can give you some advice and ideas on what you should be eating.

VEGETARIAN MENU	
BREAKFAST	Orange juice 2 Weetabix™ with milk 1 slice of wholemeal toast with butter and honey
MORNING TEA	2 cracker biscuits with sliced tomato
LUNCH	Baked bean and cheese sandwich made with 2 slices wholemeal bread (using a small tin of baked beans and a slice of cheese) 1 small tub of fresh fruit salad
AFTERNOON TEA	1 slice of fruit bun
DINNER	Chickpea and vegetable curry served with rice Side serve of cucumber and yoghurt raiti 2 slices of melon or piece of fruit such as a pear or other fruit in season
SUPPER	Cup of hot chocolate made with low fat milk

Snacks

You'll probably find that you need to snack between meals – you may start to feel hungry between breakfast and lunch. Try to keep some healthy snacks at hand so you're not tempted to open a packet of chips or lollies. Some good snack ideas are:

- Wholemeal English muffins.
- Tubs of reduced fat yoghurt.
- Wholemeal toast with yeast spread, such as Marmite or Vegemite.
- Dried fruit and unsalted nuts, such as brazil nuts or almonds.
- Wholegrain crispbread.
- A glass of vegetable juice.
- A warm glass of milk.
- A couple of prunes.
- Fruit, especially citrus fruit.
- 30g cube cheese such as cheddar.

Drinking fruit juice high in vitamin C, such as orange, blackcurrant and tomato, with your meals helps with the absorption of iron.

Weight

Weight gain throughout pregnancy is generally between 10–13kg with 1.4–1.8kg in total being gained during the first trimester. It is normal to gain about half a kilogram

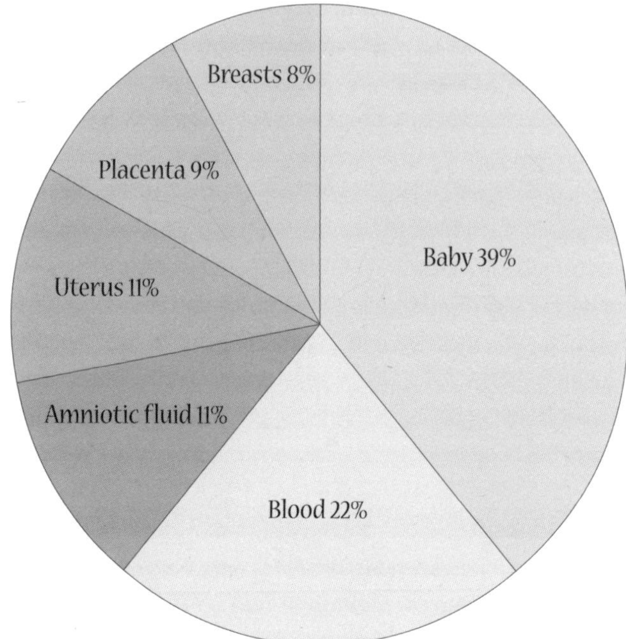

Average weight gain in pregnant women is comprised of these factors.

each week throughout the second trimester until the 8th or 9th month when it should tail off to around half a kilogram or none at all during these final months. This can vary a lot between women and depends on whether you were over or underweight in the beginning of your pregnancy.

Putting on weight too quickly or putting on too much weight can cause all sorts of problems. The extra strain on your body can accentuate back problems – you'll tire more easily, you may develop haemorrhoids, varicose veins, stretchmarks or shortness of breath, and problems with your blood pressure. It also means extra weight to lose after the birth. Please note that if you are not gaining any weight you may need to increase your food intake, and if you are overweight you may not need extra nutrients. If either of these is the case, you should see your dietitian, doctor, obstetrician or midwife.

Pregnancy Diary

The next 40 weeks will be the most unique time of your life. Never again will your body and mind go through so many changes and so many new and different experiences. Even if you have another six children, this first time will always be different. (Ask your mother about her first pregnancy and it's unlikely she'll remember much.) For this reason, consider writing a pregnancy diary, noting how you're feeling both physically and mentally. As well as being a reminder in years to come, writing feelings down, especially when you might be depressed, angry or have any other negative emotions, diffuses them and helps take their power. Seeing your feelings in black and white can also help clarify and sort them out. Don't be a slave to it though – only write when you feel like it. For example, you might make it into a kind of scrapbook with the first ultrasound pictures.

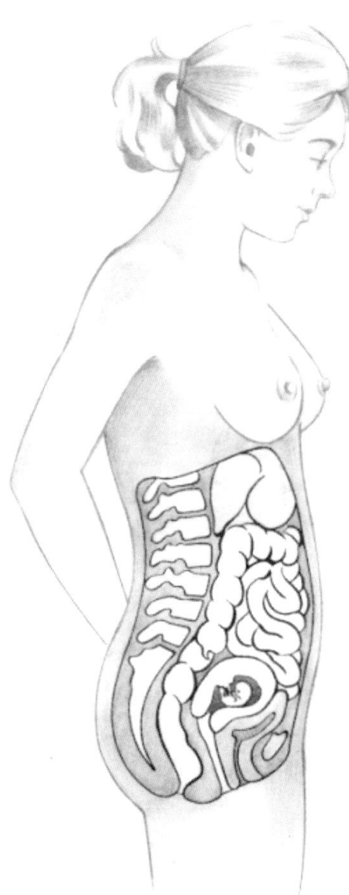

What's Happening? Week 7

As the mother, you will probably be feeling tired, emotional and may have bouts of intense queasiness or even vomiting. Your breasts may be tender and you may need to urinate frequently.

The baby is an embryo approximately 8–11mm long. All its major organs such as the heart, liver, kidneys, lungs and intestines are in place, although not yet fully formed. The heart is pumping regularly. By week 7 the systems are beginning to form. The first bone cells have appeared. Small swellings called limb buds appear where the legs and arms are developing. The placenta is functioning and the spine is formed and as it's longer than the rest of the body, it looks like a tail.

This Month's Checklist

- ✔ Start taking folic acid and watch what you eat.
- ✔ Buy a good soft, supportive bra without underwires if you don't already have one.
- ✔ Consider starting a pregnancy diary and having someone take a picture of you (and your expanding belly) each month.
- ✔ Spoil yourself!

Reality Bites

Choosing a Pregnancy Partner

Picture yourself travelling the world witnessing the sunset over the Taj Mahal, strolling the banks of the Seine, marvelling at Michelangelo's ceiling in the Sistine Chapel. Now imagine doing it all alone. Pregnancy is its own fantastic journey and should be experienced with someone else. For most women, that would automatically be her partner; for single mothers-to-be, it's simply a special person with whom you can share those exciting moments – the hormonal highs and lows, the first kicks, seeing your baby on the ultrasound screen or hearing its heartbeat for the first time.

As well as providing emotional support during your pregnancy, a pregnancy partner can learn breathing techniques to help you during labour, be at home with you when labour starts, drive you to the hospital (if you're having a hospital birth), be there to hold your hand, wipe your brow and encourage you during the birth, and they can even cut the umbilical cord. Knowing your wishes and desires about labour, they can also act as your spokesperson, communicating your needs to the midwife or obstetrician. Pick wisely though. Just as you would weigh the pros and cons of choosing a particular person to set out on a once in a lifetime world trip with, so you should with a 'pregnancy partner', choosing a friend or relative who you know will be there from the beginning to the end. After all, having experienced the birth of your child, you two will share a lifelong bond. Consider the following when choosing someone:

- Do you feel totally at ease and uninhibited with them?
- Do they have flexible working hours that will allow them to attend appointments and antenatal classes if you choose to go, as well as, of course, the actual birth.
- Can they be contacted during the day or night?
- Are you confident in their ability to convey your wishes to the midwife or obstetrician if you are unable to do so?
- Do they unequivocally support your decision to have a child on your own?

It may be wise choosing more than one pregnancy partner, so that if one person can't make an appointment, the other will be able to. The same goes for the actual birth. Many hospitals allow two or more people to attend the birth, so if all goes well, they can both be present. Also, don't automatically discount the idea of a male pregnancy partner! See Reading Recommendations on page 205 for more information.

Holy Doula!

Hiring a doula may be a solution if you have no family or support people, or if you want some extra backup. The use of a doula is quite common in the United States and studies there have shown that women who have one are less likely to have an epidural and are more likely to describe their birth experience as positive. Doulas are becoming more popular around the world but are generally not available yet in the United Kingdom.

A doula is someone who simply offers help and physical and emotional support throughout pregnancy, labour and sometimes post-partum. Unlike a nurse or midwife, a doula offers non-medical help, perhaps by communicating your needs to medical staff, by giving a massage or tucking in pillows, relieving other support members, and most importantly, staying with you throughout labour, while midwifery staff may change shifts. A doula may help in the home cleaning, running errands or just offer companionship and advice after the birth. If you're interested in hiring a doula, find out their personal experience, any training they've had, their charges, their philosophy on labour methods, their availability, and make sure to check references. Most importantly, choose someone you like and feel safe and happy with.

I hooked up with Annie through a friend of a friend who had used her and had felt very positive about the whole experience. I was really nervous meeting her the first time! I wondered if I would like her and if not, how I could turn her down without hurting her feelings. I needn't have worried, she came over and we got on like a house on fire. We had the same sort of ideas about pregnancy and childbirth and really clicked. She was also a mine of information, having had three children herself and was studying natural medicine. She was so supportive throughout and called me or came over at least once or twice a week to see how I was doing. She was fantastic at the birth. She communicated with the medical staff for me, seeming to know what I wanted before I even got it out and explaining in layman terms what the medical staff were saying. She convinced my mum to go for a walk and have a coffee when she realised she was getting a bit tired. I think though the best bit about having Annie was afterward.

I got up after the first night home, after a sleepless night, looked at the mess around me and suddenly felt totally overwhelmed at the enormity of it all. A few minutes later, there was a knock on the door and there was Annie, with a bunch of flowers and a chicken casserole. I took one look at her and burst into tears. She sat me down, and made me a cup of tea while she vacuumed and tidied, then she gave me a head and neck massage. She was fantastic. I highly recommend anyone, whether single or with a partner, to hire a doula, as long as it is 100% the right person. Susanne

Obstetrician or Midwife?

This month you will have your first visit to your GP or midwife. There are various different patterns of care, from shared care between GP and midwife, obstetrician and midwife, or a mixture of all three. Your midwife will discuss the options with you and help you decide which pattern is best for you.

Midwife Care

Midwifery is one of the oldest practising professions in the world, with midwives being specially trained to provide care during the pregnancy, throughout labour and the birth and after the birth. There are four ways you can be cared for by a midwife:

1. You can choose to have a midwife provide all your maternity care including doing your antenatal check-ups at home, assisting in the baby's delivery at home and follow-up postnatal care.
2. Shared antenatal care with a GP or obstetrician and a midwife, in which the midwife provides most of the care but some check-ups will be at the hospital or GP surgery. The birth will be in a hospital.
3. In a birth centre, where the midwife is the primary caregiver, providing care during the pregnancy and post-natally, with an obstetrician used as backup if needed.
4. Care by an independent midwife, where she provides all of your care and you pay her a fee. The birth can be at home or in a hospital.

Midwives should be (and commonly are) the primary carers for women giving birth. The doctor's role should be one of managing complications. Doctors actually have very little experience with normal birth. The role that midwives assume is one of watchful expectancy. They support rather than intervene (as is common in the medical model).

> Midwives are trained to manage complications during labour but will only use these skills or refer to medical assistance when absolutely necessary. During pregnancy I believe that midwives are the ideal carers for the majority of women. When complications arise, medical care should be sought. Sometimes then the doctor continues care or, if appropriate, care is shared between the midwife and doctor. During pregnancy the large part of a midwife's care focuses on education. The physical part of the examination only takes 5 minutes. The rest of the time is spent discussing issues important to the woman as well as informing her of what is happening to her body and what to expect in pregnancy, birth and early parenthood. Midwives aim to prepare women and their families for this exciting journey. There is a push worldwide to re-recognise and utilise the valuable skills of the midwife. In the future the midwife (I hope) should assume her rightful role of being the primary carer for women expecting a normal pregnancy and birth. Jane Palmer, midwife

Some hospitals don't grant independent or private midwives visiting rights and they may only be able to act as a non-participating support person. (See page 209–210.)

Make sure if you have private medical cover, you ask your insurer whether they cover any of the expenses of a privately hired midwife. Unfortunately, most don't and hiring a midwife privately can be expensive, costing you anywhere up to £1,500 upwards.

> I chose to have a private midwife, and gave birth at home because I think there is too much intervention in hospitals for women giving birth. I knew someone who had a midwife and talked to her, then I went to a support group to find out all about it. The midwife was fantastic – they are like teachers, knowing all kinds of things about nutrition and stuff. Mine couldn't have been more supportive – she said I could call her any time and afterwards, she came to see me every day for 10 days to help answer any questions or address any worries I had. I felt very safe in her hands and have gone on to have my second child delivered by a midwife too. Polly

One of the advantages of midwife care is that they usually have fewer women and can therefore devote more time and attention to you (approximately 30-90 minutes per visit, opposed to an obstetrician's average 10 minutes). Appointments are usually at your home or in a room at the GP's surgery, and as the majorityof midwives are female, many women feel more relaxed and able to ask questions they might otherwise feel hesitant to ask if their doctor is male.

NOTE

A midwife is a professionally qualified practitioner who is experienced in giving help or support at a birth. If you are thinking about having a home birth, some organisations offer support and advice groups for women considering this method. Refer to Useful Contacts on page 209–210 and Chapter Seven for more about home births.

Obstetric Care

Most women in the UK choose to have a midwife and GP or a midwife and obstetrician (a medical specialist in maternal and child fetal health), to look after them throughout their pregnancy and the birth. The role of the team is to advise and look after the health of both the mother and the unborn child, as well as assisting at the birth.

The advantages of having an obstetrician are that they are trained in more difficult birthing procedures and are able to perform Caesareans.

Most first time mothers feel more secure in hospitals as they are usually well-equipped to deal with any emergencies that may crop up.

Your doctor will recommend an obstetrician, and refer you to him at the hospital. If you have friends with children, ask them who looked after them – word of mouth is a good way of finding out what the options are. Alternatively, check out your local hospital and the facilities they offer. Ask for a tour of the maternity wards and labour room and ask as many questions as you can about their equipment and methods. If you're likely to have a high-risk pregnancy, you may be referred to an obstetrician who specialises in a particular branch of fetal medicine. After the birth, the baby will be seen and examined by a paediatrician, a doctor who specialises in the care of babies and children.

I chose to attend a hospital because it was my first baby and I didn't know what to expect. I wanted to be able to prepare for all possible outcomes and felt comfortable that I was in the best hands. There was also the possibility, that like my two sisters, I would have to have a Caesarean section. I was very happy with my choice and everything went extremely well. I delivered naturally in the end, but felt very safe knowing that my midwife and obstetrician were there if anything went wrong. The hospital also had a very good reputation for neonatal care in case anything went wrong. Diana

Shared Care

This is when you are under the care of both your obstetrician and a midwife or GP and midwife. Your doctor will confirm your pregnancy, refer you to a midwife for your booking-in appointment and she will discuss and organise antenatal tests or refer you to specialist treatment should the need arise. A midwife will deal with your routine check-ups during your pregnancy, and, depending on whether you choose to give birth at home or in a hospital, may also deliver your baby. With shared care, you are required to carry your pregnancy records with you for any appointments you have with your hospital doctor, midwife and GP, so that each knows what's going on and so they can provide consistent care. Your doctor and midwife will receive copies of all tests or examinations from the hospital.

The First Visit

You're pregnant! By now, the unbelievable may have sunk in, and you'll no doubt start to feel pretty damn clever and pleased with yourself, which is why your first visit to an obstetrician or midwife may be a bit of a let-down. He or she has seen it all before – hundreds of times. However, if you're lucky, you'll have someone who really loves what they do and still thinks it's all pretty amazing.

What's vital, in any case, is that you're happy and comfortable with whomever you choose. It may be short term but the relationship you have with your obstetrician or midwife is incredibly important, even more so if you are going through your pregnancy alone.

It may be worth taking your pregnancy partner for a bit of moral support at your first visit. He or she might also be a good backup, asking questions you might not think of. Once you've arrived, make it clear to the midwife or obstetrician that you are giving birth without the traditional partner and try to gauge his or her reaction. While single mothers are pretty much an accepted fact of society today, you definitely don't want to be stuck for 40 weeks with someone who secretly disapproves of or condemns what you're doing.

One single mother I know realised on her first visit that her doctor would be less than supportive of her situation. 'He had that Psalm "The Lord is my Shepherd" on a plaque on his wall, which should have given me a hint. His first question was "Where's your husband?" "In my mother's prayers", I replied, which he didn't find at all amusing. He asked me whether I had considered all my options before deciding to go ahead with the birth. I felt disapproval emanating from every pore.

Needless to say, I didn't bother going back, but found a woman doctor who was much more sympathetic.'

Whoever you choose to look after you during your pregnancy, you should never feel just like a number to be hurriedly dealt with. Your concerns should be listened to and adequate time given to ask any questions. Your doctor or midwife should be able to explain procedures, tests and any risks and side effects clearly, repeat anything you don't understand and have a patient and understanding manner.

Don't feel guilty about changing a doctor or midwife after the first visit if you're not happy – like every other service in life, you expect to get the best.

Not 9 Months but 40 Weeks

You'll soon start to refer to your pregnancy in weeks rather than 9 months. In fact the average pregnancy is 9 months and 7 days, which equals around 40 weeks. This is measured from the beginning of the first day of your last menstrual period (LMP). However, ovulation generally occurs around the middle of your menstrual cycle, meaning that when you're described as being 4 weeks pregnant, your baby has actually been developing for only 2 weeks. This second measurement can be referred to as the gestational age of your baby. You will also hear your pregnancy referred to as 'first, second or third trimester' (trimester meaning 'three months'). The first trimester includes the first 12 weeks, the second weeks 13 to 28, and the third weeks 29 to birth.

At your first appointment, which is often known as a 'booking-in' appointment, you may have the following:

- Questions about your medical history, including the father's family history. It's worth appealing to your baby's father for information about any serious family illness, genetic problems etc.
- An internal examination.
- A blood test to give you an EDD (estimated due date) as well as to check your blood group, and a test for anaemia, haemoglobin, syphilis, rubella, Hepatitis B, Hepatitis C and HIV.
- Cervical cultures for gonorrhoea and chlamydia and genetic tests, if warranted.
- Blood pressure/weight and height checks.
- A urinalysis to screen for sugar, protein, white blood cells, bacteria and anaemia.

The doctor or midwife may give you advice about eating, dietary supplements and explain what you can expect in the next few months. He or she will most probably give you a maternity record, in which all the information about your pregnancy, including results of tests, weight gain and the baby's development are recorded. This is to take away with you and to bring to all appointments, whether with your doctor, midwife, or specialist.

Some Questions to Ask

If you're seeing an obstetrician, you might like to ask:

- What type of equipment they have at the hospital he or she works at? For example, birthing pools, bean bags, birthing rooms as opposed to traditional labour theatres.
- What are his or her positions on elective Caesareans, inductions, natural births and episiotomies?
- Which (people) and how many people do they allow in the labour room, and is this still valid in the case of a Caesarean?
- Is he or she available on weekends and at night? Is there an after hours emergency number?

If you're seeing a midwife, you might like to ask:

- What do they see as their role during birth?
- How many mothers have they assisted?
- What happens if they are away/unavailable when you go into labour?
- What are their fees? (If they are a private midwife.) Do they include pre- and postnatal visits?
- Do they offer prenatal classes or can they recommend some?
- What happens if you need to be transferred to hospital (in the case of a home birth)?
- What sort of equipment do they carry (in the case of home birth), such as for resuscitation?

Further Appointments

To begin with, you will see your doctor or midwife approximately once a month until your 28th week. This will change to once every 2 weeks, up until the last 6 weeks, when appointments will be weekly. This usually involves a pretty straightforward check-up, including monitoring your blood pressure and the baby's growth.

Keep a note of any queries or concerns as they come up, so you'll remember to ask about them on your next visit.

You will be able to give birth at home if you are considered low risk. (See Chapter Seven for more information on home births.)

Birth Centres

While it may seem premature thinking about where you want to give birth at this early stage, it is worth considering all the options in advance, especially if you are considering using a birth centre, as they tend to be booked out long in advance. These offer an alternative to hospital to those women who may not feel happy about having a home birth. In the UK the majority are privately run so cost may be a drawback. See Chapter Seven for more information on birth centres.

The Doppler Ultrasound and Other Scans

At around 8 weeks your midwife may be able to hear the baby's heartbeat via a Doppler ultrasound. When you might have your first scan varies on your local facilities. It is usually between weeks 8 to 12, followed by another one to check for any problems at around week 20. Many practitioners now forgo this earlier one, considering it unnecessary in most cases, unless there is some confusion about dates and the development of the fetus.

If reality hasn't bitten yet, seeing your developing baby on screen is certain to do it. It's an amazing experience, even if it is somewhat difficult to connect that vaguely alien looking thing on the screen with an actual baby. Having your pregnancy partner there to share the event makes it even more special.

How Does an Ultrasound Work?

Ultrasound works through soundwaves bouncing off internal structures and allows technicians to see the fetus without the dangers of x-rays. There have been some concerns about the subtle long-term effects of ultrasound on the developing baby but as yet no conclusive studies have been done. Generally, ultrasound is considered safe and effective for both mother and fetus, however, if your religious or moral principles mean that you wouldn't consider a termination or treatment if there were something wrong with your baby, then don't feel pressured into it. After all, our mothers and grandmothers didn't have them!

There are two types of ultrasound – transabdominal and transvaginal. There is no pain involved in either, except that a transabdominal examination requires you to have a full bladder and because of this may cause some discomfort. The reason for this is that the ultrasound cannot 'see through' gases, which are present in the bowel. With a full bladder, the bowel is pushed up out of the way and allows for a clearer picture. The transabdominal examination involves lying on an examination table, where a gel, which amplifies the sound, is applied to the abdomen, and a transducer, which acts as a kind of visual microphone, is passed over it. For the transvaginal ultrasound, a probe is inserted into the vagina. This method usually gives better images and information, particularly in the very early stages of pregnancy and is often used to detect an ectopic pregnancy (when the fetus implants itself in the fallopian tubes).

Why is Ultrasound Used?

Ultrasound is used for many reasons, including:

1. To date the pregnancy by using the crown rump length as a measurement.
2. As a diagnostic tool to detect any fetal abnormalities or determine the causes of bleeding or to confirm any suspected miscarriages.
3. To detect the position of the fetus for amniocentesis, and chorionic villus sampling.
4. To diagnose multiple pregnancies.
5. To determine the condition of the placenta.
6. To verify the baby's position before delivery, or the size of the baby, if considering delivery before the due date.

What Will I See?

For the laywoman, scans can be hard to interpret. What looks to you like a head may actually be a spleen, and comments like 'look, he's sucking his thumb' can cause much head scratching. However, the sonographer can talk you through what you are seeing and point out the relevant bits.

This early scan is usually performed to confirm the earliest delivery date. You probably won't be able to detect the sex of the baby, but it is best to speak up sooner rather than later, just in case you don't want to know and the technician lets it slip. Also make it clear in the beginning if you want a picture to keep, as then the technician can look for the best and clearest image to freeze and print (there is usually a small charge for this).

The sonographer can usually give you some information about the scan, and may even give you a copy of the results as well as sending them to your doctor.

The 3-D Scan

Three-dimensional scans are only available in a few hospitals in the UK. These can produce more accurate information than 2-D scans; showing abnormalities or the lack thereof, even picking up small abnormalities such as cleft palates, hair lips and club feet. However the ability to obtain a good picture with the 3-D scan depends on the amount of liquid around the fetus and the mother's degree of maternal obesity. It's unknown whether in the future these scans will be used as a diagnostic tool on their own or just to gather supplementary information.

Tests

Chorionic Villus Sampling

As well as ultrasound, another test you may be offered now is chorionic villus sampling (CVS), particularly if you are aged in your mid 30s or older, or if there may be any inherited disorders or chromosomal abnormalities. Chorionic villus sampling can be used earlier than amniocentesis (see Chapter Four) as a diagnostic tool for women who may want to consider a termination if it turns out that there is something seriously wrong with the developing baby. It can also be used when there is a lack of amniotic fluid making amniocentesis difficult. Chorionic villus sampling tests are usually given between weeks 9 to 12 and check for possible genetic or chromosomal abnormalities in the fetus (such as Tay-Sachs, sickle cell anaemia, cystic fibrosis, Down syndrome, muscular dystrophy and thalassemias). Generally, these tests, apart from the one for Down syndrome, will only be performed if the family history warrants it.

The procedure is done in one of two ways – either cells are taken from a probe through the vagina into the uterus, or a needle is inserted through the abdomen. The result is to take a sample of the placental tissue (chorionic villi). In both cases, ultrasound is used to guide the doctor's instruments and reduce any risks. However, there is a slight increase in the risk of miscarriage (believed to be between 1–10%) through perforation of the amniotic sac and bleeding, as well as a slim risk of a false positive or negative result.

Nuchal Translucency Screening (NTS)

This is a relatively new, simple and painless test in which ultrasound is used to measure the thickness of the fluid behind the baby's neck. This measure, along with your age and the size of the baby, allows the doctor to estimate the possibility of Down syndrome. If results suggest you are at risk of having a baby with Down syndrome, (an estimated risk of 1 in 300 is considered high) you may be offered counselling and will have to make the difficult decision about whether to go ahead with your pregnancy or not.

There is some controversy about the accuracy of this test, with a high percentage of false positive results turning up. Concerns have also been raised about adequate training of staff who carry out the test and those who interpret it. As yet, NTS is not available everywhere, so ask your doctor or midwife about it.

Rhesus Negative

This condition occurs when some of the baby's blood crosses into the mother's bloodstream and her body consequently produces antibodies against this 'foreign' blood. If these antibodies leak from the mother's circulation back into the baby's, they will start to destroy the baby's own healthy blood cells.

Determining both parents' blood groups is important if you know you are rhesus negative. A blood test can easily confirm whether you're among the 14% of the population who are rhesus negative. If you do turn out to be negative, you need to establish with the baby's father whether he is positive. Even if you are on bad terms with the father, it's worth appealing to him, either directly or via a third party to find out. It is rare that a woman who is negative when the baby's father is positive will have problems, if the baby turns out to be also positive. Future pregnancies may be problematic too, as your body will always produce those antibodies which may attack a positive baby. In addition, the babies of rhesus negative mothers can become anaemic if they are positive inutero. Usually the rhesus negative mother is given an injection of antiserum which suppresses the creation of antibodies to rhesus positive blood after the birth of the baby.

Fetal Blood Sampling

This test, which involves taking a blood sample from the baby's umbilical cord, is used when necessary to test for abnormal chromosomes, or in the management of fetal anaemia. It is done with a local anaesthetic and a needle passed into the uterus, guided by ultrasound.

Pregnancy and HIV

You may be offered an HIV test if you think you may be at risk. If it proves to be positive, you'll probably need some medical counselling to help you decide the best course of action for both you and your unborn child.

Being HIV positive doesn't necessarily mean your child will be too, but the baby will have antibodies which will disappear after 2 years if it has not been infected. However, between 20–50% of babies born to HIV positive mothers will actually be infected with the virus.

Miscarriage

It's a sad fact of life, but up to 40% of women will suffer a miscarriage at least once in their lives. However, in most of these cases, the woman doesn't even know she is pregnant, but may simply assume she is having a slightly heavier than usual period.

With confirmed pregnancies the rate is much lower, with around 10% ending in miscarriage. It's more common in the first trimester, with the chances of miscarrying diminishing after the 12th week. Miscarriage can be due to:

- Genetic problems, for example, defects in chromosomes.
- Environmental factors, such as excessive drinking or drugs.
- Gynaecological abnormalities, such as a weak cervix or neck of the womb.
- Infections or disease.

In my 11th week, just as I was starting to relax into my pregnancy, the morning sickness finally letting up, I woke one night and found I was bleeding. I called the after hours doctor in a blind panic, who basically told me to go back to bed, keep my legs up and if I was still bleeding in the morning to see my doctor. In the morning, the bleeding had all but stopped, but nevertheless I went to my doctor, who sent me for an ultrasound. By this time, I had lain awake all night, gradually making peace with the fact that my having a baby was just not to be. I had even managed to convince myself that it was probably a good thing, my life could get back to normal, and I could go on that trip I was planning. Then, at the clinic, seeing my baby on the screen for the first time, hearing his heartbeat, I burst into tears, all my bravado crumbling under the weight of the relief that he was still there. It seemed I had a low lying placenta which, after this incident, corrected itself and I had no more problems. Amanda

●●●● In general my health was good, but between weeks 7 and 16 of my pregnancy, I experienced light bleeding on a daily basis. Investigations revealed fibroids of a significant size, and I was told that I would probably miscarry by the end of the first trimester. This news, casually imparted, was devastating. After sobbing for a day, I resolved that all I could do was stay really positive and take life one day at a time. Each day of my pregnancy felt like an achievement. I attuned myself, my body and my baby, and walked around for much of the time with my hands on my stomach, reinforcing that connection with my child and willing the baby to stay there. Dorothy

●●●● I was devastated when I had a miscarriage at 10 weeks. It took me a long time to get over it, especially as for the first few weeks I didn't even want the baby. I felt like I had cursed the pregnancy somehow. The only positive thing for me was going to a memorial service that was held at the hospital gardens. The hospital has a garden dedicated to babies who have died before 20 weeks gestation. The service was lovely and friends came to help cry with me and celebrate my baby's life. I struggle every day with his death but have given up blaming myself. Anna

Miscarriages happen, but it's important to keep it all in perspective. Every twinge, spot of blood or ache doesn't necessarily mean a miscarriage. Often, mild cramps, or a 'pulling' sensation on one or both sides of the abdomen can simply indicate the stretching of the ligaments that support the abdomen, while light bleeding can indicate that the embryo is implanting itself in the wall of the uterus. However, if you have any of the following symptoms, you should call your doctor immediately:

- Passing of clots or pinkish matter. If you can, try to collect a sample, so the doctor can easily determine whether a miscarriage has already occurred and, if so, whether it is complete.
- If you've had a miscarriage before and experience cramping and/or bleeding.
- When bleeding is accompanied by pain and is heavy enough to go through several pads in an hour.
- Light staining for more than 3 days.

Exercising while Pregnant

It's probably the last thing on your mind, but moderate physical exercise is considered to be extremely beneficial during pregnancy. In fact, one US study found that regular exercise during pregnancy could lead to a more alert and contented baby.

Today's pregnant woman is usually naturally active. She normally works (in addition to household chores) and her day runs pretty much as a non-pregnant woman's (apart from the odd mid-afternoon nap on the desk!) This can include exercise, although it's essential you check with your doctor or midwife first to make sure that it's not contraindicated in your case. The benefits of exercise are multifold. As the pregnancy progresses, you'll become less fit, due to the extra weight and strain on muscles and ligaments. So, the fitter you are to start with, the better chance you'll have of continuing a trouble free pregnancy. It will also make it easier to lose weight after the birth and can help avoid back problems, varicose veins and leave you in better shape post-partum.

As regular exercisers know, it also has psychological effects – the endorphins being released in your brain giving you a sense of wellbeing and relaxation.

During these early months of pregnancy, it's usually okay to continue with your normal exercise routine, although it's not advisable to take up any new form of contact sport or strenuous exercise. Towards the end of your last trimester, exercise should be tapered off and replaced by brisk walks and gentle stretching routines to avoid any injury to you and your baby.

BEST EXERCISES DURING PREGNANCY	EXERCISES TO AVOID DURING PREGNANCY
Yoga	Jumping, bouncing or jerky movements
Swimming	Horseback riding
Cycling on a stationary bike	Scuba diving
Callisthenics designed for the pregnant woman	Water-skiing
Walking	Contact sports such as football, boxing, kickboxing, martial arts (Karate, Tai Bo etc), excessive jogging or sprinting.

General Guidelines for Exercising when Pregnant

1. Exercise regularly (at least three times a week is preferable).
2. Eat at least 1 hour before exercising.
3. Avoid prolonged strenuous exercise.
4. Avoid overheating by not exercising in hot weather, wearing cool clothing and keeping hydrated.
5. Wear a good supportive bra and well-fitting shoes.

6. Make sure to do a good warm up and cool down of 5–10 minutes.
7. Don't exercise so your heart rate is over 140 beats per minute (bpm).
8. Always get up from the floor slowly and gradually.
9. Avoid saunas and spas which can cause overheating.
10. Don't spend too long exercising on your back, especially in later pregnancy.
11. Make sure you are consuming enough calories to compensate for those lost when exercising.
12. Avoid overstretching as your ligaments have softened and are more vulnerable to injury.
13. Try to exercise on a cushioned surface, such as grass or carpet, which are less jarring than concrete or tiled floors.

The BabyCentre.co.uk has useful information on exercise and pregnancy. See Useful Contacts on page 210 for contact details.

Yoga

Yoga is possibly one of the best all-around activities for the pregnant woman. This gentle form of exercise, which combines focus on breathing with physical stretches and relaxation, is a great preparation for both the mental and physical demands of childbirth. Yoga, practised properly, can:

- Increase your energy.
- Increase your body awareness and make you feel positive.
- Help you relax and cope with pain in birth.
- Develop useful positions for relieving any discomfort during pregnancy or labour.
- Increase general flexibility.
- Improve circulation and thus the delivery of oxygen and nutrients to the placenta.

There are many yoga classes around but it's best to join one which is specifically for pregnancy, as not all of the poses are suitable to practise during pregnancy. See Useful Contacts on page 210 for details. Alternatively, if you don't feel like joining a class, you can probably rent a video about yoga during pregnancy through your local library and there are some excellent books with instructions on how to do the various poses that are suitable for pregnancy. See Reading Recommendations on page 205.

Following are some basic yoga stretches for pregnant women:

Tailor Pose: This pose widens the pelvic canal increasing flexibility in the joints and relaxing the pelvic floor muscles. Sit on the floor with your back straight and bring the soles of your feet together, drawing them close to your body. Relax your shoulders and the back of your neck. Breathe deeply.

Sitting with Legs Apart: This pose lengthens and relaxes the inner thigh muscles and helps ground the pelvis. Sit on the floor with your back straight and open your legs as wide as possible. Breathe deeply, releasing your lower back muscles, pelvis and thighs downward with each exhalation.

The Pelvic Floor Muscles

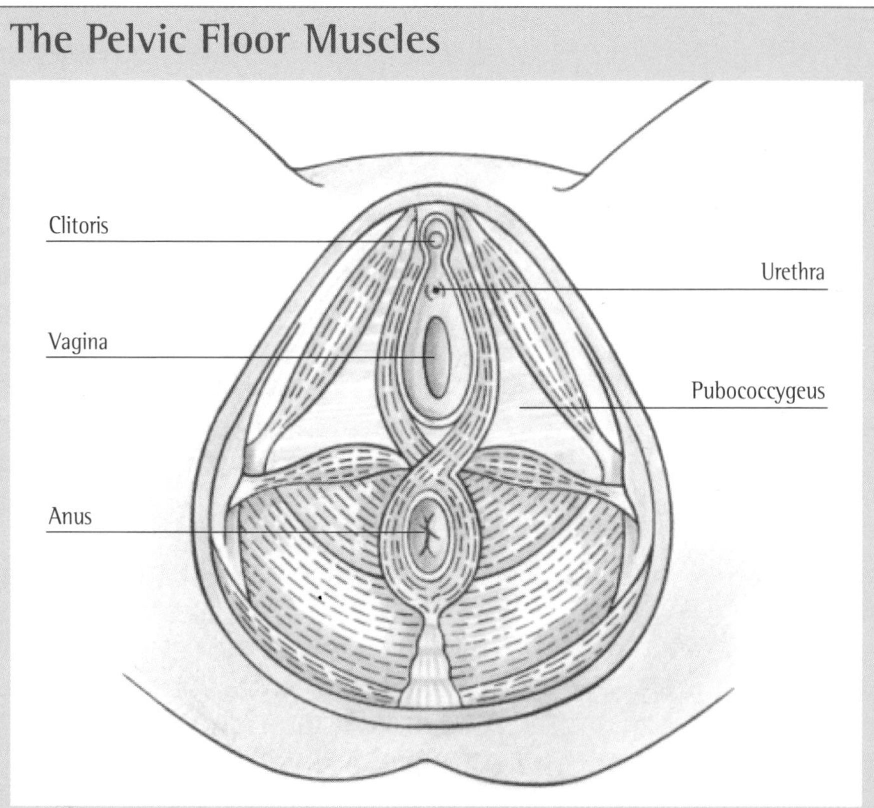

If you don't know about it already, you'll hear a lot about this very important group of muscles. The pelvic floor muscles form a kind of sling or hammock across the floor of the pelvis and support the bladder, uterus and rectum. They are put under extra pressure when a woman is pregnant due to the extra weight she is carrying. Exercising these muscles from day one will ensure that they go back into shape after childbirth and that there is no loss of urine when sneezing, laughing or exercising, as well as helping to improve the tone of the vagina and prolapse of the uterus.

To begin with, when going to the toilet, draw in these muscles and stop the flow of urine. Do this several times until you get used to feeling which muscle you need to work. You should do it as often as you can during the day, drawing up and holding for 6 seconds then relaxing, eventually increasing the time you can hold it.

Exercising in Water

Exercising in water, such as swimming or aquarobics is perfect for the pregnant woman. After lugging around all that extra weight, the joy of floating in water and having its buoyancy support you is a positive joy. Other benefits of exercising in water include the fact that as the weight is taken off all the joints, you're less likely to injure or strain a muscle.

There is an increase of oxygen to the muscles; the heart and lungs are stimulated improving the circulation of oxygen and nutrients to the fetus. Exercising in water increases muscle tone, relieves tension and builds strength and endurance. It may lessen fatigue and help you sleep better. It can also help with back problems, elevated blood pressure and fluid retention.

Like most exercising, don't overdo it, especially if you are in a heated pool. Contact your local gym or look in your paper for local aquarobics or aquanatal classes.

I go to an aquarobics class run by the hospital, which is just wonderful. I would recommend it to any pregnant woman. And the best thing is that anyone can do it regardless of back problems or pelvic problems or fitness level, etc. I just love that feeling of weightlessness; it's been a very long time since I haven't felt like a lead balloon! Kate

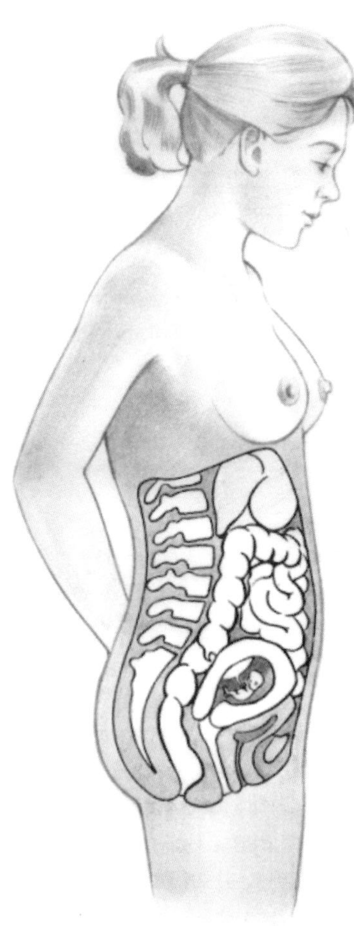

What's Happening? Week 11

You may actually start to feel better by the end of this month and in many cases, morning sickness will have dissipated. You may notice some slight swelling in your abdomen, especially if this is your first pregnancy. Your risk of miscarriage is reduced even further by the end of this month.

The embryo is now considered a fetus and measures about 6½cm and weighs about 18g. The heart is beating at around 110 to 160 bpm and 20 tiny baby teeth are being formed under the gums. The baby has its reflexes and also practises movements in the digestive tract. The ankles and wrists are formed and the ears, fingers and toes are visible. Fingernails have also formed, as have external genitalia.

This Month's Checklist

- ✓ Think about choosing a pregnancy partner.
- ✓ Get any necessary tests done if you are at risk.
- ✓ Book an appointment with a midwife or obstetrician.
- ✓ If practical, try to get some information from the baby's father regarding any genetic/family health problems.
- ✓ Work out an exercise plan and clear it with your midwife.
- ✓ Write a list of questions to ask your midwife or doctor.

CHAPTER THREE

WEEKS 12–15

Time to Tell?

Who to Tell?

By now you have probably got used to the idea of being pregnant and may even be starting to show. The risk of losing your baby now has dramatically lessened and it may be time, by the end of this month, to start thinking about telling those people closest to you, or those who need to know, about your pregnancy.

Telling the Father

Legally, you have no obligation to tell the father-to-be of your pregnancy. Whether or not you have a moral obligation is a personal decision. However, think long and carefully about the reasons for denying both his and the child's rights to know before you decide. Informing the father also gives you the opportunity to ask about any genetic or hereditary illness which could be vital for your child's health. However, if he is told about the pregnancy and he accepts paternity, he will be legally entitled to visiting rights and could eventually sue for custody. He is also obliged to pay child support (see Chapter Ten). It can be a very difficult and emotionally charged meeting and if you are worried about how he will react, consider taking a friend along for moral support. If you really don't feel up to telling him face to face write a letter through a solicitor or a third party if necessary. Try to remember it's hard for him as well. He may not feel emotionally or financially capable of being a father and to be hit with the sudden shocking responsibility of a child can be overwhelming. Remember too that while his initial reaction may be negative, once he has time to digest the fact that he is to be a father, he may feel differently.

Note that if fertilisation of your baby was from a sperm donor, the laws regarding identification of sperm donors vary between countries. In some instances, the sperm donor can indicate whether he is willing for the child to contact him. In other instances the sperm donor legally remain anonymous. However, you will usually have some idea of the donor's medical history beforehand from the fertility clinics' records.

●●●● In my experience, men expect the woman to be totally responsible for birth control. Thus we are culpable for its failure. When I told my ex I was pregnant he was ropeable. 'How did you manage that?' he asked. I had to remind him he had been present at the time. Alicia

●●●● My sister convinced me that I should tell the father. One: because he might actually be interested (I knew full well he wouldn't be!), and two: because I should find out his medical history. The second point decided me, and I did in fact go ahead and tell him. Of course, he told me to have an abortion and that he wanted nothing to do with the child. Actually, I was very hurt that he didn't have more sympathy for me; I was well and truly hysterical about the whole thing by this time! All he was concerned about was that he didn't want some love child of his bursting into his life at some point down the track. Well, I could understand that, and I assured him that I will keep him out of it, and I will not be pursuing him for maintenance. Kathryn

●●●● I'd broken up with Chris about a month before and was seeing someone else. Once I knew I was pregnant, I rang him and asked him to meet me at a restaurant nearby – our restaurant. He obviously thought it was a reconciliation, as I could see the look on his face. I didn't want to let him have false hope, so I just told him, 'I'm 12 weeks pregnant'. He looked shocked, then having done some quick mental arithmetic, realised it was his. He was thrilled, until I told him that there was no chance of us getting back together. We had a huge argument, and he walked out. He's only spoken to me twice during my pregnancy and is very bitter. Megan

●●●● His response was 'abortion' because my pregnancy wasn't planned! He then withdrew himself from the situation. He also questioned my pregnancy, my motivations, and paternity. His responses, words, and actions during my pregnancy were incredibly hurtful. He had always maintained that above everything he wanted to be my friend. He now showed very little true friendship or support towards our baby and me. Jane

●●●● I admit, it was a bit cowardly, but I let him know by letter. Sandy

●●●● When I told the father he was babbling on about something when I just blurted it out. Silence. I could see him turn a whiter shade of pale down the line. Then 'Shit'. He then went on to tell me 'he didn't want a kid'. So I made the decision to do it without him. I had put it in Fate's hands and it had been decided. I was going to have a baby. It felt right. Ngaire

Family and Friends

You will undoubtedly encounter a wide range of reactions to your pregnancy, from supportive to condemning. Be open-minded and accept the fact that going against convention often provokes a strong reaction – the single mother in particular often challenges people's morals or religious ethics. However, the last thing the single pregnant woman needs is negativity or hostility. If you encounter it from family or friends, let them know how hurt you are, then let it go and surround yourself with supportive, caring people. You may find that some people come around once the baby is born, but it may be hard to forgive the lack of support by then.

Whoever you choose to tell at this stage, whether family members or close friends, choose your moment. Explain as much or as little as you want and make it clear from the beginning what your position is on personal questions.

First I told my mother. This was very ugly! I should point out that she and I have never gotten along. But, I felt that she should know – a baby, after all, is a hard thing to keep secret unless I planned never to see my mother again. Actually, I could have done that. Generally speaking we can go for years without communicating. Anyway, she screamed at me to 'Get rid of IT!' and that I had only done this just to upset her, and what a no-hoper I was, etc, etc. I was very hormonal at the time, (strange that!), and I became hysterical myself, so I actually called one of my sisters. Well that was pretty bad too, but strangely enough, this sister and I have had a few heart to hearts in the intervening months, and I can say that we get on fairly well now. She was also responsible for persuading certain members of the family, including mother, that they should help me, and they have provided some much needed practical support ranging from buying me a car to buying a pram, car seat and cot (the 'big stuff'). So, although I still don't have any regular contact with any of them, I communicate with them through my sister, whom I do ring from time to time. Kathryn

I was still with my partner at that stage, so it wasn't really an issue. David and I were living in New Zealand at the time, so I just rang my mum and told her she was going to be a grandmother. She was thrilled. Maria

Telling my mum was the hardest thing I have ever done. She herself was a young single mum, and knew just how hard it can be. I knew one of her biggest fears was that the same thing would happen to me, and here I was, at age 20 having to ring her up (she lived 300km away at the time) and tell her I was pregnant and, judging by the father's reaction, I would most likely be single! To say she was upset would be an understatement but I am happy to say that once she came to terms with it she was, and still is, the most wonderful support I could have ever asked for. Michelle

● ● ● ● There never seemed to be an opportune moment to tell my friends – I mean, how do you bring it up? 'Oh, by the way, I'm going to have a baby', or drop it casually into conversations, 'Yeah, was feeling a bit off colour the other day, so I went to the doctor, and he reckons I'm pregnant. Anyway, are you going to have an entrée?' Eventually, I found this brilliant thing on the Internet where you can send e-cards announcing you're pregnant, so I sent everyone in my email address book a card. Unfortunately I forgot this included all my clients, the local organic fruit and veg deliverers and my ex-boyfriend! Lisa

● ● ● ● When I told my Mum she walked off without a word, at a time when anything would have been better than nothing. Two days later she was knitting and talking names and colours for the nursery wall. Ngaire

● ● ● ● My family all responded with incredible support and love, except for my 88-year-old Nanna who considered it 'bad news'. I had always considered her to be a very modern thinking woman but she couldn't get past the fact that I wasn't married and that there would be no pending wedding. She commented that I was just like Elle McPherson! At 5"1' and a stocky build Elle McPherson is the last person I relate myself to, even if she is also an unmarried mother!

All my friends were absolutely wonderful in every way. The majority were so excited because they knew I'd always loved children. At the same time, most of my friends were totally shocked because I had never been clucky for my own children. I was always more than happy and totally content to leave any maternal instincts with everyone else's children. Some friends expressed concern about sole parenting but always respected and supported my decision. I have become so much closer to most of my very special long-standing friends. I have also made some truly wonderful new friends. I am appreciative to them all. Jane

Employers

You are not required to inform employers of your pregnancy until 4 weeks before you intend taking maternity leave. However, you may need to tell them before then to request time off for antenatal check-ups etc. If you are eligible for Statutory Maternity

Pay, then you will need to obtain a maternity certificate (form MATB1) from your doctor or midwife. See Chapter Five for more information.

Your Husband must be Happy?

For most partnered parents-to-be, the news is usually something to be shouted to the world. As a single mother, you may have more hesitation. You'll probably have to deal with inevitable questions about the baby's father and people's subsequent reactions when you tell them you are a single mother-to-be. You'll face questions and comments such as, 'So where's the father then? Bastard disappeared has he?' or 'Oh, you poor love, are you going to have to cope all on your own?' They're often not sure whether you're happy about being pregnant or not and sometimes have to do a quick emotional check themselves to find out their own feelings about single mothers. While all of this confusion and emotions are flitting across their faces, an uncomfortable silence develops, before they can articulate a hesitant 'congratulations'.

Having to go through this endless times every day can be draining. Personally, if people (particularly strangers) asked me about my baby's father, I'd make up lies so outrageous they'd get the message ('the father's a Berber camel trader, we met at the annual Luxor dromedary trade fair'). Single mother Anna was more to the point. 'I'd just tell them it was none of their business! It's amazing how, when you're pregnant, complete strangers seem to think it's okay to ask you personal questions, like you're suddenly public property.' A friend Lydia was more philosophical. 'It's just human nature, people are naturally curious'. She says she didn't mind telling them her situation. 'Actually, it was sometimes quite fun to see their reaction when I told them the baby's father and I had split up – they didn't really know what to say next!' Other situations can be more difficult.

I was artificially inseminated. I told most of my friends and some of my family before I even got pregnant, but I couldn't believe the number of questions I got from strangers and acquaintances. In the beginning I told them the truth, that the father was a sperm donor I'd never met, but I got such negative responses. People would start giving me moral lectures and I even was abused by one woman. In the end, I started to get really angry at people's nosiness and told them it was none of their business, (usually in stronger terms than that!). Anne-Marie

Acquaintances are generally shocked, and I have had to come up with a suitable 'story' to explain the lack of a father to them. It's not something that I can hide! And I certainly don't tell them that he was married! I wouldn't say that such acquaintances have been negative as such, (well at least not to my face), but I think that they feel like it's not a 'real' pregnancy. That is to say, all their friends and acquaintances who have babies are in couples, and there is a certain social etiquette to how these things are done in that world. It's like I am playing dress ups, or mummies and daddies, (albeit without the daddies!) and they therefore don't take my pregnancy very seriously. I am certainly not permitted to have the ailments that 'real' mothers have, and subsequently don't get a lot of sympathy. Lucy

When I broke up with my partner during my pregnancy, people who didn't know me well didn't know whether he had 'left me in the lurch, the bastard' or if I had had an affair with someone else who was the baby's father, and therefore I was a 'bitch'. It was simply that I had had enough and having a baby is no reason to stay – but the hardest thing was that because I wasn't a partnered pregnant woman I had to always be explaining my private life to almost strangers, or else saying 'it's none of your business' and seeming rude. When you become pregnant, your stomach becomes public property and everyone touches it; when you split up your private life becomes public property and everyone wants to know. Ali

My landlord was very understanding that I had fallen behind with my rent and assured me that it was okay to gradually catch it up as long as I continued to pay my regular rent instalments. This was until he found out that I was pregnant. He then promptly tried to evict me! Strangely enough, he tried it again when I was 35 weeks pregnant – what a pig! All my neighbours agreed that he just simply couldn't handle the thought of a 'child' in one of his units. Kathryn

I can't believe how impertinent some people can get when you're pregnant. Complete strangers come up to you on the street and ask the most personal questions. Actually, strangely enough, I prefer them to the other type – the ones who leave you standing on the train at 8 months pregnant till you keel over rather than offering you their seat! In the beginning, I was quite open about admitting there was no father, because guaranteed, he always came up in conversation. The next question would invariably be, 'Well then, how did you get pregnant? Weren't you taking precautions? You had an accident? But you can't have accidents on the pill!' All of a sudden, as soon as they find out that there is no father, there is this concept that I am a no-hoper or bludger looking for an easy ride on welfare. The nicer ones at least try not to judge you, but then most of them want to offer their condolences instead! So, then I thought I would try 'inventing' a father, but that just got so convoluted and rather embarrassing, because I hate lying, and each lie would foster another one, etc. So I realised that just mentioning the presence of a father was not going to shut people's questions up, just make them take a different line of questioning. But, one thing I did notice was the more positive reactions I got when I mentioned the existence of a partner. Strangely enough it didn't matter that I was not married, it was just enough that I have a partner. Of course, I could just try telling people to mind their own business, but this just seems unnecessarily rude. Daria

Finding a place to live was very hard. I couldn't afford to keep living in the house I shared with my ex, so I needed to find something cheaper and smaller. Most places I found would only let me sign a 6-month lease and I wanted at least 12 months. I explained that I was pregnant and having a baby in 6 months so I couldn't pack up and find somewhere else then. They also looked at me as if I was social reject. (I was single and pregnant with no support in sight.) Yes, I was having a baby in 6 months but I was still employed and was going to be on full time paid leave for at least 4 months after my baby was born, then 6 months half pay before I needed to even consider getting some government support. After the baby was born I was going back to work part time, so I did have the income to pay the rent. It was hard, but eventually I found a nice place and moved in. Michelle

But I'm *not* Old

'Elderly prima gravida'. It sounded ominous, this bit of indecipherable Latin written in large letters at the top of my file that I 'accidentally' saw when my doctor left the room. Finally, after 10 minutes or so, I gathered my courage and asked him what it meant. 'Oh, older first time mother', he replied nonchalantly. Huh! I thought. Old at 32! Many of my friends of the same age were putting babies on hold for at least another couple of years. I certainly didn't feel old. I had seriously considered getting a tattoo for my last birthday. How could I be an 'elderly' anything?

Women between 30 and 34 years of age have the highest fertility rate of all age groups. There are a number of reasons why women are postponing childbirth, from concentrating on their careers and travelling the world to fertility problems, but whatever the cause, most women in their 30s and 40s have healthy pregnancies and healthy babies. However, recent studies suggest that women who postpone childbearing do face some special risks. See Reading Recommendations on page 205 for more information.

Pregnancy in your 30s and 40s

The good news:

- In about 95% of women who undergo prenatal testing their baby does not have any genetic or chromosomal disorders.
- If prenatal testing rules out chromosomal defects and the mother is healthy, the baby is at no greater risk of birth defects than if the mother were in her 20s.
- The likelihood of twins is higher especially between the ages of 35 and 39 (some women think this good!)
- Women between 30 and 40 are no more likely to have a premature or stillborn baby.
- The vast majority of pregnancies in women over 30 result in a healthy baby.

The bad news:

- First-time mothers over 30 are more likely than women in their early 20s to have difficulties in labour.
- A US study has found that women aged 40 and older were three times more likely to have a Caesarean than women in their 20s.
- The likelihood of twins is higher especially between the ages of 35 and 39.
- More women in their 30s and 40s have health problems, such as diabetes or high blood pressure, which may affect their pregnancy.
- The risk of bearing a child with certain chromosomal disorders increases as a woman ages. For example, at age 25, a woman has a 1 in 1250 chance of having a baby with Down syndrome; at age 35, this increases to a 1 in 378 chance; and at age 45, a 1 in 30 chance.
- The rate of miscarriage is greater than that of younger women – at about 12–15% at age 25 rising to 25% at age 40.
- Women over 35 are at risk of more bleeding or placental problems, such as placenta praevia in which the placenta covers part or all of the opening of the cervix; and placental abruption, in which the placenta partly peels away from the wall of the uterus before delivery.
- A 1993 study at the University of Washington, Seattle found that women who

were 40 years or older were more than twice as likely to have a premature or low birth-weight baby than women aged between 20 and 24.

Physically I think it's harder, I have old back injuries and the older I get, the more they make themselves felt. Not being pregnant at the same time as friends was probably the hardest. Not that they weren't all interested, but they weren't going through it at around the same time. As an older mother I do feel a bit left out at times, I'm not 20 or 25 anymore and I do look at things a bit differently. Ali, 43

I always thought I didn't want children. I had a 6-figure salary, holidays overseas and a full social life. Then, at 40, I woke up one day realising time was running out and I did want a child. Desperately. It was hard for me to get pregnant, and when I finally did, I just cried. Wanting a child that much makes all the difference. Merilyn, 43

Simple. I just couldn't have afforded to have a child before now. Penny, 32

I found I was much more ready and willing to give up my hectic social life, in fact it was a kind of relief. Jennifer, 36

Confidence. I just wouldn't have had enough in my 20s to be a good mother. Now I feel perfectly okay saying to the midwives and family, and anyone else who wants to give me advice, to push off if I don't agree. I have my own ideas, from how I wanted to give birth to how I want to bring up my child. Before I would have listened to everyone and not my own judgement. Caren, 41

Emotional and financial security. I wouldn't have been ready to settle down in my 20s and I don't think I could have given enough emotionally. I can also give my child more materially too. Marnie, 38

The Young Mum

Contrary to popular belief, the single mother today is more likely to be 25 rather than 15. It is estimated that there are approximately 87,000 children in England who have a teenage mother. Babies are still born to younger women, whether by accident or design. While a pregnancy may be harder on an older mother physically, being young and pregnant is a heavy, emotional burden. Having to give up a certain lifestyle before you're ready and putting plans on hold is difficult. Having a baby when you're young can mean a future where you're at home while your friends are out partying, travelling or at university; while they're out shopping for new clothes, you're shopping for a pram; while they're out splurging their first pay packet, you're trying to stretch what you have to pay the bills. It's going to be hard, but luckily there is plenty of help and support available. Looking on the positive side, being a young mum means:

- You'll have much more energy throughout pregnancy and afterwards.
- Your body will shape up much more quickly after the birth.
- Having a baby early decreases the risk of breast cancer later in life.
- You'll still be young when your children are grown up and will have time to do all the things you want.

●●●● I wouldn't have chosen to be a mum at 17, but I feel lucky now I did it, although it was much harder back then. Once Jo was in school I went back to university and finished my degree and a few years ago opened my own psychotherapy practice. I'm 34 now and while my friends are all dealing with pre-school runs and toddler tantrums, Jo starts university this year and my current partner and I are planning a 3-month overseas trip. Elisabeth, 34

●●●● I hated being pregnant. My friends would come over and tell me about the party they went to the night before and what a great time they had. It didn't seem fair, I couldn't go out or have any fun. Then when I saw Alisha for the first time, I just fell in love with her. Suddenly all the stuff I missed didn't seem important. I never really had any goals before, I just wanted to leave school as soon as I could. Now I have to look after Alisha. I have a part time job and I am studying at college. I miss her when we're not together, but I have to work hard so I can give her a future. If I didn't have her, I would probably be like my old friends are now, no job, depressed and only interested in drinking and drugs. Keri, 19

On the negative side:

- Teenagers tend to have a significantly higher number of complication rates in childbirth and pregnancy, including prolonged labour.
- Many pregnant teens do not finish their education and so are disadvantaged in the workplace.

- Many teenagers feel isolated or alienated from their families or friends.
- Teenage mothers are at higher risk of anaemia, high blood pressure and placental problems.

However, there is a good support network for teenage or younger mothers. Your doctor or midwife can put you in touch with support groups and organisations who will often help out, not just with emotional support, but often practically too, such as providing baby clothes and equipment.

Younger women don't tend to eat as well as they should, so it's vital to cut out all but the occasional junk food binge, and make sure you get the required vitamins and minerals. Ask your doctor or midwife to refer you to a nutritionist or dietitian if you feel you want some advice on eating well during pregnancy. You may find pamphlets or books in your doctor's waiting room or antenatal clinic as well.

Money, Money, Money

The bad news is that financially speaking, having a baby is possibly the worst investment you could make. According to a survey undertaken by a London magazine, it costs £291 per week, or £15,136 per year. If you're truly a masochist, project yourself into the future and add school fees, child care, extracurricular activities and the feeding and clothing of a growing child. The good news is that most babies can do without the expensive romper suits and designer prams (see Chapter Seven for tips on saving money when buying for the baby).

Nevertheless, money is without doubt one of the biggest hurdles for the single mother. No matter how much money you might be earning now, it's still only one income, compared to a typical two-parent family. It certainly gave me a few sleepless nights wondering how I was going to be able to afford to bring up a child on my own.

The key to reducing stress about money during pregnancy is to deal with it as soon as possible. Try to work out some kind of financial plan to help cover your immediate costs after the birth and get you through the first year. Take into consideration the following:

- How far into the pregnancy do you intend working?
- For how long will you take maternity leave if you intend returning to work and what will your company pay? (See Chapter Five for rules and regulations.)
- Is your baby's father likely to contribute? (He is legally required to if he is informed and doesn't dispute paternity.)
- What benefits, if any, will you be eligible for? (See Chapter Nine.)

Work out your monthly income, where you can comfortably cut costs and sort out a savings plan. If like me, you're an appalling saver, arrange for money to be moved from one account which you use for everyday expenses, to another – a 'baby' account – which can be used for everything baby-related. Shop around to find an account with higher interest rates or investigate an account where you put your money in for a specified time, for example, 3–6 months (providing you know you won't need to touch it.)

Seeing a financial adviser is also a good idea, particularly if you have any savings or want to plan a bit more long term. They can investigate fund managers, shares and stocks and recommend the best way to make the most out of your money.

Stretchmarks

Everyone hates them, but unfortunately, it is the chosen few who don't get them. Stretchmarks occur when the skin stretches during pregnancy causing small tears and the break down of collagen (a protein that gives skin elasticity) in the deeper layers of skin. Some women are more prone to stretchmarks than others, it's a kind of genetic lottery. While it's improbable that you can prevent them if they are in your genetic makeup, healthy skin is the best defence. Eating well so your skin is healthy and you don't put on weight too quickly may help too. Stretchmarks can also affect breasts and upper thighs.

It's worth doing something about stretchmarks sooner rather than later, if you think you'll be bothered by them. If you do get them, accept them and embrace them as your badge of honour, then forget them.

● ● ● ● I found cocoa butter excellent – it's very rich and really helped when my tummy was itchy as it stretched. I used to put it on after having a bath at night, and wear a tatty old t-shirt as it's quite greasy. Susie

● ● ● ● I used aromatherapy oils. A friend told me she had no stretchmarks at all and swore by neroli and lemon oils mixed with wheatgerm, apricot and almond which she'd massage onto her stomach every day. I'd often use it as a bath oil too. It didn't stop me getting stretchmarks, but they're not too bad. Liz

● ● ● ● I took the homeopathic remedy 'Clac flour' all throughout my pregnancy and didn't get any stretchmarks at all. Could be just good luck though! Sarah

Cravings

The stereotypical woman feasting on pickles and ice-cream may be just that, but as many as 90% of pregnant women do have some kind of cravings during their pregnancy and as many as 85% have an aversion to some particular food.

Cravings and aversions are due in some small part (like everything else in pregnancy it seems!) to hormones, which is why they most often occur during the first trimester when hormones are at their most active. A commonly held belief is that cravings are due to the body lacking some essential nutrients, however this has never been scientifically proven. Aversion to certain food may be due to a heightened sense of smell from a change in oestrogen levels. The most common aversions are coffee, tea, alcohol, spicy foods and strong smelling foods such as onions. Another reason for cravings may simply be emotional comfort. During the first half of my pregnancy, I found myself wanting typical childhood comfort food, such as mashed potato, custard and steamed pudding. Aversions and cravings are usually nothing to worry about, except when they cause too much or too little weight gain or result in you becoming nutritionally deficient. There is a condition known as 'Pica' which is a craving for something inedible, such as dirt, soot or chalk. If you have any cravings like this, you should see your doctor immediately, as it may be a sign of anaemia. Eating inedible things, no matter how strong the urge can lead to serious vitamin deficiencies.

Mandarins. I couldn't get enough. I'd go through about 15–20 a day. Nerida

I'm a coffee addict, but by the end of the first month, I'd want to throw up every time I smelt it. Emily

Pickled red cabbage. It had to be a particular brand though. I'd be devastated if I got to the supermarket and they didn't have any. Gina

Paddle-pops and frosty fruits. Kathryn

Lychees. I craved them all through the first 4 months. As the seasons changed and they became harder to get, I would get desperate. I tried tinned ones but they just weren't the same. Then, as quickly as that craving sprang up, it disappeared and I wanted Iced Gems. Lisa

● ● ● ● I couldn't stand the smell of McDonalds. I'd have to cross the road if I saw one and even then hold my breath. If work colleagues came in with takeaway at lunchtime and walk past my desk, I'd have to go and vomit. Helena

● ● ● ● Salt and vinegar crisps. I'd have a packet first thing in the morning and only then could I face the day. Mair

Stars and their Cravings

Catherine Zeta Jones – cake and pizza

Posh Spice – gherkins, chocolate and lobster

Mel B – fish and chips, cheesecake, ice-cream

Cindy Crawford – tacos and burritos

Uma Thurman – doughnuts

Kelly Preston – Spam (tinned ham)

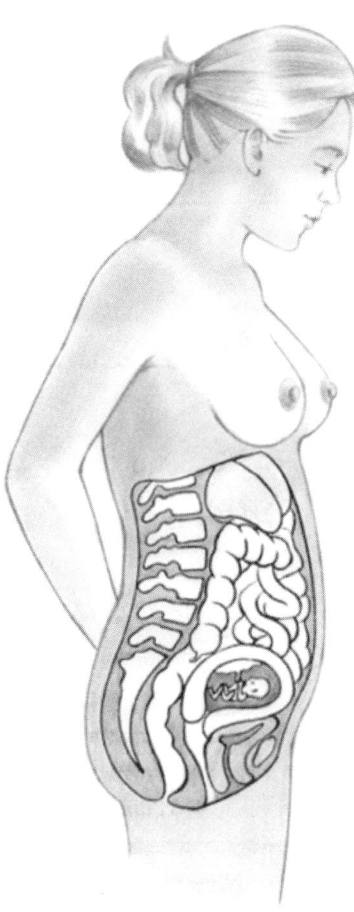

What's Happening? Week 15

You will have an increased blood flow which means your heart has to work harder. Your ligaments continue to stretch, and you may feel some aches and pains in your abdomen. A stuffy nose, due to the membranes in your nasal passages swelling because of hormones, is common now. The areola is darkening.

The baby is about 12cm long and weighs about 135g. Its body is now covered with a fine down called lanugo, which keeps its body temperature regulated. The hair on its head is becoming thicker and its eyelashes are growing. All the baby's organs are now developed. The baby's nails are well formed, and he or she is emptying his or her bladder every 40–45 minutes. Limb movements are becoming more co-ordinated.

This Month's Checklist

- ✓ Tell those closest to you about your pregnancy.
- ✓ Work out a financial plan or visit a financial adviser.
- ✓ Start using some essential oils or creams to try to lessen the effect of stretchmarks.
- ✓ Practise a relaxation technique or treat yourself to a float or massage.

CHAPTER FOUR

WEEKS 16–19

Leg Cramps and Big Pants

What the Hell was That?

Hunger pains? Butterflies? A tickle? A muscle spasm? A twitch? A definite kick! Listening to the baby's heartbeat, or seeing it on ultrasound, doesn't prepare you for the actual physical reality of feeling a living being moving inside you. Although the baby is moving almost from conception, it's only around week 12 and onwards that you'll start to feel his or her presence (most commonly between weeks 14–18).

When you may actually start to feel the baby move depends on its size, position and your size. Overweight women tend to feel movement later than slimmer women, who have less body fat between them and the baby. Women who've had another child may feel the baby move earlier, as they know what to expect and their uterine muscles are more lax making it easier to feel.

Once you've started to recognise the feeling of the baby moving you need to check its movements regularly. If you haven't felt any movement for more than a couple of days, mention it to your doctor or midwife. At this stage, the fetal movements are unlikely to cause you any physical discomfort.

Once I felt it, I knew what it was because I had read in a book that it felt like bubbles bursting and that's exactly what it felt like! Maria

The Sex. To Know or not to Know?

Everyone who knows me knew I could never not want to know. I'm infamous for my curiosity and impatience. There was no way therefore, when the sonographer asked me whether I wanted to know the sex of my baby, I was going to say no. (I actually 'knew' already, having named my baby from the moment I found out I was pregnant. The ultrasound just confirmed there was no point looking at girls' names!) Apart from pure curiosity, I felt I could really have a 'relationship' with my baby once I knew his sex and therefore his name. Other women feel differently, preferring to keep the element of surprise. It's something you'll have to think seriously about BEFORE this month's scan. Unless the baby's position makes it difficult, it's fairly straightforward for the sonographer to be able to distinguish the baby's sex now. If you don't want to know, he or she may have to swivel the screen around so you can't see. Some hospitals have a policy of NOT informing mothers of the sex of their child. In addition, this month's ultrasound will scan for abnormalities, check the baby is growing properly, and check the condition of the placenta and the amount of amniotic fluid present.

No way! I wanted it to be a surprise, a whole part of the childbirth experience is that age-old question, 'Is it a boy or girl?' Mina

I definitely wanted to know. It just seems more practical – I could buy the right clothes and decorate the baby's room appropriately once I knew the sex. Nicole

I have to admit I finally talked myself into wanting to know, (makes it easier to plan financially), but when I went for the ultrasound at 28 weeks, the umbilical cord was carefully drawn up between his or her legs. Thanks very much, bub! Actually, now I don't mind that I don't know, and figure that it will be a really beautiful surprise to take away some of the memory of that awful pain! Kathryn

Age must have something to do with it – all the older women I knew were horrified when I said I was going to find out, while the younger ones agreed it was better to know. My mum even made me promise not to tell her, she wanted it to be a surprise. Ava

I changed my mind all the time about whether I wanted to know. Finally I decided I did, but when it came time for the scan they couldn't see anything anyway. I was sort of glad that it was going to be a surprise. Sophia

Weighing it Up

There are pros and cons of knowing the sex of your baby. Consider the following.

The pros:

- It's easier to bond with the baby once you know the sex.
- You can decorate the nursery or baby's room (or corner if he or she is sleeping with you) appropriately.
- If there is a gender-linked disorder in your family such as haemophilia, it is better to be prepared.

- You can choose a name and call your baby by it when you talk to him or her inutero.
- If you really wanted one or the other sex, you'll have time to come to terms and grow to love it.
- It won't be such a shock.

The cons:

- Tests are not always conclusive and you may get an unexpected shock at the birth.
- It may be hard to keep it from people if they've said they'd prefer not to know.
- The magical element of surprise will be missing.

Predicting the Sex

Here are some old wives' tales about determining the sex.

- Pull down the skin under your left eye and look at your eyeball (the white part). If you see a vein that looks like a V or branches, your baby is a girl.
- If the expectant mother is eating and coughs, ask her to pick a number, then match the number to the corresponding alphabet letter, eg: A=1, B=2, C=3 etc, then ask her to pick a name starting with that letter. If the name she picks is a girl's name, it will be a girl; a boy's name, a boy.
- Have the mother-to-be pick up a single key. If she picks it up by the round part it will be a boy. If she picks up the long narrow part it will be a girl. If she picks it up in the middle she is supposedly having twins.
- The Mayans determined the sex of the baby by taking the mother's age at conception, and the year of conception. If both are even or both are odd...it's a girl. If one is even and one odd it's a boy.
- If the hairs on your legs are growing more quickly it will be a boy.
- If you crave salty foods, it will be a boy. If you want to eat sweet things, a girl.
- Eat a clove of garlic. If the smell of garlic seeps out of your pores, it will be a boy. If it's not detected at all, a girl.
- If you are the first born, you will have what your mother had but starting with the second, then third, then first. If you are the middle child, you will have the third, then second, then first. But if you are the last child, you will have exactly what your mother had.
- Whoever is more aggressive at the time of conception, the child will be the opposite of that sex.

- If your legs resemble tree trunks, it's a boy. If they are trim and fit, it's a girl.
- If you crave the heels of bread, you will have a boy; if you like the middle, a girl is on the way.
- If your hands start to get dry and chapped, it will be a boy; but if your hands are softer now, it will be a girl.
- You eat more if you are pregnant with a boy.
- You are more nauseated with a girl.
- If you are carrying low, it's a boy; girls are carried high.
- Suspend a gold ring on a chain over your belly. If it swings back and forth, it's a girl. If it swings around in circles, it's a boy.
- If you trip or fall over your own feet during pregnancy, it's a boy. If you are graceful, it will be a girl.
- If the heartbeat is low it will be a girl, and if it is high it will be a boy.
- If you prefer to lie on the left when resting, it's a boy, right if it's a girl.
- If your urine is bright yellow you're carrying a boy.
- If the maternal grandmother has grey hair it will be a boy.
- If you sleep with your pillow facing south it will be a girl.
- If your feet are colder than before pregnancy, it will be a boy.
- If the baby's heartbeat is 140 bpm or more it will be a boy.

Antenatal and Other Tests

Depending on various factors such as age, your medical history and any worries about the baby's health, you may be offered several tests to check that the baby is alright. However, if you have strong feelings about it, you are quite within your rights to refuse them. Be aware though, that even if you wouldn't consider a termination if there were an abnormality, knowing about it beforehand can help you prepare both emotionally and practically. See Reading Recommendations on page 207 for more information.

● ● ● ● I'm 41 and when my doctor asked me if I wanted an amniocentesis I said no. I wouldn't have aborted for Down syndrome and therefore the risk of losing the fetus due to the procedure was too high for me. The doctor then said, 'hmmm, well that's your decision, I just had one mother this morning who had a positive result for Down syndrome'. I was disgusted with her, although I was aware of the risks at my age, having an amnio would not have made the fetus less Down syndrome, just let me know about it earlier. Having made that comment she just made me worry over it that much more (and I disliked her more each time!) Although, like everyone else, I wanted the perfect child, I have worked with Down syndrome children – it's difficult for the family but I would cope. The thought of receiving a favourable amniocentesis report a few days after you have miscarried following the procedure is not something I wanted to deal with. Alison

● ● ● ● Waiting for the results of my amnio was the worst two weeks of my life. I had only just come to terms with becoming pregnant when I was told I should consider an amniocentesis because of my age (38). During this time I constantly replayed scenarios in my head about how I could cope with a disabled child and felt heart-wrenching guilt because I knew I didn't want to just 'cope'. Then I would have nightmares about having to go through a termination or labour. I was so stressed I couldn't concentrate on anything or sleep. My hair fell out and I lost weight. Finally the big day arrived and terrified I sat in the waiting room with a kind friend who had come to support me. When the doctor gave me the good news that everything was alright I burst into tears and couldn't stop crying for the next hour. Then I went home and had the best sleep I'd had in months. I really feel for other women who have to go through that! Trish

Amniocentesis

This test is most frequently done on women aged over 35 who are more at risk of having a baby with a chromosomal abnormality such as Down syndrome, if there is some family history of chromosomal abnormalities, or if other tests have shown something abnormal. It's usually done between weeks 16 to 18. An amnio involves having a long fine needle inserted through your abdomen into the uterus from where a sample of amniotic fluid is taken from around the baby (which, apparently isn't as bad as it sounds). Ultrasound is used to guide the needle. The results, which can detect neural tube defects, Down syndrome, some intellectual disabilities and chromosomal abnormalities are very accurate, but can take up to 3 weeks to come through. There is also a slight increased risk (about 1 in 200) of miscarrying after the test. Because of the amount of time it takes for the results to get back, you may be up to 20 weeks pregnant and will most probably have to undergo an induced labour, if you want to terminate the pregnancy.

AFP

Alpha-fetoprotein (AFP) is routinely offered at 15–18 weeks. This simple blood test measures the level of alpha-fetoprotein, a protein produced by the fetus.

Abnormal levels indicate the possibility (not existence) of Down syndrome or a neural tube defect such as spina bifida, which can then be confirmed by ultrasound or amniocentesis. Only a couple of women out of 50 with high readings will out to have an affected fetus. Other reasons for a high reading may be that there is more than one fetus, or the pregnancy is further along than originally suspected.

When blood is taken for the AFP test, it is also used to check levels of the hormones oestriol and hCG. This test significantly boosts the detection rates for Down syndrome, picking up about 80% of neural tube defects and 70% of Down syndrome. However, the test will often return a false positive screening.

About 3% to 5% of women who have the screening test will have an abnormal reading, but only about 10% of those women will have a child with a genetic problem.

When Something's Wrong

If tests show that there's a suggestion that something's wrong with the baby you will be informed as quickly as possible, and tests will be repeated so there is no margin for error. Counselling will be offered and all options discussed. These may include:

- Treatment, where possible. Often, with today's new brand of super medicine and depending on the severity of the condition, there may be something that can be done, or
- Termination. On other occasions, the defect or abnormality may be so severe that termination may be offered.

If the news is bad, you will probably be offered professional support, from a genetic counsellor, specialist midwife or therapist, who can help you work through the myriad issues you have to deal with. Emotional support is also vital, and you should take your pregnancy partner to any further appointments.

Remember though, in less than 6% of all live births is there any sort of defect. Half of these are non-life threatening and many can be corrected with surgery.

There's More than One in There

For some women the words, 'There's more than one in there', usually uttered by a smiling ultrasound operator, can strike a chill into the heart. For others, it means a double celebration. You may have suspected something, and this is just confirmation, or it may come as a complete and utter heart-stopping shock.

Fraternal twins are twice as likely to give birth to twins, as are women over 35, as often more than one egg is released.

How Twins Happen

Normally, a woman's body releases only one egg from her ovary, however, twins can be conceived through the woman's body releasing two eggs, which are then fertilised by two separate sperm. Identical twins occur when one egg fertilised by one sperm divides, resulting in two babies with the same genetic makeup. Unlike fraternal twins, identical twins share a placenta, although each has separate umbilical cords.

If having a baby on your own is twice as difficult, the reality is that for the single woman bringing up not one but two or more babies is going to require even more help and support. Not just with feeding, clothing and baby paraphernalia, but both the pregnancy and delivery might go ahead in a different way.

Carrying more than one baby does have a higher risk of complications than a single pregnancy and it's usually recommended you see an obstetrician. If you have complications or are carrying triplets, you may be referred to a specialist obstetrician who has received additional training in maternal fetal medicine and specialises in high-risk pregnancies.

Your Body and Twins

You'll need to be more careful of your nutrition, consuming an extra 1250kj a day, supplementing your diet with extra vitamins and minerals and resting more, to take care of the extra pressure your body is put under due to extra weight gain etc. You'll probably be scheduled to see your doctor more often, for example, every other week from week 20, then weekly after week 30.

You may find you have morning sickness for longer and worse than other women, due to the extra hormones in your body, and other pregnancy-related problems, such as backache, haemorrhoids, and high blood pressure. You need to rest more and the chance of having a Caesarean is higher. You are also twice as likely to deliver before 37 weeks, and as a result, multiple birth babies are likely to be smaller.

How You Might Feel

It's normal to feel ambivalent about carrying twins or more, to worry about the physical, emotional and financial aspects of having more than one child at a time, particularly as a single mother. You may feel you need some counselling and practical advice. The Twins and Multiple Births Association (TAMBA) can supply over-the-phone counselling and advice for mothers-to-be of multiples. In addition, they also produce a newsletter, with second-hand equipment for sale, such as double prams (see Useful Contacts on page 210).

See Reading Recommendations on page 205 for books about having twins.

Hormones

One minute you may be in floods of tears just watching an advertisement on TV, the next you're feeling high as a kite. Hormones, which are chemicals released by the body's glands to help it prepare for pregnancy and birth are to blame for most of our emotional and physical changes during pregnancy. But what are they and why do we need them?

Oestrogens

- Essential for your reproductive system to function normally.
- Prepare the body for pregnancy by suppressing other hormones.
- Help the fertilised egg to implant in the uterus.
- Help the embryo to receive nourishment.
- Essential for the development of the female sexual organs in the fetus.

Endorphins – The 'Happy Hormones'

- Calming. Help you deal with stress during pregnancy.
- Released when giving birth, endorphins help control the pain threshold.
- Can often give you a natural 'high' in pregnancy and birth.

Relaxin

- Produced by the placenta, it relaxes and softens ligaments and joints, its purpose to allow the baby to get through the birth canal.

Progesterone

- This female hormone is produced in the placenta after week 10 and is necessary for the pregnancy to reach full term.
- Prepares the uterus for the fertilised egg.
- Prevents the woman from going into premature labour by stopping the involuntary muscles from contracting strongly and bringing on an early labour.
- Contributes to breast changes.

Prostaglandins

- Stimulate the uterus in late pregnancy causing contractions.
- Help to 'ripen' the cervix.

Adrenalin

- Activated by stress or excitement, it increases your heartbeat, blood flow to the muscles and opens the airways which improves breathing.
- Stimulates contractions during labour.

Oxytocin

- Stimulates contraction of the uterus during labour and after birth.
- Helps the milk glands to produce milk.

Prolactin

- In conjunction with other hormones, stimulates the growth and development of the breasts.
- Helps the body create a milk supply.

Sex during Pregnancy

Many women find their libidos fire up during pregnancy, while others lose their sex drive altogether. Some find they can orgasm for the first time, many becoming multi-orgasmic. If you feel like having sex, there is absolutely no medical reason not to, unless advised by your doctor. The fetus is cushioned safely in its amniotic sac and sealed inside the uterus and so it can't be hurt. When you have an orgasm the baby can't feel it, but will get a euphoric hormone rush as you do. You may feel the contractions of the uterus more than pre-pregnancy, due to its enlarged size. If you do have sex, make sure you use condoms to protect yourself and your baby from disease. If having oral sex, don't let your partner blow air into your vagina. This could cause an embolism, which could potentially be fatal.

Vaginal secretions often change in pregnancy, and lubrication may increase in volume or diminish. If you feel a bit dry, use a lubricant.

When having sex, you may find the missionary position restrictive or uncomfortable. Instead try these positions:

- Your partner lies on top, but keeps the weight on his arms, rather than on your abdomen.
- Lie on your back at the side or foot of the bed with your knees bent, and

your bottom and feet perched at the edge of the mattress. Your partner can either kneel or stand in front of you.

- Lie side-by-side in the spoon position, which allows for only shallow penetration. Deep thrusts can become uncomfortable as the months pass.
- Get on top. It puts no weight on your abdomen and allows you to control the depth of penetration.
- Enter from a sitting position, which also puts no weight on the uterus. Try sitting on your partner's lap as he sits on a chair.

Eek, What's Happening to my Body?

You'll probably be fatter. Your hair might be thicker, or it could have thinned somewhat. If it was curly, it might now be straight and vice-versa. You could have skin as soft and unblemished as a baby's bottom, or have a face full of teenage-like eruptions. You could be ravenous, or still unable to stand the thought of food. Your breasts will probably be fuller and the areola bigger and darker. You might find that you are more energetic and vital or you could still be hitting the pillow at 8.00 p.m. You may notice a dark line down the centre of your abdomen. This is known as the linea nigra and will fade after childbirth. Your belly button may have popped out and will stay that way until after the birth.

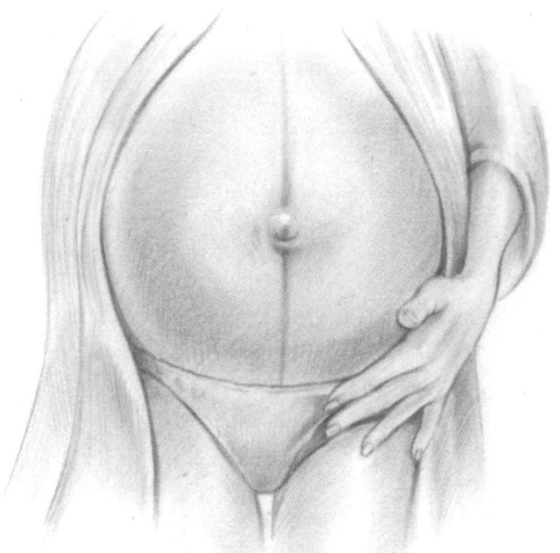

A dark line called the linea nigra may appear down the centre of your abdomen during pregnancy.

Some women revel in the changes their body is going through, others are ambivalent, feel self-conscious, depressed or pine for their pre-pregnancy selves. Whatever your feelings, role models such as Demi Moore and Cindy Crawford have shown us that it's possible to be beautiful and pregnant and to even go back to how we were after birth. (Admittedly, bags of money and a personal trainer probably help!)

Most of these changes aren't permanent, and will disappear if not during the pregnancy, then after the birth. If you feel brave enough, get a friend to take regular photos of you, to document your changing body and serve as a permanent reminder – you may not appreciate the beauty of your body now, but you may feel differently in years to come.

Pregnancy may make you Smarter!

Although you may often feel like you're too often exhausted and living in a permanent state of forgetfulness, research by neuroscientists at the University of Richmond and Randolph Macon College in Virginia, USA have found that dendrites (special brain cell structures) doubled in pregnancy, as did the number of glial cells, which act as communication conductors. In a study performed on mice, it was found that the pregnant mice were more energetic, curious and more fearless. They learned mazes quickly and made fewer mistakes, and that these effects were long lasting.

Smilers, Starers and Tummy Touchers

It's fascinating to see how other people react to your changing shape. You'll suddenly find yourself the object of fond smiles from grannies, understanding ones from mothers who've 'been there' and solicitousness from just about everyone. Suddenly people start holding doors open for you, rush to pick up dropped objects and constantly inquire about your health. while others will just want to reach out and touch your 'bump'. Some women find this annoying, patronising and intrusive, others revel in the attention. Whatever your feelings, a pregnant woman is often an object of beauty and mystery for men and awakens strong feelings of solidarity in women, so try to have patience with the smilers, starers and tummy touchers!

Big Pants

Depending on how big you are, you may find it increasingly difficult to fit into your regular clothes by the end of this month and it may be time to start thinking about changing your wardrobe. It's not necessary to run out and buy a whole new wardrobe of special pregnancy outfits, but you might find things like maternity trousers and jeans especially tailored to go over the bump are more comfortable. The good news is that maternity clothes aren't what they used to be – frumpy, bow-adorned tent dresses and unflattering dungarees that make you look like a Play School presenter. Today's maternity clothes are fashionable, even occasionally funky, and best of all, bumps are 'in', so there's no need for loose, baggy clothes.

Lycra and stretch jersey that proudly emphasise, rather than cover up your state, might have little old ladies tut-tutting, but they are now the accepted norm. There are maternity shops in most major cities and usually big department stores stock maternity wear. If you find it hard to get out to shop, many offer mail order or Internet shopping. (See Useful Contacts on page 211 for details.)

Cheapskate Maternity Tips

- Beg, borrow or steal from post-pregnant friends.
- Buy a capsule wardrobe such as the 'pregnancy survival kit' which contains four pieces – leggings, skirts, and long and short sleeved tops.
- People notice your bump more than what you're wearing, so don't worry about wearing the same thing over and over. Just add different accessories.
- There is an increasing number of second-hand maternity shops around and you'll find that many of the things they sell are barely worn.
- Maternity swimmers aren't really necessary, as long as your costume has plenty of Lycra to stretch over your tummy and wide enough straps for good bust support.
- Stretch jersey is a great fabric. It is low maintenance, comfortable, usually cheap and you can often wear it afterwards too.
- Buy a belly belt. This great invention which buttons into your jeans, skirts and trousers allows you to extend your clothes to suit your expanding tummy. It's available from major department stores and maternity shops.
- If you have to look smart for work, wear a maternity dress with a tailored pre-pregnancy jacket or little cardigan unbuttoned over the top.
- Sarongs are great for casual wear to accommodate a growing belly. When you get too big to tie it around twice, do the one-and-a-half tie. (Put it on and gather the material in your right hand. Wrap the other piece around as far as it will go, then grab a bit of the material and tie it to the first bit. Wrap the excess around as far as it will go and tuck into the waist.)

Dressing Tips

- A pregnant woman's body temperature is often a bit up and down, so wear layers you can strip off as you get hot.
- Look for pants with a waistband that cradles the belly or is big enough to stretch over it.
- If you haven't bought a good maternity bra, buy one now, made from 100% cotton with wide straps and adjustable hooks at the back to accommodate your growing size.
- Support pantyhose may not look sexy, but then neither do varicose veins. Wearing them will help with the blood circulation in your legs and hopefully prevent varicose veins.
- Most women feel more comfortable with pants that go over the bump or bikini style ones that sit under it. You can often buy special maternity ones with added support.
- You may have to invest in new shoes, to accommodate your bigger feet, which may have grown a size thanks to fluid retention and the joints loosening up in your body. Choose comfortable flat shoes with wise chunky heels. Slip-ons make it easy as you get bigger and you can't see your feet anymore to tie laces! Wear air-cushioned trainers when possible.
- Make sure not to buy anything restrictive around your midsection.

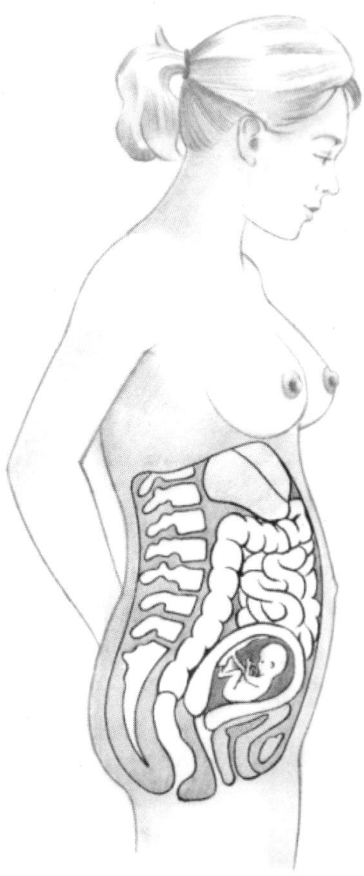

What's Happening? Week 19

Your belly button may pop out now and stay that way until delivery. You might find yourself feeling a bit breathless as your lungs are compressed by the internal organs being pushed up. You may need to urinate more frequently, due to the pressure on your bladder.

The baby is approximately 25.5cm long, about half its birth length. It is swallowing amniotic fluid, which helps it exercise its digestive muscles. The baby's movements are more complex and it may be sucking its thumb. Lanugo forms from sebum and skin cells to create vernix (a creamy white substance believed to help protect the baby inutero). Vernix will cling to the lanugo and in the creases. Your baby may now have a pattern of being awake and asleep (usually opposite to yours!)

This Month's Checklist

- ✓ Look into buying a few comfortable maternity pieces to supplement your wardrobe.
- ✓ Keep note of any unusual symptoms you may be having and report them to your doctor or midwife.
- ✓ Try some gentle aerobic exercise such as swimming or walking.

CHAPTER FIVE

WEEKS 20–23

Halfway There

Work

Thank goodness things have changed since our mother's day when the pregnant woman was required to leave work, often never to return. Today, most healthy pregnant women work throughout some, if not all, of their pregnancy and there are strict regulations governing employer's attitudes towards them.

If you haven't told anyone at work yet, now might be the time to think about it. Apart from stopping the speculation (or simply fuelling the gossip!) it gives your employer plenty of notice to have you train someone to take over your role while you are on maternity leave, or allows them to think about hiring a temp. You may also need to take time off work to attend appointments.

It's probably best to make an appointment with your immediate boss and/or personnel officer and to be prepared for a number of reactions – from total support to resentment or anger. Statistics show that the most discrimination against women happens when they are pregnant.

Your Requirements

Whether you have full time, part time or casual employment:

- You are not legally required to inform your employer of your pregnancy until you are 24 weeks pregnant.
- If you do inform your employer unofficially now, you need to put it in writing.
- Four weeks before the date you have given to leave, you need to inform them of how long you intend having off.
- You need to provide your employer with a maternity certificate confirming you are pregnant and your expected date. The total time allowed away from work is 26 weeks. If you have worked for your employer continuously for 26 weeks into the 15th week before the week your baby is due, you may be able to get additional maternity leave, which lasts for 26 weeks from the end of ordinary maternity leave.

- It would be useful to write to your employer 4 weeks before you intend to return informing them of your return to work date.
- If you decide to resign from your job while on maternity leave you must give 2 weeks notice, or one month's notice if you are paid monthly.

● ● ● ● I did not make any official announcement at work until week 18, because of my concern with regard to the viability of my pregnancy, and also uncertainty as to how the news would be received in my workplace. I was employed in a professional and responsible position, and there were no precedents for single mothers in that particular environment. Dorothy

Sources of Income

There are various sources of income available for women during pregnancy and they all have different requirements for qualification. You should access the Department for Work and Pensions website for the most current information (see Useful Contacts on page 211).

Statutory Maternity Pay (SMP) is paid to you by your employer. You must be employed in the 15th week before the week your baby is due and employed for at least 26 weeks into the 15th week before your baby is due. You can choose when you start SMP as long as it is not before 28 weeks. SMP is paid for up to 26 weeks.

You may be able to claim Maternity Allowance if you cannot get Statutory Maternity Pay if you are self-employed or earning over £30 per week (see Useful Contacts on page 211–212).

Employer's Requirements

- Your employer cannot dismiss or retrench you because of your pregnancy.
- Your employer must provide a larger size uniform if they normally provide a uniform.
- Your employer cannot transfer you to another job 'out of the public eye' because you are pregnant.
- You cannot be prevented from receiving a promotion because you are pregnant.
- Your employer must inform your replacement that their job is temporary.
- Your employer must give you back the position you held before maternity leave or if it no longer exists, one at the same level and salary.
- If you went on to part time work during or after the pregnancy, your employer must reinstate you to the original full time position afterwards.

- If your job is a risk to your pregnancy, your employer must adjust your duties/position accordingly.

Discrimination

If you think you are being discriminated against because of your pregnancy, seek immediate advice from your union or one of the contacts under Useful Contacts on page 211. The Department of Trade and Industry publishes *Maternity Rights: A Guide for Employers and Employees* (PL958) which can be downloaded from their website. Discrimination includes:

- Not hiring you because you are or might become pregnant.
- Not giving you access to training or promotion because you are pregnant.
- Trying to make you take maternity leave before you want to.
- Not employing you because you are suspended from work for health and safety reasons connected with your pregnancy.
- Discriminating against you because of your shape.

●●●● Because I work with the elderly, most responded quite guardedly. They were polite but didn't initiate conversation about it. One woman would ask me, as an aside in a whisper, how my pregnancy was as if it was a big secret (a bit hard to keep secret when one's tummy is bulging!) Another woman commented that she didn't know I was married. When I told her I wasn't she then asked how had I fallen pregnant! Jane

●●●● My boss at work, strangely enough, was very supportive, and assured me that I could work as long as I felt comfortable. Kathryn

●●●● I was doing temp work at the time, and one of the jobs I was sent for was for a 3-month maternity cover! I really needed the work and was worried about telling them, but had no choice as I was starting to show. I needn't have worried, they were great. Turns out the girl I was replacing was replacing someone else who got pregnant, so my chair was nicknamed 'the pregnancy chair'. They never made an issue of my pregnancy, despite the fact that I was very much in the public eye and having to deal with major big-wigs and were wonderful when I had to take time off to go to appointments and the like. Helen

The Work Environment

It is medically accepted that some workplaces and occupations do represent a health risk for pregnant women, possibly causing miscarriage, stillbirth or premature birth.

These include:

- Working with chemicals or toxins in workplaces such as operating theatres, photographic labs, dry cleaners, dental surgeries, chemists, cosmeticians and factories.
- Jobs which require heavy lifting or strenuous activity.
- Working with animals or meat which could expose you to Toxoplasmosis.
- Working in unhealthy environments, such as pubs, where you are exposed to high levels of cigarette smoke.

Most offices and workplaces are non-smoking these days so exposure to cigarette smoke should be minimal. Make sure if you sit for long periods of time that you have a comfortable chair with good back support. Put a small cushion in the small of your back if you need extra support. Take frequent short breaks, stand up and walk around or do under the desk foot and leg exercises to keep the circulation going. Air-conditioning and heating are very drying, so make sure you drink lots of water throughout the day. Forget the high heels, wear comfortable flatties instead.

If you have any concerns that your work environment have affect your health during pregnancy, speak to your doctor or midwife who can tell you whether your job is okay for your condition. If you're worried about your work environment or any hazards involved in your job, contact your union, who may be able to give you some more information. Your employer is required to move you to another position at the same pay if it's found you are exposed to hazards (see Chapter Five for more information on work and your rights).

If you are unemployed, you will need a letter of confirmation of your pregnancy and due date from your doctor or midwife, so you will be exempted from looking for work with out having your benefits cut off. If you are on income support, Jobseeker's Allowance or getting Working Families Tax Credit, you could claim a Sure Start Maternity Grant. You will need to get the grant form from your local Job Centre Plus Office.

Visual Display Units (VDUs)

You may have heard some information about the effect of radiation from your computer on the unborn baby. It's a contentious subject, but as yet, studies have uncovered very little concrete evidence. However, do ask your doctor or midwife about any recent research and if it makes you feel safer, have an electrically conductive filter placed over the screen.

Travelling when Pregnant

Travelling may be necessary for your job, or you might want to take a last, relaxing holiday before the birth. This trimester is probably the best time to travel. Usually, morning sickness has passed and you're often feeling more energetic. However there are some things to consider before you plan a trip:

- The climate. A pregnant woman's metabolism is faster, causing her body temperature to be higher. Therefore travelling to a hot climate may make you feel uncomfortable and tired.
- The altitude. The lack of oxygen at high altitude may be hard to adjust to.
- The location. Going to a Third World country where hygiene is low and disease rife is a bad idea for a pregnant woman. It may be difficult to drink safe, clean water, and medical help may be hard to come by if you experience any problems. Also, most vaccinations are not recommended for pregnant women.(Check with your doctor or NHS Direct for safe vaccines.) Travelling vast distances, no matter by which method can also be very draining.

Driving

When wearing your seat belt, make sure it goes across your thighs and above your 'bump', rather than across the middle of it. If you were in an accident, the pressure from the belt could hurt the baby if it were across your middle. If you're driving long distances, make sure to have frequent stops to stretch your legs, go to the toilet and have something to eat. Carry nutritious snacks with you. If you have to drive a lot, try a cushion in the small of your back for extra support.

If you're lucky enough to have a car with an adjustable steering column, you may be able to put it slightly higher for your comfort. If you're a passenger, put your seat back as far as it goes and try to put your feet up on something, such as an overnight bag.

Train Travel

A great alternative to driving, or taking a bus, is a train, as it allows you to get up and walk. Make sure to take a sleeper if you are travelling a long distance. You may want to bring snacks, such as fresh fruit and juice, in case the buffet car doesn't have any.

Flying

Most airlines require you to have a doctor's letter confirming it's safe for you to travel after about 24 weeks. This is usually given unless there is some problem with high blood pressure or a threatened miscarriage early in the pregnancy that could cause you to go into premature labour, due to the change in air pressure. Some international airlines won't let you travel after 32 weeks regardless. Following are some tips when flying long distances:

- Before planning a long haul flight, okay it with your doctor.
- If you do have to fly long haul, try to break it up with a stopover half way.
- Make copies of your medical notes and carry them with you.
- Contact the embassy/tourist board of the countries you will be visiting for details of the locations of hospitals and carry them with you just in case.
- Carry a list of names and numbers of people you want to be contacted in case of problems.
- Check your travel insurance and/or private medical cover to see if it covers a hospital stay in a foreign country for a pregnancy-related problem.
- You won't be allowed to sit in the emergency exits of planes if you are pregnant, so try to request a bulkhead seat a week or so beforehand by ringing the airline and telling them you're pregnant.
- When you get on board, seek out a flight attendant and tell them you're pregnant, and if they could find you a seat with a couple of spares next to you, where you can stretch out, you'd be very grateful. If this is impossible, ask for an aisle seat, so you can get up and down easily to go to the toilet.
- Don't overpack and use a suitcase with an extending handle and wheels.
- Wear layers in case you get hot or cold.
- Get up and walk around every 2 hours and do foot exercises, such as rotating your ankles frequently.
- Ask your midwife about wearing anti-embolic support socks.
- Drink lots of water.
- Try to get some rest. Take earplugs and an eye mask if necessary.
- Wear loose comfortable clothing. Massage sandals are a good idea too, or shoes that are adjustable such as with velcro fasteners, in case your feet swell.

● ● ● ● I flew from England to Australia at 7½ months. Some carriers wouldn't even take me, and once I found one who would, I had to get a doctor's certificate, with my due date and a confirmation there were no problems in my pregnancy. How this was supposed to stop me going into premature labour, I don't know! The flight was pretty bad because it was packed and they wouldn't let me sit in the emergency exit seats where at least I could have put my feet up. I walked around a lot and tried to do some exercise, but still ended up with ankles twice their normal size. I'm really glad

I decided to stop over a night in Singapore. I got off the plane, and the wonderful hostess arranged a ride in one of those little buggies for me, so I didn't have to walk down endless airport corridors. I left most of my stuff in an airport locker, jumped into a taxi and was soaking in a warm bubble bath in a luxury hotel in no time. My flight didn't leave until the next evening, so the following morning, I went downstairs to the 'beauty spa' and had a facial and reflexology, which helped the swelling in my ankles no end. I ended up arriving looking great, glowing and relaxed after having a good night's sleep. Mind you, I never would have survived doing it straight through. Allison

Common Complaints

Some women never have any problems during their pregnancy; others have everything going and feel like their body's falling apart. Here are some of the myriad complaints you might (or might not!) suffer during your pregnancy. Remember to see your doctor if any of these complaints become unbearable.

Hyperemesis Gravidarum

Fairly rare in pregnancy, this condition causes excessive vomiting, often lasting the entire 9 months, rather than in the case of morning sickness which usually ends after the first trimester. In severe cases, it can lead to dehydration of the mother, a lack of nutrition and possible damage to the baby. Before an announcement of hyperemesis gravidarum is made, other tests will be done to rule out other causes of vomiting, such as gastrointestinal disorders or an ulcer.

Treatment of hyperemesis gravidarum must be undertaken by a health professional and may include dietary modification, hospitalisation and intravenous feeding in severe cases, stress relief techniques and a general edict to take it easy. Eat smaller, more frequent meals, and avoid fried fatty foods which are harder to digest. You may find it aggravated by dairy products and might need to swap to soy or rice milk (preferably calcium enriched).

Heartburn

Blame hormones for this one. They soften the sphincter between the oesophagus and stomach, which lets stomach acid back up into the oesophagus causing a burning sensation. This tends to get worse in later pregnancy as the growing baby pushes all your organs up. Suggestions to relieve heartburn include:

- Eating smaller meals more often. Also avoid spicy food and oily things.
- Eating yoghurt after a meal.
- Milk.
- The homeopathic remedy, Mercurius Solubilis.
- Try to sleep propped up, which will stop the contents of the stomach rising into the oesophagus.
- Drink a glass of water with a teaspoon of cider vinegar before eating.

Fainting and Feeling Light-headed

This is common during pregnancy, as most of the blood supply is around the lower body and the brain may become temporarily deprived of oxygen. Suggestions to avoid fainting or light-headedness include:

- Avoid standing for long periods of time.
- When resting, lie on your side as opposed to your back and always get up slowly.
- Don't take very hot baths and try to avoid the heat as much as possible.
- Eat small protein-rich snacks throughout the day so your blood sugar isn't low.
- Try a few drops of Bach Rescue Remedy as soon as you start to feel dizzy.
- If it persists, discuss it with your doctor or midwife.

Constipation and Haemorrhoids

Digestive problems caused by hormonal changes, iron tablets and a lack of fibre in your diet can result in constipation, which in turn can lead to haemorrhoids. These are varicose veins of the rectum and can affect up to half of all pregnant women. They are mainly caused by straining and pushing and can be itchy, painful and cause bleeding. Following are suggestions to prevent constipation and haemorrhoids:

- Do regular exercise, especially squatting.
- Drink 8-12 glasses of water a day.
- Get plenty of fibre in your diet.
- Avoid long hours of standing.
- Avoid straining your bowels.
- Drink prune juice.
- Make sure your iron supplement contains vitamin C to help with absorption.
- Buy a commercial preparation bought from the chemist that alleviates these conditions.
- Use ice packs.
- Take warm salt baths.

- Try the homeopathic treatment, Hamamelis.
- Apply comfrey ointment to the anal area three times a day.
- Apply wet baking soda to take away the itch or add it to your bath.
- Apply comfrey or yellowdock root ointment to your anal area.
- Take Psyllium husks for a gentle, natural laxative effect.

Leg Cramps

These plagued me throughout my pregnancy, usually waking me in agony at 3.00 a.m. They are pretty common during pregnancy and can be caused by a lack of calcium, circulation changes, or the extra weight you're carrying. Suggestions to relieve leg cramps include:

- Regular exercise.
- Massaging the area when cramp strikes.
- Magnesia Phosphorica 6X (use the homeopathy treatment or tissue salts).
- Extra calcium in your diet.

Coughs and Colds

You might have to think twice about reaching for a bottle of cough medicine because of the drugs in it. Prevention is therefore better than cure. To alleviate coughs and colds during pregnancy:

- Eat well and include lots of food high in vitamin C in your diet.
- Get plenty of rest.
- Eating garlic or onions can help with infections, but only eat them if they don't give you indigestion.
- If you feel really stuffed up, use a humidifier with a couple of drops of eucalyptus essential oil.
- Drink hot water with lemon and honey.

Varicose Veins

Varicose veins are due to the increased blood flow and relaxation of the muscular walls of the blood vessels, which make it more difficult for the blood to reach the lower body. They may be partly hereditary, but if you are careful they can usually be avoided. To avoid varicose veins:

- Massage can be used as a preventative measure but not once they have already appeared.
- Wear supportive stockings such as those made specially for pregnant women and try to avoid standing for long periods of time.

- Get regular exercise.
- Eat a good diet with lots of garlic, onion, ginger and capsicum which break down the clotting agent in blood.
- Keep your feet raised whenever you can.
- Eat horse chestnut which may help increase the flow of blood.

Anaemia

A lack of iron resulting in anaemia is very common during pregnancy. Anaemia is a lack of red blood cells in your bloodstream and can make you feel very listless. If you suspect you may be anaemic, tell your doctor or midwife, who will do a blood count to measure your haemoglobin and may prescribe iron tablets. To avoid anaemia:

- Try eating lots of iron rich foods such as leafy greens, parsley, and avoid caffeine as it can interfere with the absorption of iron.

Carpal Tunnel Syndrome

Lots of women find themselves affected with this during pregnancy. Carpal tunnel syndrome, which is usually in the wrist, is caused by a trapped nerve and can be very painful. It can affect you particularly if you do a lot of repetitive tasks such as typing. Suggestions to relieve carpal tunnel syndrome include:

- Massage.
- Acupuncture.
- If you regularly use a computer, get a wrist rest.

Swollen Ankles

Your potassium/sodium level is affected by oestrogen, making your ankles retain fluid. It seems to get worse in hot weather or when standing or sitting for long periods of time. Apart from being unsightly, this is not usually a problem, but if you feel your ankles are unduly swollen, if the problem persists for more than 24 hours, or if it's accompanied by swelling of the hands and/or face, see your doctor or midwife. To avoid swollen ankles:

- Wear support pantyhose and flat shoes.
- Keep your feet up when possible.
- Lie on your left side to reduce pressure to the major blood vessels.
- If you can still reach your ankles, massage with an oil base with a few drops of peppermint essential oil.
- Drink lots of water.

Headaches

Some women find they get headaches more frequently throughout pregnancy. The problem is that you can't run to the medicine cabinet as you normally would. Try to analyse what may be causing the headache; common causes include tiredness, stress and dehydration. Hormones are also to blame. Try some relaxation techniques, drink plenty of water and massage the base of your neck and shoulders with a few drops of lavender oil added to almond oil. If headaches persist, visit your doctor or midwife.

High Blood Pressure

About 2% of women will develop high blood pressure during pregnancy. Your doctor or midwife will be constantly monitoring your blood pressure through the pregnancy. Usually, your doctor will recommend rest, and perhaps calcium supplements, but if the elevated blood pressure is accompanied by swelling, excessive weight gain, or protein in the urine, they may be indications of pre-eclampsia (also known as HDP – hypertensive disease of pregnancy or PIH – Pregnancy Induced Hypertension). The danger of pre-eclampsia is serious to the unborn child. Clots and fatty acids can build up in the placenta causing it not to function correctly and premature labour may occur. Should pre-eclampsia become severe, and become eclampsia, it can cause fits, and possibly coma. Apart from high blood pressure and protein in the urine, which a doctor or midwife would easily pick up, signs to watch out for include:

- Severe headache.
- Nausea.
- Vomiting.
- Pain in the abdomen.
- Swelling of hands and feet.
- Weight gain.
- Blurred vision or visual disturbances.
- Fever.
- Rapid heartbeat.
- All over itching.

Gum Bleeds

Don't panic if your toothbrush suddenly turns pink. Bleeding gums are common in pregnancy. Because of hormones, gums often become inflamed, and tend to bleed easily. They can become prone to infection, too, so brush gently and practise good oral hygiene. A visit to the dentist may be a good idea, as it will be more difficult once the baby's born, but tell the dentist you are pregnant, as there are some procedures which shouldn't be performed on pregnant women, such as x-rays and procedures that involve the mother lying down for too long.

Bleeding gums can be a sign of vitamin C and bioflavonoid deficiency, so make sure you include lots of fresh fruit and vegetables in your diet. NHS Dental treatment is free while you are pregnant and for 12 months after the birth (see Useful Contacts on page 212).

Nasal Congestion

Extra oestrogen softens and thickens the mucus membranes causing this common complaint. It's more common in winter, when heating systems dry out the air. It's important not to use nasal sprays or medication unless prescribed by your doctor.

To alleviate a runny nose:

- Place a dab of Vaseline in each nostril, which will help lubricate them.
- Use a humidifier to counteract the dry air.
- Inhale the steam from a couple of drops of eucalyptus oil in hot water.
- Take a ¼ of a teaspoon of salt and mix with 250ml water. Dissolve well and put two drops in each nostril. Wait 5–10 minutes then gently blow your nose.

Nose bleeds are also common during pregnancy, as your increased blood supply puts pressure on the small delicate veins in your nose. Blowing your nose gently and keeping the mucous membranes well hydrated by drinking plenty of water may help reduce nose bleeds.

Fears and Dreams

Vivid dreams are common during pregnancy. It's a way of the subconscious dealing with worries and fears. Often you'll dream of your baby and common themes seem to be leaving it somewhere, or forgetting it. These are normal 'can I really cope?' manifestations. Other common themes are the fear of something being wrong with the baby or the fear of childbirth itself, worries about how you will cope with such a radical change in lifestyle, how your body may 'never be the same', what is going to happen to your career? Listen to your dreams and try to work out what you're really worried about, so you can deal with it. Keeping a dream diary and writing down your dreams as soon as you wake can be useful in getting to the bottom of those sometime cryptic subconscious messages.

Bringing up a baby alone is one of the issues that is going to constantly rear its ugly head, both in conscious and unconscious hours. Don't try to be a superwoman – voice your fears to supportive family and friends, and physical ones to your doctor or midwife.

Fears about giving birth are normal too. Just remind yourself, that if childbirth were so terrible, women would never have more than one. Education is the best defence. Try to arm yourself with as much information as possible – speak to other women about childbirth and perhaps try to get yourself a childbirth video. Demystifying childbirth and knowing your options can go a long way to diffusing any panic.

● ● ● ● I was at a fun fair and had just got off some ride. I was laughing and talking to someone about the ride and how much fun it had been. All of a sudden, I looked down and there was this little person, a baby with an old man's face. 'You're not going to be a very good mother are you?' he asked. With horror, I realised I had forgotten my baby at home – I'd left him lying in his cot. I started running home panicking, then I woke up. Cathy

● ● ● ● I dreamt about coming home from the hospital with the baby. I was feeling great, and couldn't wait to start my new life. I opened the door and walked into the baby's room. To my horror, it was completely empty. I had forgotten to buy baby things. I didn't even have a nappy or a cot. Alison

● ● ● ● I had nightmares at least three or four times a week. I would be climbing the Eiffel Tower with the baby and slip, dropping her. 'Mama' she'd scream as she fell and I'd wake up. Sometimes I'd dream I was bathing her. I'd have her in the bath and turn around and do something else. When I turned back, she was blue and floating on the surface. I usually woke up then, desperate to go to the toilet. Francesca

● ● ● ● I found that my mind was most active at night and before I went to sleep, I'd lie awake, worrying about everything; that my baby would be deformed, that I wouldn't bond with it, that I'd hate being a mother, that birth would be unbearably painful. Invariably, I'd have nightmares, usually about giving birth to a monstrous bloody lump of flesh or sometimes Siamese twins. Larissa

Stress and Pregnancy

Work, finances, your changing body, the health of your unborn baby, the birth, day-to-day living and worrying about doing it all on your own – pregnancy can be stressful! Add a good dose of hormones, and it can be an explosive mix. Not only can stress manifest itself at night in the form of insomnia and bad dreams, but it can also invade your waking hours.

Stress is not good for anyone, but it's even worse for pregnant women. In the short term, a high level of stress can cause fatigue, sleeplessness, anxiety, poor appetite or overeating, headaches and backaches. Long term it can affect your immune system, cause high blood pressure and heart disease. Studies also suggest that high levels of stress may pose special risks during pregnancy, including possible miscarriage.

In one study, middle class women who experienced high levels of pregnancy-related anxiety (such as worries about the health of their baby or fear of labour and delivery) were significantly more likely to deliver prematurely. This seems to be due to stress releasing more hormones, which trigger labour. It also appears likely that this increase in hormones can constrict blood flow to the placenta, so the fetus may not receive the nutrients and oxygen it needs for optimal growth. Stress also may exert its adverse effects indirectly by affecting the pregnant woman's behaviour. For example, women who are experiencing high levels of stress may not follow good health habits. They may not eat properly, or they may react to stress by reaching for cigarettes, alcohol or illicit drugs, all of which have been linked to low birth-weight and the increased risk of birth defects.

Stress Reduction Techniques

Some techniques that may relieve stress include:

- Exercise.
- Deep breathing.
- Floating.
- Massage.*
- Acupuncture.*
- Reflexology.*
- Having a good support network.
- Aromatherapy.
- Homeopathy.*
- Herbal remedies.*
- Hypnotherapy.*
- Meditation.
- Visualisation and affirmations.
- Eating healthily.
- Getting enough rest.
- Avoiding cigarettes, alcohol and drugs.
- Stress management classes.

* Make sure you see qualified professionals.

I really recommend seeing social workers. Mine put me in contact with a support class which I still keep in contact with, and flooded me with all sorts of useful information and contacts. I was able to make use of a lot of these resources, and thus have things ready for my baby at a time when I couldn't have been poorer. I also found the emotional support invaluable. In addition, she put me in contact with organisations who provide respite care for single mothers, or any mother with a particular need for respite. It was absolutely wonderful, as babysitting was and is a luxury that I can't afford. My visits to the social worker did stop though, once I left the hospital. I have to admit that I didn't relish the thought of seeing her to start with, but realising that all the odds were stacked against me anyway, I decided to accept any and all help that was available. It felt very strange speaking to her at first and I certainly did feel more than a little 'hopeless', but boy was it worth it in the long run. Kathryn

Now Listen

Although protected and buffeted by the outside world by amniotic fluid, internal organs and the mother's abdomen, many studies have shown that the embryo does receive sound without much distortion or interference from background noise. What's so amazing is that some studies have demonstrated that listening begins at 16 weeks, 8 weeks before the ear is structurally complete!

It is believed that sounds have an amazing impact on the developing fetus, and a simple 5-second burst of music or sound, such as a laugh or cough, can cause changes in the heart rate or movement of the baby, which can last for up to an hour.

Studies have also shown the effect of classical music on premature babies to be significant with faster weight gain than babies who were not played music. So why not try playing gentle relaxing music such as Brahms and Mozart on your tummy? You can buy small tape recorders from electrical stores that look like a Walkman but actually play music out loud. Lie down, relax and turn the music on to a low volume placing it on or around your navel. There are even companies who produce music compilations specifically for this.

Of course, a mother's voice is the most powerful of all sound experiences, as it's transmitted through her own body. Therefore talking to your baby is important. Try to set aside a time when you feel relaxed and talk to him or her in a soothing, calm manner or sing lullabies or nursery rhymes. You might feel a bit stupid at first, but you soon get used to it and it helps somehow to build a relationship with your child. I imagine it must also be a tremendous comfort after the trauma of birth and being delivered out into a big cold world to hear a familiar voice.

A Stretching Regime

Stretching during pregnancy can prepare you for birth by strengthening and loosening the joints that are used the most in labour. It improves posture, relieves muscle tension, swelling, backache, and can relieve tension. Make sure not to 'bounce' into a stretch, hold a stretch for too long, or overstretch. During pregnancy a hormone called relaxin increases joint laxity, which means there can be a risk of overstretching. Tips for stretching include:

- Start gently and don't push yourself.
- Hold each stretch for a minimum of 10 seconds.
- Breath deeply during the stretch.
- For best results stretch daily.

See Reading Recommendations on page 206 for books about stretching and exercise during pregnancy.

Shoulder Stretch:

Kneel on the floor on a yoga mat or other soft surface with your knees about 20cm away from a wall. You can put a cushion between your knees if you think you need extra support. Spread your knees and turn your feet, toes pointing towards each other. Drop your shoulders down while lifting your arms above your head. Straighten your arms and place them about 6in (15cm) apart and as high up on the wall as you comfortably can. Hold the stretch for a few minutes while breathing deeply. Make sure to gently lower your shoulder blades away from the back of your head and neck for this stretch to be effective. This stretch relaxes the shoulders and stretches the muscles which support your breasts. If you find your back aches, move closer to the wall.

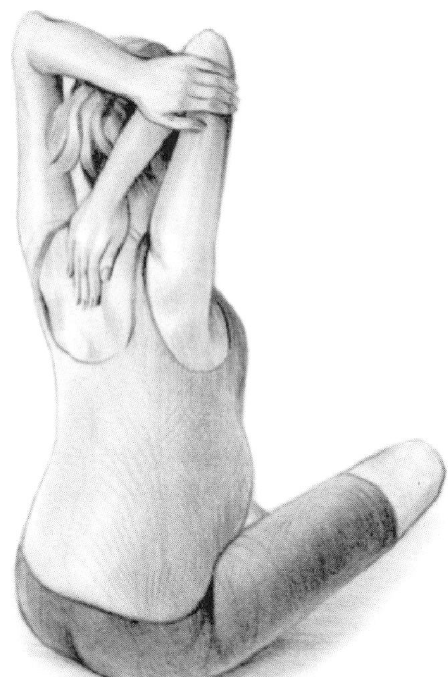

Arms and Shoulders:

Sit cross-legged on the floor, lift your right arm and stretch it to the ceiling. Bend it at the elbow and drop your hand down your back. Put your left hand on your right elbow to push it further down your back. Stop when you feel the stretch, hold, then release gently. Remember to keep your back straight.

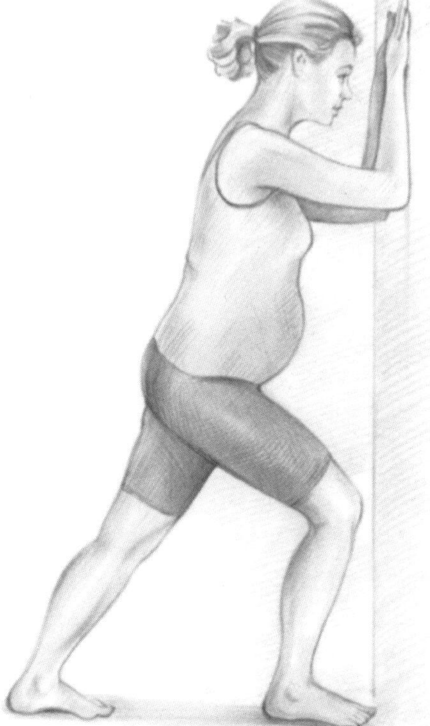

Calf Stretch: Stand facing a wall at arm's length. Bend elbows and rest your forearms against the wall. Leaning forward, place your head on your hands and bring one foot forward, sole flat on the ground, keeping the knee bent and relaxed. The other leg should be kept back with the knee straight. Feet are parallel with both heels on the ground. Breathe evenly, feeling the stretch in the back of the leg. This exercise is particularly good for relieving cramps in the calves.

The Cat: This is a great one for easing aching backs. Kneel on all fours, with your arms in alignment with your shoulders. Breathe in, then as you breathe out, drop your head forward and arch your spine. Hold for a moment, then breathe in again, bring your head back up and relax back into the neutral position.

The Cat: This is the wrong neutral position. Ensure your back is always straight.

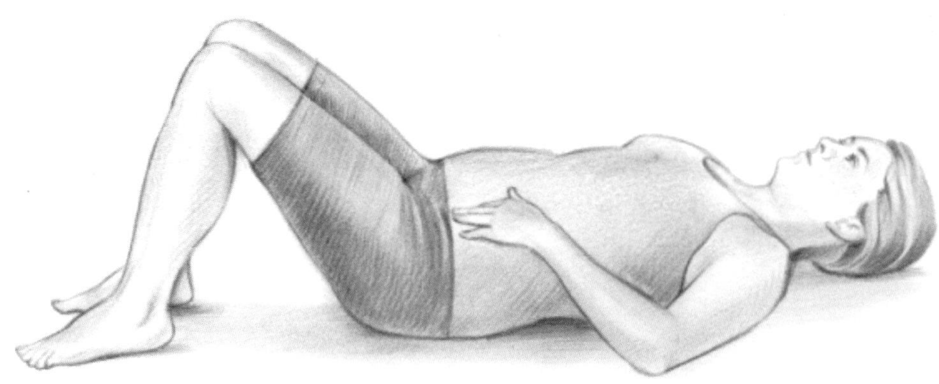

Pelvic Tilt: This helps reduce stress on the spine and will strengthen the pelvic floor muscles. Lie on your back, knees up, feet slightly apart. Press the small of your back into the floor so it flattens out, while tilting your pelvis upward and gently squeezing your buttocks together. Rock slightly back and forth while squeezing, then release your buttock muscles.

Rocking: Kneel on your hands and knees on a soft surface, knees a comfortable distance apart. Inhale and move your weight forward onto your hands without arching your back. Exhale and move your hips back toward your heels and relax.

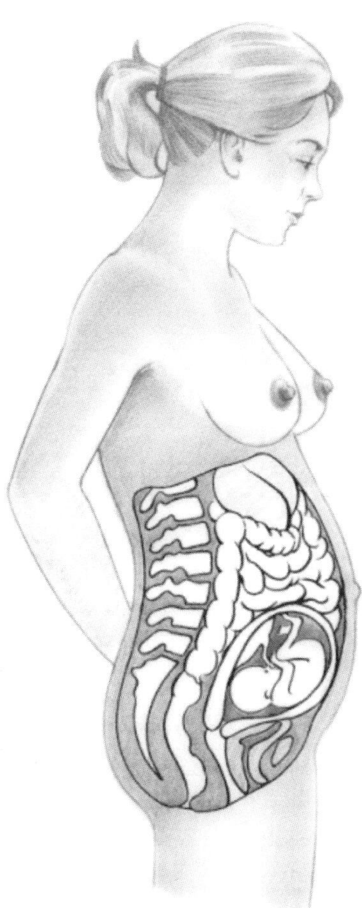

What's Happening? Week 23

Your belly might start to itch around now due to the stretching skin. You might also find the skin darkens in patches on your nose, cheeks or forehead. This will disappear after pregnancy. You may have gained between 4½–7kg. You may also have a surge of energy and vitality.

The baby may have developed its own sleeping pattern now. Unfortunately, it's usually the opposite to yours, as it sleeps while you're active, due to the rocking sensation as you move around, and then wakes when you lie down and there is more room in the womb. Its hearing is now fully developed. It measures around 33cm and weighs about ½kg. The fetus continues to grow rapidly and it now has its own individual fingerprints.

This Month's Checklist

- ✔ Consider telling your employer of your pregnancy, if you haven't done so already.
- ✔ Work out a daily regime of stretches to keep you supple and allay back pain.
- ✔ Think about whether you want to use the father's surname for the baby.
- ✔ Set aside some time to 'talk' to your baby and to perhaps play soothing music.

You're Calling it *What?*

Kickboxing or Caress?

Around this time of your pregnancy, when there's still plenty of room in the womb, is often when the baby moves the most. For some women, it may be as if the baby's practising for the Olympic gymnastic team, while others feel only the occasional gentle prod. The average number of movements is around 10 in a 12-hour period but don't panic if it's less than that – you just may not be feeling them. Some babies are also naturally less active too. You'll probably find that on days when you're busier, the baby is likely to be less so, lulled to sleep by all that movement. When you're resting or sleeping on the other hand, you're likely to feel the baby more as it has more space and is usually awake.

Recent research has suggested that from 28 weeks onward, it may be a good idea to record movements twice a day, once in the morning and again at night, particularly if you don't seem to have put on any weight or become any bigger. That way if there's a problem, it may be able to be investigated and rectified. Call your doctor if you've noticed an absence or slowdown of fetal movement for more than 24 hours after week 22, and if you've felt fewer than 10 movements per hour after week 28. Your baby may simply be in a different position, but it might also be in distress. You may need an ultrasound to confirm everything's okay.

It's pretty difficult to remember how many movements you may have felt over a 12-hour period, or to lose count, so it's a good idea to make a kick chart.

How to Make a Kick Chart

Draw a simple graph, with a vertical and horizontal axis. At the top of a piece of paper put the days of the week in columns. Along the left-hand side put the hours in half-hour blocks ranging from when you wake up to 12 hours later and rule off in rows. Every time you feel a movement, fill in the appropriate square. It's not really necessary to keep counting once you reach 10. Some days this may take minutes, at others hours.

		A TYPICAL KICKCHART																				
		WEEK 38							WEEK 39							WEEK 40						
		M	T	W	T	F	S	S	M	T	W	T	F	S	S	M	T	W	T	F	S	S
A.M.	9.00																					
	9.30																					
	10.00				■																	
	10.30																					
	11.00	■									■										■	
	11.30		■	■								■								■		
NOON	12.00					■													■			■
P.M.	12.30																					
	1.00								■				■									
	1.30																					
	2.00													■								
	2.30							■							■							
	3.00						■															
	3.30																	■				
	4.00																					
	4.30															■	■					
	5.00																					
	5.30																					
	6.00																					
	6.30																					
	7.00																					
	7.30																					
	8.00																					
	8.30																					

Less than 10 movements felt by 9pm

	M	T	W	T	F	S	S	M	T	W	T	F	S	S	M	T	W	T	F	S	S
9										■						■				■	
8								■													
7			■																		
6																					
5																					
4																					
3																					
2																					
1																					
0																					

NOTE

The closer to the end of the pregnancy you are, the more important are the baby's movements, or lack thereof – it could indicate fetal distress.

At 7 months, my baby was really active, especially when I took a bath or lay down for a while. I was at work, doing a presentation one afternoon, when I suddenly realised I hadn't felt the baby move since the night before. I found it really hard to concentrate and rushed through the presentation, so I could sit down at my desk and try to figure out whether it really had been that long, or I'd just been too busy to notice. I spent the rest of the day, with my hand on my stomach, desperately willing him to move, but nothing. That night by 9, I still hadn't felt any movement and called my doctor, who told me to come in first thing in the morning. I spent practically all night awake, panicking, thinking that my baby was dead and imagining the horrific scenario that lay ahead. At 6.00 a.m. I gave up and decided to have a warm bath. I'd just lain down in the water, and kapow! I was kicked so hard it nearly took my breath away. I was so relieved, I cried. I kept my appointment anyway, and a scan revealed everything was absolutely fine. Alana

When Something is Wrong

It's the most devastating news that any woman could ever receive – that her baby has died inutero. There are several reasons why a baby may die in its mother's womb – it could be the result of a placental insufficiency (see below), or an incompetent cervix which starts to dilate long before it should (sometimes due to a previous late abortion or repeated miscarriages). Whatever the reason, it won't make the pain and loss any easier to bear and you should make sure you are with your pregnancy partner or close friend when dealing with the news.

What Happens when your Baby has Died?

If your labour has already started or you are due shortly, the labour will proceed as normal. If not, you may be given the choice of being induced (see Chapter Nine) or going home and waiting for labour to start spontaneously. Methods used to induce labour include a pessary, where a tablet containing hormones is inserted into the vagina, and a D&C (Dilation and Curettage) where under local or general anaesthetic the cervix is artificially dilated and an instrument called a curette is inserted to remove any embryonic tissue and endometrial lining.

Whichever you decide on, think seriously about seeing your baby afterwards – it's been proven that the grieving process is much helped by actually seeing your baby, holding it and naming it after the birth. By law, babies born after 24 weeks are required to be registered, which means you will have to have the baby formally buried or cremated. The hospital will also give you the choice of taking your baby's body for burial or you can let the hospital take care of the arrangements. This will usually mean the baby's body is cremated on site and its ashes scattered in a memorial garden in the hospital grounds.

My pregnancy was progressing well. I'd been really healthy – no problems, no morning sickness or anything. Then one day at work, I had this sensation of wetting myself. I went straight to the toilet and discovered I was bleeding. I felt like ice and a colleague, noticing my face as I walked out of the toilet, asked me what was wrong. I asked her if she could take me to the hospital. They took me straight for a scan and everything seemed okay, I could see this tiny little figure moving around. The doctor told me everything was fine. Two weeks later, I was booked in for a regular scan. The doctor kept freezing the screen and although I couldn't see anything, I could just sense from his face that there was something wrong. He then turned the heartbeat monitor on, and nothing. He turned to me and I read his face before he said the words, 'I'm sorry, I think your baby has died'. He bought in another colleague to check and I held my breath, hoping it was just some horrible mistake, but the second doctor just shook his head sadly. Then I was examined and they told me that as the baby was 14 weeks, it would be difficult to do a D&C, and I would have to go through labour. They booked me in the next day. I went home, and just lay like a stone on my bed all night, feeling revolted that I had a dead baby inside of me that I was going to have to give birth to. The next morning, the midwife sat down and talked me through what was going to happen, and what my baby would look like. She said I could take photos and make foot or handprints of the baby and gave me a little quilt to hold the baby in that I could also keep. After talking with her, my baby seemed so much more real, a baby, not just a dead body to be got rid of. An hour later, the doctor gave me a pessary to start labour and I waited and waited, praying it would be quick and all over soon. But before I was due to have the second pessary, I started to bleed very heavily and it was taken out of my hands. After all my mental preparation to meet my dead baby, I would have to have a D&C anyway. I spent a sleepless night in the maternity ward feeling incredibly lonely, crying and listening to all the other babies cry. Afterwards I went into a severe depression; a year later I can only now just see light at the end of the tunnel. Melissa

Helping the Grieving Process

Most women who have been through this terrible experience agree that taking photos of the baby helps. Just remember, you don't have to develop the film until you feel ready, but not having this memento of your child may cause deep regret afterward.

Ask your pregnancy partner, friend or relative to see the baby with you; it will make it easier for them to grieve with you if they meet the person you are grieving for. Having a funeral or memorial service can help by validating the existence of the baby as a separate human entity and makes grieving easier. Although you mightn't feel like it when the death occurs, there may be a time when you want to visit your baby's grave. If you feel unable to cope with funeral arrangements, ask for help from a friend or family member. Support groups such as SANDS (Stillbirth and Neonatal Death Society) offer advice on arranging funerals for babies. If you choose to have the baby cremated at the hospital, most hold memorial services for these babies about once a month in their chapels, which you can attend.

You may return from hospital to find that some well meaning friend or relative has removed all evidence that a baby was expected to be coming home with you. Although it may not seem like it, some women say that it helps the grieving process to have to pack away those reminders of your baby yourself. If you don't, it may make it seem less real and harder to let go of.

Talk about your child as often as you need to. If family and friends find that difficult, find a support group in your area where you can meet people who feel the way you do and understand what you are going through. Make sure to seek counselling if it becomes too much to bear.

●●●● I have joined SANDS. It is an association that was set up to help people suffering miscarriage, stillborn and neonatal death. Paula

●●●● All I can suggest to you is to build memories for yourself, keep everything from your time in hospital. If you have no pictures of your child ask someone to draw what you imagine your child would be like. I have a box of things to help me remember such as cards. Can I finish by saying that life will never be the same again but you will find a new place to exist in this world. Give yourself time, give yourself space, give yourself all the love you can. Jane

The Placenta

It's been attributed almost magical powers, animals eat it (and increasingly so do we!) to aid healing, and it's long been used in beauty treatments and face creams. This amazing mass starts to form at around 4 weeks, when it attaches to the uterus and starts producing hormones.

By week 13 the placenta is almost complete and the umbilical cord is attached to it, pumping blood into the baby's circulatory system. The placenta allows oxygen, nutrients and antibodies to pass from you to the baby. It also produces the hormones that control your pregnancy and is used as a 'filter', removing the baby's waste to your body for disposal. Occasionally in pregnancy there can be problems with the placenta. These can include:

Placenta Praevia

This simply refers to the position of the placenta in the uterus. Placenta praevia means the placenta is attached to the lower half of the uterus, covering or partially covering the opening of the uterus. It's fairly common early on in pregnancy (it occurs in 1 in 200 births), but it usually moves up of its own accord. If it doesn't there is a possibility of haemorrhage, and should it stay in this position, vaginal birth will be impossible. The major symptom of placenta praevia is painless bleeding which is bright red in colour, ranging between light and heavy, which may disappear and come back. Treatment often includes increased bed rest and cutting down of activities, although if bleeding continues, hospitalisation and complete bed rest is recommended; careful monitoring through scans; as well as treatment with vitamin and mineral supplements. Transfusions may also be an option. If severe, you may be on complete bed rest until week 36 when, providing the baby's lungs are sufficiently developed, a Caesarean may be performed.

Placenta Abruptio

This occurs when a tiny part of the placenta has detached from the uterus. It happens in about 1 in 4 pregnancies and is most common in mothers who smoke, who are older, take drugs, have hypertension, have been involved in an accident or have taken aspirin. The severity of the bleeding and the associated pain depends on how much of the placenta has separated from the lining of the womb. If bleeding is severe, you may be hospitalised and the same treatment as for placenta praevia is applied. You may also be advised to have complete bed rest, with no getting up except for bathing and using the toilet. When the abruption is severe, i.e. when more than half of the placenta separates from the uterine wall, immediate medical attention and delivery are necessary.

Placental Insufficiency

Placental insufficiency is when the placenta is not functioning correctly, which can lead to inadequate growth in the baby. Sometimes changing your diet will help, as well as bed rest, which will allow a better flow of blood through the placenta to the baby. In extreme cases, stillbirth may be a result. Placental insufficiency can also be a problem as the placenta ceases to function normally once you're about 10 days past your due date. For this reason you may be induced (see Chapter Nine) if you are more than 10 days overdue.

I didn't fit the usual case study at all. I didn't smoke, drink or do drugs and I hadn't been involved in any kind of accident. It started at 29 weeks and I was told I had to stay in bed as much as possible for 4 or 5 days. I was told to avoid sex (that was easy!) and just take it gently. The bleeding stopped fairly quickly, although it did happen again a couple of weeks later. A scan showed that the placenta was really low, covering most of the opening to the uterus, so I had to have a Caesarean in the end. Cathy

NOTE

Recent studies have shown that placental problems may be linked to a lack of folic acid.

Perineal Massage

As far as massages go, it probably rates as a big fat zero on the relaxation scale. The perineum is the bit of skin between the vagina and the anus and despite being fairly elastic, during childbirth it's prone to tearing with the effort exerted in pushing the baby out. It's been suggested that by massaging this area, slowly making this piece of skin more supple, it may help prevent tears or the need for an episiotomy, in addition to aiding in the healing process. An added advantage, say advocates, is that you will feel fewer stinging sensations as the baby crowns. This will familiarise you with this sensation, meaning you're more likely to be relaxed during the birth.

However, many midwives and obstetricians believe that perineal massage is neither useful nor necessary. They ascertain that as long as the mother's perineum is supported during crowning, and her pushing is properly timed, there should be no problem. It's up to you to decide: ask your midwife, doctor, or friends with children if they think it's of benefit. If you do decide to do it, try to do it a couple of times a week increasing to once daily as your pregnancy progresses. To perform perineal massage:

1. Wash your hands thoroughly and make sure your fingernails are cut. In a semi-sitting position, spread your legs apart (you might like to use a mirror for the first time). Put a little light unfragranced massage oil, like avocado, vitamin E or a water-soluble lubricant, such as KY Jelly, on your fingers and thumb and around your perineum.

2. Spread your legs and insert your thumbs inside your vagina. Press the perineal area down toward the rectum then to the sides. Gently continue to stretch until you feel a slight burn or tingling.
3. Hold the stretch until the tingling subsides and gently massage the lower part of the vaginal canal back and forth.
4. While massaging, hook your thumbs onto the sides of the vaginal canal and gently pull these tissues forward, as your baby's head will do during delivery.
5. Finally, massage the tissues between the thumb and forefinger back and forth for about a minute. Make sure you're firm but not too vigorous, as this can cause bruising or swelling.

A good diet with supplements of zinc, vitamin C and fatty acids such as fish oil, evening primrose or flaxseed oil may increase your skin's elasticity.

Urinary Tract Infections

Pregnant women are more vulnerable to urinary tract infections (UTIs) and you may find that you experience this unpleasant condition for the first time. The reason is that the urinary tract dilates, so the urine may become stagnant. Also the kidneys have to function much harder than normal in pregnancy, as they have to cleanse a great deal more blood. UTIs need to be treated promptly, because if left untreated, they can result in low birth-weight babies or even premature birth. If you feel any symptoms, such as a burning or stinging sensation when you pass urine, if you have a temperature and low back pain or pain when you apply pressure over your kidneys, you may have a UTI or kidney infection. Usually this means taking antibiotics, which can in turn lead to thrush, so prevention is the best cure.

Avoiding UTIs

- Drink plenty of fluid.
- Wear cotton underwear.
- Avoid refined sugar and sugary foods.
- Eat plenty of acidophilus yoghurt.
- Empty your bladder frequently.
- Always wipe from front to back after going to the toilet.
- Wash the area after sex.

Oh, My Aching Back!

It's a classic pose; the pregnant woman standing, belly out, rubbing the small of her back. Some lucky women find that a chronic bad back is actually relieved during pregnancy, while others who may have never suffered a back problem are suddenly burdened with one. Backache during pregnancy can be caused by various factors, including the extra weight gained, poor posture, or stretching ligaments. Even if you're having no problems with your back during pregnancy, it's vital to look after it so you don't have any problems after the baby is born – you're going to be doing a lot of bending and picking up over the next year or so! Here are some helpful suggestions for preventing and relieving backache:

- Gentle exercise – particularly stretching such as 'The Cat Stretch' and pelvic rocking (see Chapter Five).
- Make sure not to cross your legs when sitting.
- Swim.
- Sleep with pillows under your knees, which will take the pressure off your back. Make sure you are sleeping on a good, firm mattress.
- Don't wear high heels and try to stay off your feet for long periods. Wear flat shoes, preferably ones with cushioned soles.
- A warm wheat pack is soothing.
- Osteopathic treatment is safe during pregnancy and can bring great relief. Make sure you find a qualified practitioner.
- Use herbal rubs, such as tiger balm.
- Try to have regular gentle massages with a qualified therapist.
- A handful of Epsom salts in the bath.
- The homeopathic remedies, pulsatilla, arnica or rhus tox may help.
- Acupuncture (but see a professional).
- Avoid lifting any heavy objects.

Standing

Standing in correct posture is important when you are pregnant, as it can reduce back pain. When standing it is important to keep your chin level (as if you have a string attached to the middle of your head which is being pulled upwards). Make sure your shoulders are dropped and relaxed and pull in your abdomen, rather then standing with a sway back. Squeeze your buttocks so that your pelvis tilts and your weight is centred over your hips. Spread your weight evenly on your feet and stand with your feet shoulder-width apart.

Bending

Don't stoop over low surfaces. Bend down from the knees or raise the surface. If possible, kneel instead of bending.

Sitting

Try not to sit down for long periods – tempting though it may be! Make sure your chair is comfortable with plenty of back support. Put a rolled up towel or small cushion in the small of your back for extra support. Try to keep your feet up as much as possible, or rest them on a footrest.

Lying

Try not to lie flat on your back, it can put extra pressure on large blood vessels and make you feel faint. Instead, lie on your side with a small pillow under your stomach and another between your knees.

Lifting

Try to avoid heavy lifting. If you do need to lift, bend your knees and hold the object close to your body. Don't hold your breath. If you find you need to do this, the load is probably too heavy.

Gestational Diabetes

Glucose screening is usually performed around weeks 25 to 28 and is a routine test to establish whether you have pregnancy-induced diabetes, which can result in overly large babies, difficult deliveries and health problems for you and your baby. This test involves having a very sweet drink, then an hour later, doing a blood test to determine the blood sugar level. If the test is positive and a high level of sugar is found in the blood you may undergo a second 3-hour glucose tolerance test. If this test is positive then a diagnosis of gestational diabetes is made.

Gestational diabetes is a form of diabetes which affects around 5.8% of pregnancies. During pregnancy, the woman's body is under continuous demand to supply an ever-increasing amount of insulin, up to three times higher than normal. In women with gestational diabetes, a hormone produced in the placenta is thought to cause insulin resistance. Usually, this type of diabetes disappears after the birth and can often be controlled in pregnancy through diet and exercise. There is some controversy as to whether this test should be routine, as some members of the medical profession believe that the expense involved and the small number of women who test positive don't warrant it; instead they believe, it should be offered to women considered to be at risk.

Who's at Risk?

- Women who have a family history of diabetes.
- Women who are more than 20% heavier than their recommended weight.
- Women who have high blood pressure.
- Women who are carrying multiple fetuses.
- Women who are over 25.

Effects of Gestational Diabetes on the Baby

When properly controlled, there is little effect to the unborn child, however if poorly controlled, it may result in a large birth-weight baby, the excess glucose from the mother being stored as fat in the unborn baby. After delivery the baby's own glucose levels may drop, requiring an intravenous glucose infusion, and jaundice (yellowing of the skin), can occur.

Effects of Gestational Diabetes on the Mother

During the pregnancy, ketones (an acid by-product formed when the body's fat stores are being used for energy) can pose a problem. If blood sugars are not controlled, ketones develop and actually eat away at the body's own energy resources. If there is a problem controlling the blood sugars, then a ketone urine test should be done each morning. There is also a risk of developing type 2 diabetes later in life. Gestational diabetes during a pregnancy is also likely to appear again in later pregnancies. Other documented risks include:

- Premature labour and delivery.
- Caesarean deliveries, especially when the baby is very large.
- Pre-eclampsia, which is pregnancy-induced high blood pressure.
- Urinary tract infections.
- Hydramnios, which is creating too much amniotic fluid.

Treating Gestational Diabetes

It's important that you follow a diet recommended by your doctor. He or she may refer you to a nutritionist. Good nutrition and gentle exercise, along with daily monitoring of glucose levels, are usually enough to keep the diabetes under control.

The Name Game

Practically from conception, it's something everyone wants to know. 'What are you going to call it?' Admitting you haven't thought about it yet is guaranteed to disappoint family and friends, who are dying to go off and discuss or ridicule your choice, or feel put out if you aren't naming the child after them.

Naming a child is one of life's biggest decisions, and a huge responsibility for any parent. Some women don't even want to think about names until meeting their baby; others have had favourites for years.

One advantage of naming your child early in your pregnancy is that the bonding process can start to take place while your baby is in the womb. If you don't want to name it yet, don't worry, nicknames work just as well. However, if you do want to start thinking about a name, knowing the sex of the baby makes it a lot easier. Today, there are a huge number of resources to help you out, including myriad name books (see Reading Recommendations on page 208) and websites (as well as helpful family members dropping ever so subtle hints!) Things you might want to think about when choosing a name are:

- Is it easy to make fun of? (There was a 'Wayne King' in my town!) Children are cruel, and you don't want to saddle your child with a name that will be the butt of playground jokes.
- Think about the stereotypes the name may evoke.
- Make sure the initials don't spell anything undesirable, eg. Alexander Samuel Smith (Ass) or Polly Imogen Garrett (Pig).
- Does the name have a positive connotation for you? You're going to be saying it for a long, long time, so make sure there's no-one in your past with the same name you disliked.
- Is the name rhythmic? Generally it's better to avoid names where the first and last names have the same number of syllables.
- Do you have a common last name? If so, it may be better to use an unusual or long first name, eg. Anastasia Jones.
- Is it easy to pronounce or spell? The names may look great, but your child doesn't want to have to go through life having to correct people's pronunciation or constantly spell their name, eg. Siobhan. On the other hand, if you've chosen a common name, an unusual spelling may be just what you need, eg. Gemima Jones.
- Be conscious of nicknames and variations. If you're thinking about a long or

particularly 'grown up' name, think about choosing one that you can use a variation of as a child, such as Madeline/Maddy.

- Avoid fad names, which will be out of fashion sooner than the child's out of nappies.
- If it doesn't sound too odd and you want to use your own surname rather than the father's, you could consider putting the father's surname as a middle name or second middle name, eg. Joshua Harrison Evans.
- Try not to have too many of the same letters in the name, eg. Robyn Robinson.

The Playground Test

Go to a crowded playground and yell out the name you have chosen. If it feels uncomfortable or if everyone looks at you or if two or more children respond, you might want to rethink your choice!

The Surname – Yours or His?

As if trying to think up a first and perhaps middle name is not enough, the single woman has to also consider the child's surname – yours or his? Reasons to give the baby your surname include:

- Less confusion.
- Yours sounds better than the father's.
- Your baby was conceived through artificial insemination/donor insemination.
- You're not sure who the father is.

Reasons to give the baby the father's surname include:

- For your child to have some bond with its father.
- You like the sound of his name better than yours.
- The father intends to have a role in bringing up the baby.
- You intend to establish paternity and child support.
- Tradition.

Stars and their Children's Names

Ocean Alexander, Sonnet Noel, Isabella Summer – actor, Forest Whittaker
Blue Angel – musician, Dave 'the edge Evans', U2
Homer – Matt Groening, creator of The Simpsons
Hud, Speck Wildhorse and Justice – singer, John Mellencamp
Free – actor, Barbara Hershey
Earving III – basketball player, Magic Johnson
Hopper Jack – actors, Sean Penn and Robin Wright
Jett – actors, John Travolta and Kelly Preston
Alfie and Gulliver – actor, Gary Oldman
Fifi Trixibelle, Peaches Honeyblossom, Pixie, Heavenly Hiraani Tigerlily – TV personality, the late Paula Yates
Memphis Eve – singer, Bono, U2
Brooklyn Joseph and Romeo – singer, Victoria Beckham and soccer player, David Beckham
Rio Riley – actor, Sean Young
India Raven – actor, Catherine Oxenberg
Lourdes and Rocco – Madonna
Missy – musician, Damon Albarn, Blur
Michael Samarie (daughter) – actor, Conni Marie Brazelton, ER
Camera (daughter) – tennis player, Arthur Ashe and photographer, Jeanne Moutoussamy
Zephyr (son), Lyric (daughter) – director, Robby Benson and Karla DeVito
Sailor Lee (daughter) – model, Christie Brinkley and architect, Peter Cook

I decided to give Kit both our names as surnames, but not to hyphenate them, which I think is a bit pretentious. In a way, I wanted to thank her father's family, as they were really supportive during my pregnancy after David and I broke up. Maria

I had always liked the name Jacob and so as soon as I found out I was pregnant, I decided that was what I would call him. Unfortunately, 'he' turned out to be a she and it wasn't until the 9th month I decided to call her Elizabeth, after my aunt who was so supportive during my pregnancy. Julie

Poor Lily didn't have a name until she was 6 weeks old! I just couldn't make up my mind when I was pregnant and when she arrived still nothing struck me. I live in a small town and every time I'd take her out, everyone would be coming up to me to have a look and ask if I'd thought of a name yet. They were more scandalised about the fact that I hadn't named her than being single. Then the woman at the newsagent suggested Lily. I went home and thought about it and decided I really liked it, and tried it out, calling her Lily for a few days. It suited her, so Lily it was. Jodie

I thought for a long time about whether to use my ex-partner's surname and convinced myself it was the best solution – it would give my son some connection to his father, and besides, his surname sounded so much better than mine. In the end I changed my mind though and decided it would be easier to use mine, that way, there'd be less difficult questions. Grace

I love my grandmother, and we're very close so I thought it'd be nice to name the baby Ruby after her. I didn't tell her until after my daughter was born and she was horrified! She told me she'd always hated her name and couldn't believe I'd saddle my child with it. She still won't call her by her name, but always refers to her as 'darling'! Belinda

Lack of Sleep

While it may seem good practice for the sleepless nights to come, not sleeping well can leave you feeling listless, cranky and not inclined to look after yourself. Unfortunately during pregnancy, the odds are stacked against you having a good night's sleep – there's aching legs and cramps, sore backs, racing minds and indigestion, just to name a few, but being prepared, taking things easy, and trying some of the following suggestions may help you get a decent night's sleep:

- Eliminate caffeine (found in tea, coffee, soft drinks and energy drinks) from your diet, as it's a stimulant and will keep you awake.
- Try to get into a routine of going to bed and waking up at the same time every day.
- Don't eat a big meal immediately before going to bed – it will be hard to digest and may sit in the stomach, causing indigestion. You may find it easier to eat more frequent smaller meals anyway.
- Don't drink too much before you go to bed or you'll be going to the toilet all night.
- Invest in a fan if you don't have one, but don't have it blowing right at you.

- Sleep on your side if possible with a pillow under your tummy and one between your knees. This takes pressure off your back.
- Take a warm bath before bed with a few drops of lavender essential oil.
- Leg cramps are a common cause of nightwaking. Make sure your diet has adequate calcium and try doing some gentle calf stretches before going to bed.
- Only engage in gentle exercise in the later stages of pregnancy and don't exercise just before bed time. The natural high will keep you awake.
- Feng Shui says you should keep your bedroom for sleeping. Don't watch TV or work in your bedroom.
- If you really find you can't get to sleep, don't fight it lying in bed with your eyes shut tight trying to will yourself to sleep. Get up and make yourself a milky drink or cup of chamomile tea.

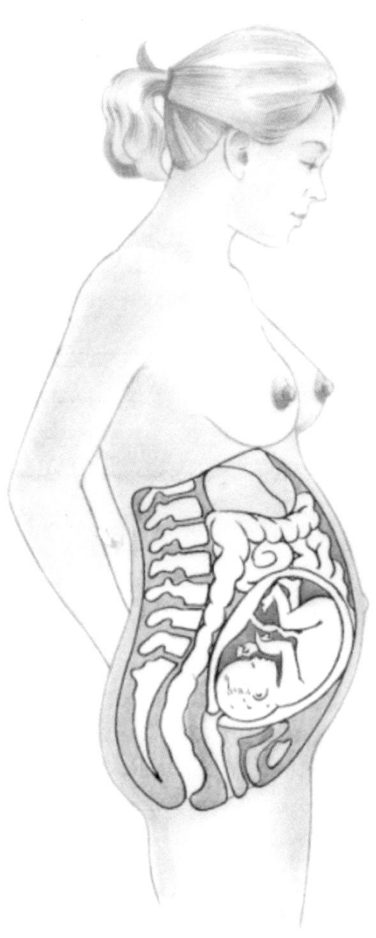

What's Happening? Week 27

You may find you have a thick, white vaginal discharge. There may also be a lower abdominal ache from stretching ligaments. You'll probably feel more fetal activity if these movements haven't already begun. Your breasts may feel much bigger and heavier. Your abdomen may feel itchy as the skin stretches over your growing bump.

Your baby's eyelashes and eyebrows have grown, as has the head hair. Although it isn't fully formed, the baby is capable of sustaining life with intensive care if born at the end of this month. Its skin is thin and wrinkled. The baby weighs about 0.9kg and is about 37cm long. The eyes may be prominent and are open when the baby is awake. The baby is sucking its thumb and opening and closing its eyes.

This Month's Checklist

- ✔ Start a kick chart to record the baby's movements.
- ✔ Start regular perineal massage.
- ✔ Think about whether you want to give the baby your surname or the father's.
- ✔ Don't forget to make an antenatal appointment for 2 weeks from now, instead of a month. This will continue until week 36 when they become weekly.

CHAPTER SEVEN

WEEKS 28–31

Giving Birth – Your Options

Antenatal Classes

You and your pregnancy partner might want to think about joining an antenatal class at this stage of your pregnancy. The purpose of these classes is to inform and prepare you for what your body is going to go through during labour and to learn strategies and techniques for managing this. Classes can also help you choose the method of birth you want to have if you haven't decided yet, and can be invaluable for your pregnancy partner to know how to help you during labour. Other benefits of classes include the opportunity to meet other mothers-to-be, to discuss and compare notes, to ask any questions you might have forgotten to ask your doctor or midwife. You may also have access to literature, videos and other information. A tour of your local hospital will probably be included. You will probably learn about breastfeeding and may also get to learn about resources in your area, such as the National Childbirth Trust.

On the negative side, this may be a time in your pregnancy when your single status is very visible and you may feel a little uncomfortable surrounded by couples. However, times have changed and you may find you're not the only single woman there. Some women find the information given at classes incredibly useful, while others find they have learnt nothing new. Just remember, whether you decide to go or not, your body will always instinctively know what to do!

Finding a Class

Unless you live in an isolated area, chances are there are usually a large number of antenatal classes for you to choose from. Your local hospital usually runs them, as do organisations such as the National Childbirth Trust, as well as independent midwives. If you have a particular birth philosophy in mind (such as a home birth), talk to your midwife to see if they run classes or can recommend one. If you haven't made up your mind yet, try to talk to other pregnant women (or log on to an Internet chat room if you don't know any) and get their recommendation, or ask your midwife or doctor.

Before joining a class, try to glean as much information as possible about the curriculum and the instructors' philosophies. Ask if you can sit in on a class before signing up – that way you can ascertain whether you are going to feel uncomfortable in the company of so many couples and whether you think the classes are worthwhile. Don't forget to ensure the class schedule fits in with your pregnancy partner, if you have one. A good class and a good teacher should:

- Be progressive. You should learn something new each week, not simply repeated information.
- Be informative and relaxed.
- Have breathing and relaxation exercises included.
- Be knowledgeable and hopefully have experienced childbirth themselves!
- Give you some insight into the physical and emotional aspects of labour.
- Not talk down to you or withhold information.
- Provide room for discussion and questions.
- Not automatically assume that all the women have a partner.
- Stress the idea of choice in childbirth and not make you feel there is only one way.
- Provide information about Caesarean sections and explain all the methods of pain relief during labour.
- Have no more than 10 women and their birth partners in the class.

●●●● I am going to antenatal classes at the hospital. Just the regular ones, no Lamaze classes or anything! I'm finding them really good, but I feel so tired these days I feel pretty unmotivated to go. Kathryn

●●●● Useless, but maybe because I think I read a lot, I found them quite basic. The class was also huge, with 30 couples. I got more from books. Sophia

●●●● I only went to one. To tell you the truth, I felt really out of it being on my own. Everyone else was part of a couple, and I felt like everyone pitied me when I had to have the instructor as my 'partner'. Stevie

●●●● Great. Watching the childbirth videos was a bit shocking, but I am glad I knew a little bit more about what to expect. Rebecca

●●●● I liked my teacher at first, but then it all started to get a bit too much like brainwashing.

It was constantly assumed that we all wanted a natural (i.e. drug free) birth and that anything else was because we were 'unprepared' or 'unfocused'. She talked about Caesarean for about 30 seconds. I wanted to hear about all the options, to keep an open mind about what I might choose to do or have at the birth, but I felt this intense pressure to conform. Rowena

I hated it and stopped going after a couple of times. Once my mum went with me, and another time a friend came, but I just felt stupid the whole time, surrounded by five loving couples. Kylie

I was lucky. I had a brilliant class and there were a few other single women there too. Our teacher was fantastic and we all had a great laugh, which I think helped us all get over some fears. Some of us have kept in touch too which is great. Marika

Do-it-yourself Antenatal Education

Chances are your mother didn't go to antenatal classes. Most definitely your grandmother didn't. Yet they probably wouldn't rate their births as any worse than the woman who attends antenatal classes today. While there does seem to be a bias towards attending classes, it's a personal decision. Some women simply don't have time. Others may feel intimidated by being single in a sea of couples. Perhaps they simply feel too tired to attend on evenings or at weekends. Maybe they just don't think they're necessary. For whatever reason, if you decide not to attend antenatal classes, with a little planning, and a bit of self education, it's possible to arm yourself just as well. There are a huge number of informative and well written books, videos and easy to digest magazine articles available that can help you learn how to cope with whatever labour might bring.

Childbirth Methods

There are various methods in which to give birth (as outlined below). Each have their advantages and disadvantages, so it is worthwhile investigating all your choices before making a decision. There is a profusion of books dealing with childbirth choices, but as new developments and methods in the practice of midwifery and obstetrics occur so quickly (relatively speaking), it's worth checking the publishing details inside the front cover to see when the book was written. Make sure you get something new-ish, or you may end up believing that a 'normal' delivery is done in stirrups after a pubic shave and an enema! Ask other women which books they used and if they still have them. Scour second-hand bookshops where you can often find good as new, up-to-date books at less than half the original price.

If you feel overloaded with information and long to digest just small amounts at a time, pregnancy magazines are excellent. They usually contain real women's birth stories as well as informative and interesting articles, ideas and tips. Unfortunately, you'll find little specifically aimed at the single woman and they do tend to be somewhat repetitive, so don't bother buying a new issue every time it comes out. (See Useful Contacts on page 213 for more details.)

In addition, videos can offer further information. You certainly won't find a section dedicated to them in your local video shop, but they are out there. The bad news is that labour and birth videos tend to retail between £50 to £70 as they're aimed at facilitators of antenatal classes and childbirth education providers. If you want to save money, ask other pregnant women whether they want to get together to buy one to share. Alternatively, better libraries may stock them, although they do tend to be out of date. If you're confident ordering via the Internet and have a credit card, the US offers a much better variety, where even with international postage added on you'll generally find they still beat what's available in the UK. (See Useful Contacts on page 214 for more details.)

Lamaze

Pioneered by Dr Ferdinand Lamaze, this is the oldest, most common technique for reducing the stress and pain of labour and delivery. Lamaze focuses primarily on breathing techniques and relaxation. The aim is to 'decondition' women about the pain of labour, teaching them instead to see contractions as helpful stimuli. They stress replacing 'unproductive behaviour' during labour and delivery, such as anger and screaming, with more 'helpful actions', such as deep breathing. Lamaze suggests that doing this makes pushing more effective and less painful. Exercises are taught for antenatal and use during labour. Lamaze doesn't discourage the use of drugs or medical intervention.

The Bradley Method®

Rather than the quick panting breaths emphasised in Lamaze, the Bradley Method® or 'husband-coached childbirth' teaches slow, deep abdominal breathing. It also stresses the importance of a good diet and exercise during pregnancy. Instead of using distraction as a pain reliever, it teaches the woman to 'look within' and work in harmony with her own body. Medication is not encouraged and medical intervention is kept to a minimum. Many users of the Bradley Method opt for home births.

The Leboyer Approach

Leboyer emphasises the idea of gentle birth; of making the baby's transition from womb to the outside world as trauma free as possible. Quiet tones are used while staff and support people are speaking, lights are dim and the baby is placed directly on the mother's chest once it is born. Additionally, the cord is not cut until the placenta is delivered.

Active Birth

This method, created by childbirth educator Janet Balaskas is based on hatha yoga, and focuses on moving around and changing positions during labour. It encourages the woman to respond as her body tells her to, rather than what might be convenient for the medical profession. Balaskas was probably fundamental in changing the way women give birth – she believes that standing, kneeling or squatting are the ideal positions rather than lying flat on your back. We have her to thank in part for hospitals now providing such equipment as squatting bars, and beanbags. The importance of stretching exercises and support from your partner is also stressed. Her ideas have now been incorporated into many antenatal classes.

Water Birth

A study published in the *British Medical Journal* has shown there is no greater risk associated with water birth than there is with women who delivered conventionally. Women who choose to have a water birth go through labour and deliver their babies in a birthing pool heated to body temperature. Becoming more popular in Britain, many hospitals now have their own birthing pools. Alternatively, you can hire one and use it at home. See page 128 for more information.

Plan A

I remained blissfully ignorant of this latest fashion for the pregnant woman, which had winged its way from the US to us, until a pregnant friend asked me if I'd 'done my birth plan yet?' Personally, I've yet to meet anyone whose birth has ever gone exactly to 'plan', but writing down any ideas you have about the birth of your baby not only helps the medical and non-medical support people involved, but it also clarifies what kind of birth you would like to have (in an ideal world). The only danger with writing a birth plan is feeling disappointed or cheated if things don't go according to 'plan', so try to think of a birth plan as a rough guide rather than written in stone.

How to Write a Birth Plan

Things you might want to consider when writing a birth plan include:

- Do you want mobility or do you want to be in bed?
- Do you want to wear your own clothing, or a hospital gown? (If giving birth in hospital.)
- Do you want to be able to use the shower or bath?
- What kind of pain medication do you want, if any?
- Do you have a preferred position for giving birth? (See Chapter Nine)
- How do you feel about an episiotomy?
- For home births, what are your plans in case transport is needed?
- How long do you want to wait before going to hospital once contractions start? If you are having a home birth, how long do you want to wait before calling the midwife?
- Who do you want at the birth? (If you are giving birth in a hospital or birth centre check how many people they allow into the delivery room.)
- What do you want in the way of equipment? For example, birthing balls, stools, a beanbag, squatting chair, or a birthing pool.
- How do you feel about having students or residents present?
- Do you want to wait until the umbilical cord stops pulsating before cutting it?
- Do you want an enema?
- Do you want to be continuously fetally monitored?
- Do you want to be induced if overdue?
- Do you want a Caesarean?
- What about the use of forceps?
- Who do you want to cut the cord?
- Do you want the baby to be given to you immediately?
- Do you want music, dim lighting, aromatherapy oils burning? (If you intend giving birth in a hospital, invest in an electric aromatherapy burner, available from most large department stores, as you won't be allowed to have a naked flame in the delivery room.)

Make sure to give a copy of your birth plan to your pregnancy partner.

TIP

If you have access to the Internet, there are a few websites where you can print out a pre-designed birth plan (see Useful Contacts on page 214 for details).

Hospital or Home?

You may find it's automatically assumed you are going to give birth in a hospital, and the statistics in Britain probably feed this assumption – only 2% of women give birth in their own homes. Just compare this to the Dutch system, where ¼ of all births are at home! Many believe the 'medical management' of birth is to blame, others think home birth is largely unsupported by doctors. (You'll find most doctors refuse to attend a home birth for reasons of legal liability.)

Don't let yourself be put off if you think a home birth is really what you want – remember that women have been giving birth at home since time immemorial. Arm yourself with all the facts; research and investigate – talk to other women and perhaps attend one of the support groups for women considering home births to hear first hand experiences.

If you do decide to go ahead, you'll need to discuss this with your midwife. Active natural birth is encouraged, with the mother moving around as much as possible with little medical intervention from the midwife as considered safe. Water births are also very popular at home births as well.

The midwife will take over your care, visiting you in your home, often monthly, fortnightly, and then weekly as your pregnancy progresses, doing your medical check-ups as well as providing you with as much information as possible about home births and discussing your desires for the birth. When you go into labour, you'll call her and she along with a student or additional midwife will attend to you throughout the birth. You should consider a home birth only if your pregnancy has been considered 'low risk'. You will be advised to go for a hospital birth if you have any of the following problems:

- Diabetes, heart problems or high blood pressure.
- The baby is in a breech position (head up, feet down) or transverse (baby lying across the uterus).
- There is evidence of fetal distress.
- When there are multiple fetuses.

Home Births – The Facts

Below are some interesting statistics and facts about home births in Britain:

- Pain relief is allowed to be administered by midwives at home births, such as Pethidine or Entonox.
- Less than 2% of all births are at home.
- Midwives will transfer you to hospital by ambulance, if necessary.
- The cost of hiring an independent midwife ranges from about £2,000 to £7,500.
- The midwife will notify the birth and you will then be able to register your baby and obtain a birth certificate.

The Advantages of Home Births

- You'll be in familiar, comfortable surroundings.
- You won't be disturbed afterwards by hospital timetables.
- You won't have to share a room.
- The baby can arrive in a warm, friendly environment.
- You can have as many people present as you wish.
- The baby will be used to your home.
- The labour will be allowed to progress naturally without any unnecessary medical intervention.
- You can be free to behave however you want without fear of disturbing other women.
- You won't have to move from a bed to a delivery room and back again.

The Disadvantages of Home Births

- Facilities for an emergency Caesarean will be as far away as your nearest hospital.
- You will not be able to have an epidural.
- Sophisticated resuscitation equipment will not be close at hand.
- You will probably feel more inclined to rest less and want to do more in your own home after the birth.

I knew I wanted a home birth before I even fell pregnant. I'm a midwife and having worked in hospitals and having seen the level of intervention I wanted none of it. I also think that drugs confuse women, who need to be clear headed at this time, as well as the effect they can have on the baby. I didn't tell any of my family, until I was 32 weeks or even the obstetrician, who I saw twice, because I knew I would be met with a brick wall. I did have some concerns through my pregnancy and had to confront these fears one by one. My midwife was great for this. As well as the normal antenatal checks, she really made sure I knew everything, patiently answered all my questions and helped to alleviate any concerns, so I was really well informed about what I was going through. I hired a birthing pool (which was unfortunately still in its box when I went into labour at 37 weeks!) However, we got it set up and I had a very short labour (4 hours) where I delivered in a semi-upright position on my hands and knees in the pool. Although my family wasn't happy at the time, they now agree it is the best way and I wouldn't do it differently if I had another child. Kerri

I knew a few people who had had home births and they told me about their experiences with a midwife. I must add here that I strongly believe that the support you receive when pregnant and during labour and birth has an enormous impact on the outcome of your birth, and how those around you make you feel about it has an enormous impact on your mothering skills and self-esteem and confidence generally. I had mostly positive reactions from people around me. But I chose to be in the company of people who weren't going to give me a hard time about our decisions. I had a few people say 'home birth, aren't you brave!' and I would sometimes comment but mostly just think, 'No, hospital birth, aren't you brave!' I looked forward to the visits with the midwife and got to know her really well throughout the pregnancy. I had complete faith in her, as she did in me. She helped me to trust my body and to truly experience the wonder of pregnancy and childbirth. I must also add that midwives also do home visits everyday for the first week after your baby is born to give support with breastfeeding, to check your health and the baby's, to change a nappy, make a cuppa, and put a load of washing on – whatever it is you feel you need. They also visit you a few times in the second week (or as needed). I recommend home birth to all women who feel passionate about natural birth.

The only advice I can give is that if any woman does not feel comfortable about home birth, I strongly recommend that they make arrangements for a midwife to care for them during pregnancy, birth and the postnatal period in the hospital. I think a woman and a midwife who know each other really well are a great team and continuity of care undoubtedly provides for a positive birthing experience. Ellen

An Alternative to Home Births

The Birth Centre

These are becoming increasingly popular among women, but unfortunately are available primarily in bigger hospitals in large cities or towns. They are still a new-ish development, and the majority are privately run. Birth centres offer an alternative for the woman who doesn't want to give birth in a hospital, yet doesn't feel comfortable with a home birth. They are much more flexible about how you choose to give birth, and usually offer equipment such as pools, birthing balls, squatting bars etc. They tend to encourage more active participation in birth, with as little medical interference as possible.

Women who have given birth in a birth centre report that they have more input to decisions during labour and the birth. Birth centres have a friendlier, less 'hospitalised' feel, with much lower intervention rates. Active birth and early discharge are encouraged. The only drawback for using a birth centre is cost.

A Water Birth

Talk to any women who have had a water birth and you'll find they probably can't recommend it highly enough. Many hospitals and birth centres today have birthing pools available for labouring women. Alternatively, if you're giving birth at home, you can hire one (ask your midwife for names of companies who do this). Birthing pools typically measure around 1.6m wide x 0.6m high and hold approximately 115L of water heated to 37°C. While many women spend time in a birthing pool during labour, a true water birth is one where the baby is delivered in the birthing pool. You need to be aware that you will be unable to have any form of medical pain relief, such as an epidural, with a water birth. The benefits of a water birth include:

- The calming effect of the warm water will help your body create endorphins, which are natural pain killers.
- Being relaxed will also make your labour more efficient and less likely to require medical intervention.
- The buoyancy of the water will take the pressure off your abdomen.
- It may be easier moving around in water to find a comfortable position than on 'dry land'.

Basically giving birth in water is almost identical to an active 'land' birth. Your midwife will check how dilated you are before getting into the pool. She can monitor your heartbeat and do all your examinations while you are in the water. The baby can safely be born under the water (after all it's been cosily ensconced in nice warm fluid for 9 months) and the midwife will tell you whether it's preferable for you to deliver the placenta in or out of the pool (she may need to check for tears or blood loss). If you are thinking of hiring a birthing pool, you probably need to have it delivered 21–28 days in advance, just in case.

My child's birth was an incredibly powerful and empowering experience which has changed me in so many ways that I wouldn't even know where to begin. She was a water birth (the pool was a large blow up children's pool). It was a 2½-hour labour and the midwife didn't make it on time due to traffic on the M4 motorway. My girlfriend (another home birther) remained incredibly calm as I birthed the baby. Our midwife arrived about 5 minutes after he was born and we were all ecstatic. Jo

What is a 'Natural' Birth?

You'll undoubtedly hear this term often throughout your pregnancy. According to the Royal College of Obstetricians and Gynaecologists, a 'natural birth' is one in which 'the labour starts by itself and is not assisted by breaking the waters or the use of drugs to stimulate contractions, when no drugs are used for pain relief, where the baby is delivered normally without an episiotomy or sutures and where the placenta is passed without the use of drugs to hasten its delivery'. This is the type of birth most women would wish for in an ideal world, but for the majority it is impossible to achieve. Giving birth is painful. Women who claim that it isn't were probably unconscious at the time! See Reading Recommendations for more information on different methods of childbirth.

Labour Pain

For first time mothers it can be really difficult to anticipate what levels of pain and discomfort they can tolerate without medical, or other, relief. Try asking a woman who has given birth to describe the intensity of the pain and in all likelihood they'll find it impossible. It's a unique feeling and the amount of pain varies widely from woman to woman. Labour pain is actually caused by the reduction of the blood supply to abdominal tissues surrounding the uterus and also by the pressure on the mother's pelvis or spine from the baby. As is generally always true, worry and anxiety may also exacerbate the pain and discomfort which is why most antenatal classes today include some form of relaxation and breathing techniques. While wondering how you might cope with the pain of labour may keep you up at night, there are four points to remember:

1. The pain is finite; it may not seem like it, but it will end.
2. Each pain, each contraction, brings you closer to meeting that wonderful new life you've been nurturing for 9 months.
3. It will all be a vague, hazy memory afterwards.
4. There are a wide range of options to help you cope with the pain.

While many women prefer not to use drugs, because they don't want their perceptions of the labour process and the delivery of their baby to be affected, others feel pressured into having a 'drug free' birth. Try to keep an open mind about both options and do what you want. If you choose to have some medical pain relief don't feel bad about wanting the pain to end; having a more fulfilling birth experience is not 'unnatural'.

Types of Pain Relief

Pethidine

Pethidine is a derivative of morphine, and is often injected into the thigh or buttocks. It works by acting on the nerve cells in the brain and spine. It is the most widely used pain-relieving drug and is usually given in doses of 50 to 150mg either via a drip or an inter-muscular injection. The effects last between 2 to 4 hours, and it is usually given once labour is well established. The amount of pain relief varies widely between women, some finding it very useful in helping them relax and better able to cope with the contractions. Other women find it can make them sleepy and a bit 'spaced out'.

The downside of pethidine is that it can cross the placenta and enter the baby's bloodstream. This can make the baby sleepy, have trouble sucking, or infrequently have breathing difficulties, although these are usually short term effects. It can also make the mother feel nauseous and cause their blood pressure to drop.

I had pethidine after 16 hours of labour which didn't do much, except make me a bit 'heady'. It didn't take away anything from my body, but afterwards I did feel it was the wrong thing to do, because I needed that side of me clear, so that I could control what was going on. Carol

Gas

The gas that you may be offered is a mixture of nitrous oxygen and pure oxygen. The gas doesn't effect the baby and may offer temporary relief between contractions. You may feel nausea, a feeling of 'spaciness', but the effects last only minutes.

● ● ● ● The first mouthful of gas made me so sick, I vomited for about 10 minutes. Even today I remember the weird, cold taste of it and feel really nauseous all over again. Yoko

Caudal Anaesthesia

This numbs the vagina and perineum after an injection into the spinal area around the sacrum and might be used if the mother has to undergo a vacuum extraction or forceps delivery.

Pudendal Nerve Block

The pudendal nerve is in the vagina, near the pelvic region. By injecting an anaesthetic into this area, the lower part of the vagina is numbed, and although used infrequently, the mother may have such an injection if she is to have an episiotomy.

Epidural

This is an anaesthetic injected as needed into a fine tube that has been inserted into a space between the spinal cord and the dura (the membrane covering the spinal cord) into the area containing the spinal nerves. The most widely used anaesthetic in labour, the epidural is seen by many women as an absolute godsend. After a local anaesthetic to numb the area, a fine, hollow needle is inserted into the epidural space (the region around the spinal cord inside the spinal column). A catheter is threaded inside the hollow needle, and anaesthetic syringed down the catheter. The injection prevents pain spreading from the uterus by

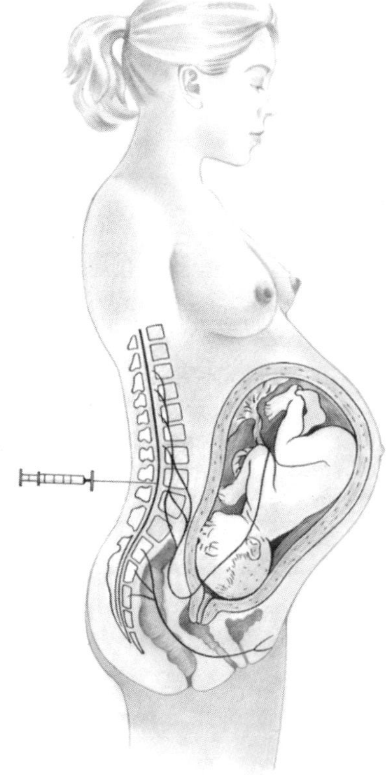

An epidural blocks the nerve roots that lead to the uterus and lower part of the body.

acting as a nerve block in the spine and, ideally, removes all sensation from the waist to the knees, whilst keeping the mother fully alert. It may be allowed to wear off a little toward the end of labour so the woman can push when needed. It can also be used in Caesareans so that the mother is able to remain conscious during the birth. The advantages of an epidural are that it offers complete pain relief throughout labour, yet the mother will be awake and alert and can rest during the first stage so that she has more energy when the time comes to push her baby out into the world.

The disadvantages are that you need to lie still for 5 to 10 minutes while the epidural is being set up. It'll then be another 10 to 20 minutes before it takes effect. It may not always be effective – some women find that only one half of their body has been anaesthetised, or there is a part of their body which the anaesthetic hasn't reached. An epidural may also temporarily lower your blood pressure, resulting in a decreased flow of blood to the placenta. This is dangerous for your baby, so you will need a drip in your arm before you have your epidural so that fluids can be administered quickly if there is a need to boost your blood pressure. The loss of sensation may also make it harder for you to push your baby out. In addition, a few women find they get a very bad headache after the epidural; and some studies suggest a correlation between epidurals and the need for a forceps or ventouse delivery. Finally, you'll have to have a catheter inserted into your bladder, as you won't be able to empty it yourself until the effects wear off.

●●●● I wish I had known that there would be a time when it was too late to administer an epidural. I was keeping that option for when it really got too much, and after a couple of hours with just a shot of pethidine, I couldn't stand it anymore and begged them to give me an epidural. 'Sorry, it's too late for that now, we need you to be able to push'. Luckily it was only another 25 minutes of incredible agony before my son was born. Natalie

●●●● I had an epidural. You can't feel anything in your lower body at all. It certainly took away the pain. I couldn't feel anything, not one thing, your legs are completely and utterly numb. It's weird, because you can't really consciously push, but your body seems to do it automatically. I think the epidural slows down the labour too. I also had to have a vacuum extraction. Jessica

A Spinal Block

A spinal block is a type of regional analgesic. An anaesthetist injects the pain killing medication into the fluid between the outer two membranes that cover your spinal cord. Like an epidural, the drug reduces sensation from your waist down but can only be given once. The advantages of a spinal block are that it's faster to set up than an epidural, and the pain relief is rapid and lasts a few hours. The disadvantages are that you have to keep still for 5–10 minutes while it's set up, the loss of sensation may make it harder to push, it may lower your blood pressure, and you may get a bad headache.

Acupuncture

Some women find acupuncture a very effective form of pain relief and certainly, unlike most pharmaceutical forms of pain relief, it won't effect the baby. Acupuncture works by inserting very fine needles into certain points, which stimulate the nerves, blocking the pain pathways. It's important to try acupuncture before labour, to see if it is suitable for you and to build a relationship with your acupuncturist. The advantages of acupuncture are that it is drug free and you'll remain alert, and the baby will not be affected. The disadvantages are that your acupuncturist may not be allowed into the delivery room, and your movements may be restricted once the practitioner has inserted the needle.

● ● ● ● I had my first child without anything, no type of pain relief at all and when I fell pregnant the second time, I couldn't face the thought of doing it with any form of pain relief and I was pretty anti-drugs. I had been seeing Andrew, an acupuncturist throughout my pregnancy, for things like backache and swelling and found it so effective, I decided to use him during labour as well. He was fantastic, as well as acupuncture, he did massage, which freed up my support person to do other things and was a great relief. The acupuncture seemed to make the contractions more regular and effective and the birth was over in a little more than an hour. He charged me less than £200 despite being on standby to come to the hospital any time of night or day. Kylie

Hypnosis

Hypnosis can often achieve remarkable results in controlling pain. Hypnosis is simply a state of deep relaxation, which can be self-induced or produced with the help of a practitioner. To use self-hypnosis during labour, you will have to see a practitioner to learn the skill. The advantage of hypnosis is that it is drug free. The disadvantages are that some people cannot be hypnotised, and your therapist may not be allowed into the delivery room.

TENS (Transcutaneous Electric Nerve Stimulation)

This involves electrode pads attached to the skin close to the area of pain. A painless current is passed through, stimulating the nerve endings to block the pain pathways to the uterus and cervix. The current also stimulates the mother's production of endorphins (pain killing hormones). The advantages of this treatment are that it is drug free, and the woman herself controls the amount of pain relief she needs. The disadvantage is that you must be familiar with the system so you know how it works.

Visualisation

This involves creating positive images in the mind, to calm fear and anxiety. It is drug free and the woman remains alert. However, it may take some control for a woman in labour to concentrate on positive images.

Caesareans

According to Greek mythology, Apollo removed Asclepius, founder of the famous cult of religious medicine, from his mother's abdomen. Numerous references to Caesarean section also appear in ancient Hindu, Egyptian, Greek, Roman, and other European folklore.

22% of women in the UK will have a Caesarean. Some women choose them (elective Caesareans), others may not have much choice. Non-elective Caesareans are usually due to:

- Cephalo-pelvic disproportion (the baby's head is too big for the mother's pelvis).
- Breech births (bottom or feet first), multiple births, or transverse lie (when the baby is lying crossways in the mother's womb).
- Placenta praevia or placental insufficiency.
- Fetal distress.
- Medical conditions such as diabetes, pelvic abnormalities, hypertension, and infectious diseases or pre-eclampsia.

Emergency Caesareans may be performed if:

- There is severe bleeding in labour.
- The baby can't easily be delivered with forceps.
- Severe eclampsia or pre-eclampsia is evident.
- Fetal distress is evident (the baby's heartbeat has become abnormal).
- There is a failure of labour to progress.
- The cord is prolapsed (when the cord descends into the vagina).
- The baby is extremely premature.

Other women, when thinking about their labour actively, decide to have a Caesarean.

If this is your decision, don't let anyone make you feel guilty or bad about it. It's your body, your birth and your baby.

The advantages of having an elective Caesarean are, obviously, a pain free labour; a lack of post birth complications such as a prolapsed uterus; lack of vaginal slackness or numbness due to scar tissue from an episiotomy. The disadvantages include the fact that the operation is just that, an operation, and post-partum recovery time is slower and more painful – you will probably need extra help at home lifting and carrying, bonding with your baby may be more difficult, and you will have scarring. There are also complications that may occur, such as blood clots in the legs, pain following the operation and difficulty resting your baby on your tummy while breastfeeding.

I'm a very small woman. I'm only 150cm tall, and was around 50kg when I fell pregnant . As the pregnancy progressed it became apparent that I was carrying a large baby. In addition, she descended and engaged two-fifths only to pop up again. At 39 weeks, and still not engaged, an ultrasound was conducted and it was estimated that she was 3.9kg. Given that, and the fact that she still wasn't engaged, we decided to go ahead with an elective Caesarean. Imogen was born just on term and weighed in at 4.1kg. Kathryn

What is a Caesarean?

A Caesarean is the surgical opening and removal of the baby from the abdomen. Your pubic hair may be clipped or shaved, you might have a suppository to help you empty your bowels, and you may be administered antibiotics to guard against infection and an antacid to neutralise stomach acid. You'll have a drip inserted through which fluid or drugs may be administered and a catheter to help you drain your bladder. You'll have a blood pressure cuff out on your arm to keep a constant check on your blood pressure and electrodes on your chest to monitor your heartbeat. An epidural or spinal block is given which will numb you below the

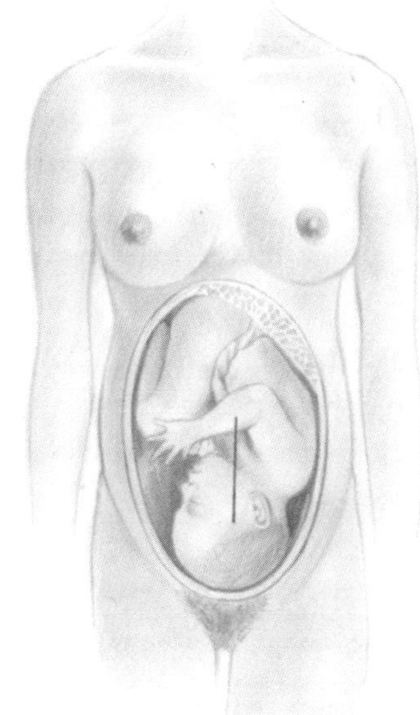

The 'Classical Mid-line' or vertical uterine incision.

waist and a screen is put over your chest. An incision of about 15–22cm is then made just below your public hairline and the baby is then lifted from the abdomen. Once the cord is cut, the placenta is removed and you'll be stitched back up. The whole procedure, providing there are no complications, takes about 1½ hours.

While you should feel no pain, a Caesarean may feel uncomfortable and rather like someone is rummaging around inside you. You may feel a pulling sensation. You probably won't see much of the action as there is a screen between you and your abdomen. However you can request for the screen to be lowered to see the moment the baby is lifted out. Once your baby is born and has been thoroughly checked, he or she will usually be placed on your chest while you're being stitched up. This may not occur if you need some help with breathing or special care for other reasons and are taken to the Intensive Care Unit. The baby may be given to your pregnancy partner while you are taken to a recovery room and monitored. You are then reunited with your baby when you return to the postnatal ward.

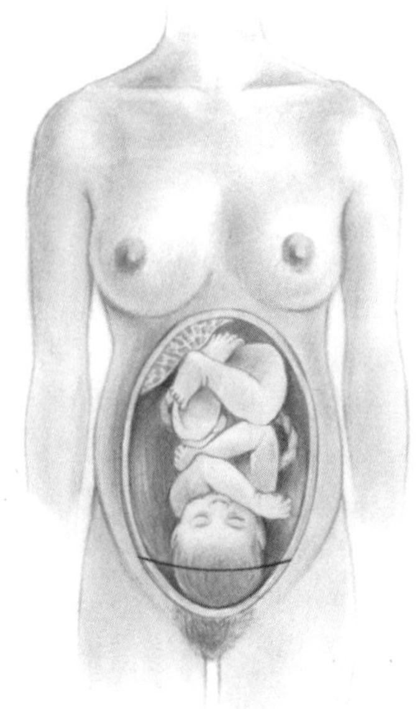

The 'Bikini Incision' or transverse uterine incision.

Your support person or people can be present during the birth, although with a Caesarean, it tends to be restricted to one person as there is usually at least six medical staff present.

How Long will I have to Stay in Hospital?

Usually about 5 days, to allow your stitches or clips to be removed, although you can go home earlier and have the midwife remove them. If you don't have anyone to help you at home, stay in hospital and recover as long as you can.

After a Caesarean

For the first week, and even after that, it may be hard to lift and care for your baby. If at all possible, try to have someone at home with you for the first week.

These days, the Caesarean incision is usually made below the pubic hairline so you won't see it once the hair has grown back. It will start off looking red and raised, but will fade over time to silver. It may be a little uncomfortable and itchy for a few weeks. You're not supposed to drive for at least 6 weeks after the birth.

● ● ● ● I had a terrible time afterwards, I couldn't even get off the bed, I was doped up to my eyeballs so the next day I asked to be taken off the drip. I couldn't walk, and to make matters worse I got mastitis when I got home. I had abdominal pains for several months afterwards. Helen

● ● ● ● The pain afterwards was very manageable with paracetamol and codeine. My hospital stay was 5 days, although I would have been greatly glad to leave after three. The only physical effect that was troublesome was the feeling that I'd lost my stomach somewhere, and not being able to cough easily. I was up and about doing light tasks (like baby care!) pretty much after I got home. I guess it took about a month before I felt normal again, but I suspect that this was more related to having a newborn baby than to having a C-section. I don't feel that I missed out by not having a natural birth, I ended up with a healthy child, and that is all that matters to me. Sally

● ● ● ● I didn't have any problems with recovery at all. Even during the hospital stay, I hardly used pethidine for pain relief, mainly just paracetamol. I have never felt different about having a Caesar as you hear some women do. Jodie

Just Tricking – Braxton Hicks Contractions

You may have started to notice (and worry about) an odd feeling, a tightening across your abdomen usually lasting about 20 seconds. These practice contractions are known as Braxton Hicks contractions and usually begin sometime after week 20, although you may not feel them until sometime after that. This 'limbering up' of the uterine muscles in preparation of childbirth is usually felt as a tightening, beginning at the top of the uterus and spreading downward. Braxton Hicks contractions are important as they ensure good blood circulation through the uterus.

Braxton Hicks contractions are not generally painful, although often uncomfortable. If you feel more than four in an hour, or if they are accompanied by pain or a discharge of any sort, contact your doctor immediately as you may be in pre-term labour, which can often be halted.

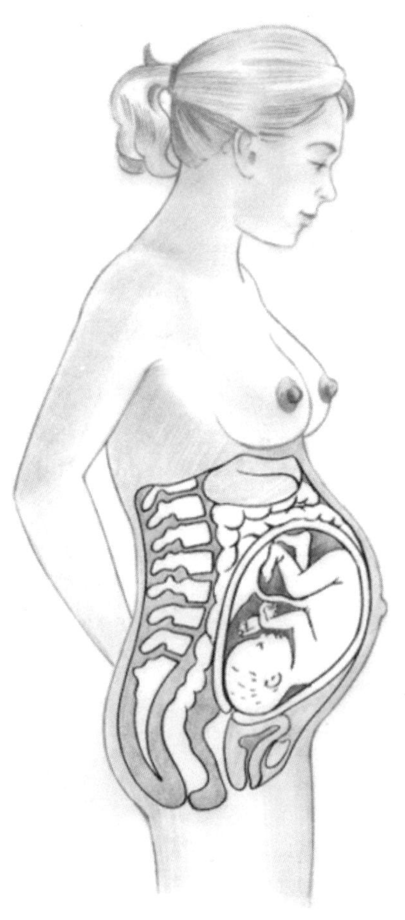

What's Happening? Week 31

You may find you feel a little breathless as the baby grows and the internal organs are squeezed into a smaller space. You may also find your libido fires up; you might also feel dizzy or light-headed because of the progesterone lowering your blood pressure and the diversion of blood to the uterus. You've probably put on between 9kg to 12kg and may have felt a Braxton Hicks contraction.

Your baby's movements will peak this week and it may have changed positions and turned upside down. Most of the wrinkles are disappearing from your baby's face, and there may be a lot of hair on its head! The weight gain has been substantial recently with the baby putting on about 2 pounds of weight, mostly fat and muscle tissue, since last month. It can now hear quite well and is learning to recognise your voice. Your baby is about 24cm in length.

This Month's Checklist

- ✓ Check out your local antenatal classes, or local library for a DIY approach.
- ✓ Investigate your birthing options and consider writing a birth plan.
- ✓ If you are having a home birth, discuss this with your midwife.
- ✓ Investigate prices and arrange delivery of a birthing pool if you want a water birth.
- ✓ You will need to supply your work with a maternity certificate confirming your pregnancy and your EDD (estimated due date).

Ready, Steady...Spend

Shower Power

You may get a raise of an eyebrow by one of your older female relatives, but the baby shower, a fairly recent US import, looks like becoming a part of prenatal tradition. At a baby shower, family and friends gather to eat and drink and celebrate the imminent arrival of your newborn with gifts for the baby (and if you're lucky for you too!) At the moment in this country, this usually occurs at the point when you either stop working or go on maternity leave. It's often suggested that alcohol not be served in deference to the mother, but I reckon there are not too many mothers-to-be in the world who'd begrudge their friends a glass of champagne!

It's most usual to have a baby shower in the last 2 months of pregnancy – which is sufficient time in case of an early arrival, yet doesn't seem too...umm premature. Usually, a friend, relative or pregnancy partner arranges it for you, but you could always drop heavy hints if no-one seems to be making moves! Guests tend to be all-female and include all generations, but that's by no means a hard and fast rule. If you have close male friends who won't be bored by labour horror stories and a gaggle of oestrogen-fuelled women excited by smocked baby nightdresses, by all means invite them. Often a shower is a surprise so you won't know who's coming anyway!

Some people believe you shouldn't invite friends or relatives who are having fertility problems or have lost a baby, but think about whether these women might feel more hurt at being left out. Just approach them quietly with sensitivity, telling them you'd love for them to come, but understand if they feel unable to.

It's usual to receive things for the newborn, such as nightdresses, packets of nappies (cloth or disposable), bunny rugs, toiletries, and soft toys. If you're lucky you might also find that people get together and buy some of the bigger or more expensive items you may need. If you know about the shower, make a list of things you need and either give it to the person arranging it, or if this feels too mercenary, leave it 'lying around' somewhere conveniently in sight!

Incidentally, if you are going to have a baby shower, wait until after the event before buying clothes or equipment for your baby.

Buying for your Baby

Newborn baby clothes are so adorable; the temptation is to buy everything you clap your eyes on. Add to this an unspoken desire as a single woman to prove to the world that you can provide for your baby well...and you may as well set fire to those £50 notes.

Consider how fast a baby grows. Would you pay £30 for a pair of pyjamas you knew you weren't going to fit you in a month? Be strong. Shop with a tightwad friend who'll set you straight about the need for designer label romper suits and handcrafted oak cradles. See Reading Recommendations on page 208 for more information on buying goods for your baby.

Clothes

The essential items of clothing you need for your newborn baby are:

- Six towelling or fleecy stretchsuits.
- Two cardigans or knitted jackets.
- Six singlets or bodysuits.
- One or two hats.
- Four pairs of socks.
- Two bibs.

Before using any new baby clothes, wash them in a gentle detergent, as some contain irritating starches to keep them looking 'crisp' in the shops.

Equipment

Equipment that you require for your newborn includes:

- Car seat or baby carrier.
- Pram.
- Baby bath.
- Baby nail scissors.
- A couple of face flannels.
- Liquid soap-free wash.
- Two large soft towels.

If you're going to Breastfeed

If you are going to breastfeed your baby, you will need:

- Three nursing bras.
- A packet of breast pads.
- A breast pump.

If you're going to Bottle-feed

If you are going to bottle-feed you will need:

- Six bottles and newborn teats.
- Sterilising kit/steamer.
- Bottle brush.
- Baby formula.

Nappies

If you're going to use cloth nappies, you should have:

- About three dozen nappies.
- Pins or fasteners.
- Liner pants.
- A bucket with lid for soaking.
- Soaking powder such as 'Napisan'.

If you're going to use disposable nappies, you should have:

- Newborn-sized nappies.
- Nappy sacks.
- Change mat.
- Baby wipes.
- Protective cream for preventing nappy rash.

Optional Extras

Other items to consider include:

- A carry sling.
- Mattress protector.
- Cot (plus a new mattress, fitted sheets and cellulose blankets if winter)
- Baby monitor.

Useful Hints before Buying

- Ask other parents what they did and didn't find useful and which brands they particularly recommend. Some websites also have bulletin boards or chat rooms where you can ask other mums for their recommendations.
- Make a list.
- Don't try to do all your shopping in one go, you'll exhaust yourself.
- Take a note pad and pen with you.
- Once you've seen something you like, and have noted the make, model number and price, ring around the baby shops to compare prices. Tell them if you can get it cheaper elsewhere as often stores will match or beat their competitors' prices.
- Ask shops if they are going to be having a sale in the near future.
- Try buying things such as creams, lotions and nappies online (see Useful Contacts on page 214 for details).

● ● ● ● My baby is 7 weeks old and I found that when I was pregnant with him there seemed to be so much to buy. I put by what I could, which helped, and tried to buy something each time I did the grocery shopping like breast pads, maternity pads, wipes, cotton buds or things you may want for your labour. It was easier on the budget that way. Erica

● ● ● ● Second-hand and recycled baby clothes stores sell great stuff and are so much cheaper than the big stores. Also they often sell toys second-hand and the majority of times things are in excellent condition. Local papers are also a winner for finding some of the expensive stuff! Kylie

Buying Second-hand

Buying second-hand, or having things given to you, can be a great relief on the ever-burgeoning baby budget, however, there are some things you should always buy new because of the ever-changing safety recommendations. What is considered suitable at one time may be considered positively dangerous in 5 years time. Things may have also been recalled due to faults and the owner hasn't heard about it or bothered to return it. One of the best sources of second-hand equipment is your local weekend paper, which usually has a classified section selling baby goods. Increasingly too, there are websites where you can buy over the Internet – a very convenient way of saving you time and energy! (See Useful

Contacts on page 214 for details.) Items that are safe to buy second-hand include:

- Bottle steriliser (microwavable bottles are very convenient).
- Bottles.
- Breast pump.
- Pram (but check it carefully).
- High chair (check the five-point harness is still intact, and if not, buy a new one).
- A baby bath.
- Clothes (check for fire resistant fabrics).

Items that you shouldn't buy second-hand include:

- Bottle teats.
- Mattresses.

Second-hand items you should buy with caution include:

- A car seat. Check the webbing for fraying, and the year of manufacture, which is moulded into the plastic back or beneath the harness adjuster at the front. Don't buy it if it is over 10 years old, or shows any sign of wear or of being in an accident.
- Cots (ensure that they comply with British Standards Institute Kite Mark requirements).

Buying Safely

- Always ask for proof the item is made according to British Standards Institute Kite Mark, which ensures that it meets standard minimum safety and design requirements.
- Take a tape measure with you when you go shopping so you can check the size of gaps and openings of items accurately. Heads can get caught in gaps over 85mm, fingers between 5–12mm and legs between 30–50mm.
- Make sure furniture, such as dressers or change tables are free of rough surfaces, sharp edges, points and protrusions, and check that they are sturdy and secure.
- Test locking devices thoroughly. They should lock firmly and securely and be simple to operate.
- If you buy a cot or baby basket second-hand, buy a new mattress.
- Check the fire rating on babies' clothes (printed on the inside label) before you

buy and make sure you buy the highest fire retardant or resistant ones possible.

- If a cot you want to buy has wheels, make sure at least two are lockable.
- Mattresses should be firm, well-fitting and have no more than a 25mm gap between the mattress and cot sides. Sides must be at least 500mm above the top of the mattress and the thickness should not exceed 100mm.
- It's not recommended that newborns have pillows or cot bumpers, so don't bother buying these.
- If you buy a change table, make sure it has raised sides so the baby can't roll off, and check that it is stable.
- Prams should have a five-point harness and be sturdy with easy to use locks.
- If you're buying a car seat second-hand, don't rely on the owners to tell you the truth about its age and condition. Check yourself that there are no tiny frays in belts or evidence of repair and always check the date of manufacture (see above).

Buying Frugally

There is an awful lot of pressure on women to go into shopping overload. Pregnancy magazines are full of ads for the latest 'must haves', all supposed to somehow make your life easier. The truth is that no piece of equipment can replace a pair of warm arms, or make your baby sleep through the night and he or she most definitely won't care if they are dressed in Baby Target instead of Baby B'gosh. Save that money for essentials later on and take advantage of what could be the least expensive time of your child's life. Tips on saving money when buying equipment or items include:

- Instead of a change table, invest in a waterproof padded change mat which you can use to change the baby on the bed or floor. You can also buy a chest of drawers with extra-wide tops that you can put change mats on.
- Try buying online. Online supermarkets offer substantial savings on products like nappies and creams and lotions, and best of all, they deliver to your door! (See Useful Contacts on page 214 for details.)
- Instead of baby wipes, it is cheaper to use cotton wool. Newborn poo is very runny and easily cleaned. Baby wipes contain a lot of chemicals designed to keep them moist which is not good for baby's delicate skin. Warm cotton wool as well as being softer and kinder to their skin, is much more cost effective.
- Forget those cute baby towels – they are small and not useful for very long. Instead, wash one or two of your own and keep just for the baby's use.

- If you can't afford a bottle steriliser or haven't managed to find one second-hand, sterilisation tablets, while not as convenient, are cheap and easy to use.
- If you are going to breastfeed and will be returning to work, it may be worth hiring an electric breast pump to express milk. These can be hired by the month from larger pharmacies, medical suppliers or the National Childbirth Trust. If you'll only be leaving your baby occasionally, it's probably cheaper to invest in a hand held pump.
- Cloth nappies cost about £7 less a week to use than disposables (see table below), but whichever you decide to use, start stocking up whenever you see them on sale.
- Cheap disposable nappies are usually a false economy – they need to be changed more often as they are less absorbent. Instead buy better quality in bulk, which is usually more cost effective.
- Start saving plastic shopping bags to use in nappy bins if you are going to use disposables.
- Limit your size 0–3 months to just a few; babies grow out of these sizes more quickly than anything else.
- Things seem to cost twice as much if they have a picture of Peter Rabbit on it and come from a baby store. Save your money and buy things such as nappy buckets, bins and baskets to put babies' toiletries in at places such as hardware stores, or discount shops.

●●●● My favourite was a snuggle bed, which is a tea-tree mattress with slightly raised sides which either sits in a cot (most babies seem to find the wide spaces of a cot a little scary) or could go on the bed. I used it as long as 6 months, until he couldn't fit into it and used to take it when I went visiting, so that my baby could have a sleep anywhere, without lugging around a carry cot. Fiona

●●●● My bath thermometer. I was always scared that what felt lukewarm to me was far too hot for my daughter. It wasn't expensive at all and it had the right temperature for a baby's bath water marked on it. Natalie

●●●● Definitely my sling, it was excellent and going out was so much easier without a pram. In fact, I didn't even have a pram for the first 3 months! Josh loved it and inevitably fell asleep rocked by my body moving and heartbeat I guess. When he was older, I turned him around so he could watch the world go by. Get the best one you can afford though – I found some of the cheaper ones I tried on very uncomfortable. Jenny

● ● ● ● I found this thing that you put in the bath, which was like a little recliner lined with towelling you sit in the bath and lie the baby on. It was the most useful thing I bought. You have both hands free to wash the baby, she can't slip around and you can use them in an ordinary bath instead of buying a baby bath. It cost less than £10. Sophia

● ● ● ● A friend gave me a huge pile of her children's cloth nappies. I actually used disposables, but I found them lots of use for everything from slinging over my shoulder when burping my son to lining the change mat. Margaret

Cloth versus Disposable Nappies

There's no avoiding this particular purchase. The only decision you need to make is whether you want to use cloth or disposable nappies. It's a highly debated subject with endless studies producing conflicting results as to which has less impact on the environment. (This could be due to the fact that most of the studies are sponsored by interested parties such as nappy manufacturers!)

The disposal of baby wastes by whatever means is damaging to the environment (it takes 200–500 years for a disposable nappy to decompose). Both cloth and disposable nappy systems impact adversely on the environment in different ways.

So, in the end it comes down to personal choice. There is no denying that today's disposables are remarkable, with new technology ensuring babies stay completely dry and thus nappy rash free. However, there is the problem with...errr disposal.

Which Nappy?

DISPOSABLE NAPPIES	CLOTH NAPPIES
Expensive	Cost effective (using cloth nappies can save you around £2000 for 30 months of nappy wearing
Plastics and chemicals such as absorbent gel which is difficult to break down	May need to use large quantities of bleach and washing powder containing phosphates

DISPOSABLE NAPPIES	CLOTH NAPPIES
Environmentally unsound, forests are felled and replaced with trees planted and intensively managed using pesticides and fertilisers. The average baby will use 6,500 nappies before potty training	Can be reused for years
Time efficient. No soaking, washing, drying	Increased cost of water, electricity and wear and tear on your washing machine
Most keep baby drier than cloth	More labour intensive time needed for soaking, washing and drying
	May need to change baby more often
	Some areas offer a home delivery service for cloth nappies, delivering clean and collecting used for recycling. It is worth investigating whether this type of service is available in your area

Nappy Fact

A baby will use anywhere between 5000 and 8000 disposable nappies until they are toilet-trained. This is the equivalent of up to five trees.

Premature Labour

Babies born between 20 and 37 weeks are known as 'premature', or 'pre-term'. Around 5% of babies born in the UK are born pre-term. A baby born weighing less than 2.5kg is considered to have a low birth-weight. Babies who weigh less than 1.4kg are considered to be a very low birth-weight. The further to term a baby goes, the greater the chances of survival. However, where once babies born less than 25 weeks had little chance of survival, today slightly less than ½ of these will survive, with the odds increasing as weeks pass. Going into labour prematurely can be caused by:

- The membranes, the amniotic sac in which the baby is growing, rupturing early due to an infection.
- Cervical incompetence (when the cervix opens too early). If this occurs early on in the pregnancy, the doctor may put in a cervical stitch, to hold it closed until week 37.
- Multiple pregnancy, when the pressure of more than one baby on the uterus can start labour.
- A problem with the mother or baby, such as gestational diabetes, high blood pressure, or the baby not growing properly in the womb.
- Infection of the uterus, cervix or urinary tract.

Other risk factors include:

- Drug abuse including alcohol, nicotine and street drugs.
- Heavy physical exertion, such as lifting or long periods of standing.
- Inadequate nutrition.
- A hormonal imbalance.
- Stress.
- When the mother is younger than 17 or older than 35.
- Infections such as rubella or chorion amnionitis (amniotic fluid infection).
- Placenta praevia and placental abruption (see Chapter Six).
- Fetal abnormality.
- Excess amniotic fluid (polyhydramnios).

How to Recognise Premature Labour

With Braxton Hicks contractions to trick you up, it might be difficult to recognise if you are really in labour or not, however, real contractions tend to be more regular than Braxton Hicks. If in doubt, it's best to contact your doctor or midwife. Following are some warning signs that may be an indication you're going into premature labour:

- Lower back pain.
- Abdominal cramps with or without diarrhoea.
- A change in vaginal discharge, such as a thick mucous plug known as a 'show'.
- Rupture of membranes resulting in a trickle or flow of fluid from your vagina.
- Aches or pressure in the abdomen.
- Pelvic pressure.

If you suspect you are in premature labour, particularly if there is fluid leaking from your vagina, call your doctor or midwife immediately. Treatment depends on how far along you are. Sometimes, premature labour can be halted with bed rest, at other times medication may be used. In some instances, surgery to close the cervix may be an option.

If labour continues, steroids may be given to the mother to help develop the baby's lungs. (Premature babies treated with steroids inutero are likely to be healthier than those who are not.) If your doctor or midwife suspects you are in premature labour, and depending on how early you are, you may be moved to the best hospital equipped to care for premmies.

What Happens When a Baby is Born Prematurely?

As soon as the baby is born, it will be subjected to a health check to monitor its breathing, colour and overall activity. If the baby has breathing difficulties, it may have a tube inserted into its lungs to help, and it may be put into an incubator to help keep them warm.

Most premmies will be transferred to a special care unit once it is stable. Depending on its condition, you may have time for a quick stroke or kiss. If your hospital doesn't have sufficient facilities to care for your baby, you may both be transferred (depending on your condition).

What Problems Will a Premature Baby Have?

Babies who are born at a younger gestation than 37 weeks, often have problems because they're not yet fully developed. They sometimes suffer jaundice as their livers are not yet fully developed. They may have breathing difficulties, due to the lack of a chemical known as surfactant, which is necessary for lung development. They often have a low body temperature, are prone to infections, they may have hypoglycaemia or low blood sugar levels and difficulties in sucking or nursing. They may be on a ventilator to help them breathe; they might be sedated to keep them calm and stop any movement which could cause tubes to fall out. Premature babies might be given antibiotics, corticosteroids to help with lung development and may be in an incubator to regulate their temperature. As a baby's sucking reflex doesn't develop fully until 32–36 weeks, they may have to be fed through an intravenous drip or a tube straight into their stomach.

What Will a Premature Baby Look Like?

Your baby will naturally be smaller than if he or she was born at full term. Often premature babies still have a covering of lanugo, a fine downy hair over their bodies. Their skin may be yellow due to jaundice or may seem almost transparent, with veins clearly visible below the skin.

How You Might Feel After the Birth of Your Premature Baby

Going into early labour can be a big shock. You may feel totally unprepared, both physically and practically. You may feel numb and disconnected from what is going on around you. You may find it hard to eat or sleep and to comprehend what you may be told about your baby's condition, or to accept the severity of your baby's condition if they have problems. You may feel helpless and awkward, in the way, and scared of hurting your baby with all those tubes. Give yourself time to adjust and talk to the nursing staff to allay any fears about touching or inadvertently hurting your baby. Most importantly, talk about your feelings – get help and support. (See Useful Contacts on page 214 for details.)

Tayla was born by emergency c-section at 35 weeks. My membranes actually ruptured at 32 weeks, and so I had 3 weeks of jabs, boring bed rest and hospital stays to try and keep her in there a bit longer. Halfway through the 35th week, they did tests which confirmed she had got an infection (to be expected with early ruptured membranes), and that there wasn't enough amniotic fluid left. After a horrendous 11 hours in labour, they did an emergency c-section as she was starting to be in some distress. I guess the worst thing was that when it was all over and she had been 'pulled out', there was no holding, playing or peaceful quiet time – none of that wonder and joy of looking at your newborn, counting her fingers and toes. I was in the theatre with eight medical staff and Tayla was just whisked away to have some oxygen. It was a sad time for me, lying there, being stitched up knowing I couldn't hold my baby and I have to admit shedding a few tears. It was when I got back to my room later that it really hit me though, and I got really upset that my baby was not with me. I couldn't stop crying and asking what was going on down in NICU where the baby had been taken. I felt so helpless and although my best friend, who was there throughout, was great, it would have been such a relief to have a partner, who I guess would be the only person who could really feel as I did – someone I could share the burden of my fear and sadness with. I kept asking whether I could go see her, till finally the midwives got fed up and wheeled me down to NICU. She was still in her humidicrib and I could only touch her through the holes. I felt so sad and cheated at not being able to hold her but she was everything I could have hoped and dreamed for, she just took my breath away. Of course she was pretty small. She was in NICU for 4 days, and then came in with me. Unfortunately she had to go back in when she went bright yellow with jaundice. She had to be under the ultraviolet lights as much as possible, coming to me only for three hourly feeds a day (she surprised everyone by breastfeeding like a trooper). There were some pretty rough patches over the next week. I got to know all the other parents with babies in NICU and together we suffered through the highs and lows. Tayla had to have a lumbar puncture at 48 hours old and her poor tiny heels were so sore looking from all the heel pricks they had to do. Altogether, she needed to stay in hospital for another 2 weeks, until she got over her infection. The relief as we were driving away from the hospital was incredible. I'll never forget putting my little girl into the car, knowing she was finally healthy and best of all mine, to take home and start our life together. Fiona

Child Care

It may seem strange to start thinking about this before your child is even born, but many single women find that they have to go back to work quite early on to make ends meet. The majority of nurseries have long waiting lists, so it's important to investigate all the options now and get your baby waitlisted.

There a few different options for child care: nursery-based, home-based, or having your baby looked after by a family member. Whichever method you choose really depends on your own personal feelings (and often finances). It is worth checking with the Department for Work and Pensions to see what benefits you are entitled to. You may be entitled to claim Working Families Tax Credit, Child Maintenance Bonus or New Deal for Lone Parents (see Useful Contacts, page 212).

How to Choose a Nursery

Obviously you need to choose somewhere near home or work. The price often varies from centre to centre. You should look out for and ask about the following factors when choosing a child care centre for your baby:

- Is the atmosphere relaxed and happy?
- Are you welcome to visit at any time?
- Is there an orientation process for new children and parents?
- Do carers spend time talking to and encouraging the children?
- Are the staff appropriately qualified?

- Are the premises clean and safe?
- Do the staff give you a big welcome when you arrive?
- Do toilet-training, nappy changing and rest times meet individual needs?
- Is there a wide range of toys and activities for the children?
- Does the service/carer have a planned program of day-to-day activities for the children?
- Is information readily available about the service's/carer's policies, e.g. discipline, hygiene procedures?
- Do you feel welcome to discuss your child and child care policies with carers?
- Are cultural differences recognised and accepted?
- Do snacks and meal arrangements meet individual needs?
- Will your child's individual needs be met?

To this, I would personally add, 'trust your instinct and visit as many centres as you can', so you begin to build a picture of what good child care is.

Registration

The Office for Standars in Education (OFSTED) approves and regulates childcare services in England. They register and inspect childcare services.

A typical full-time place at nursery now costs over £110 per week (£5,700 per year).

Types of Child Care

Long-term Day Care

Long-term day care centres usually operate between 7.00 a.m. and 6.00 p.m. and care for 35 to 40 children aged from birth to school age, although some won't take children until they are 12 months. You can use them all day or part-time, although the fees are usually fixed so you pay a per day rate regardless of hours. Children are usually divided into separate groups, according to age and should have a ratio of one carer per four children at the youngest age.

Childminder Schemes

The Children's Information Service (CIS) will have a current list of registered childminders in your area (see Useful Contacts, page 215). Childminders can provide a home-from-home atmosphere, caring for children of all ages. Do visit them before your baby is born, if possible, and preferably while there are children present so that you can see how the childminder cares for them. Always request references and, where possible, contact the referees to discuss any issues you may have. Usually childminders are for children under school age, although they may also provide after school care. Numbers are limited, depending on the age of the children, but there are rarely more than four or five children in total. The beauty of a childminder is that the hours are flexible and can even include overnight stays. They are also extremely reasonably priced and cheaper than nurseries. All carers are registered and there are very stringent checks on carers and their houses, as well as frequent unannounced visits by OFSTED administrators.

Although a 'stay at home' mum, I decided that my son and I needed an occasional break from each other. My ex and I discussed our options. Our son was two-and-a-half years old and we decided that he needed extra attention and one-on-one care. We put him with a childminder. As soon as we walked into the lady's house, my boy was happy. He ran off and played. He is now 5 and going to school but still goes to her and sleeps over once a fortnight. It is a good idea for us both, because he is still in a family environment and gets to spend time with her husband so he has a male role model (his Daddy lives away these days). I don't regret placing him with a childminder and think it was the best option for us all. Kellie

I chose a childminder, because Jasmine was only 6 weeks old when I went back to work and I wanted her to be somewhere that she would get lots of personal attention and be in a home-like environment. Sophia

When I actually decided to go back to work, it was pretty much a spur of the moment decision. Once I made the decision, I went back to work the very next week and I needed to find somewhere quite quickly. Ultimately, I chose a childminder because of my son's age. I thought that a family environment would be more suitable, we found a lovely mother and daughter 'team' and my son took to them straight away. It was so much easier going off to work knowing he was happy with the childminder. Tash

● ● ● ● I used a childminder to look after my child on my return to work, although progressively phased out this care and introduced him to anursery when he was 2. To leave him so soon was heart-wrenching, but financially I had no choice. The initial childminder was not a huge success, but the second family became like de-facto grandparents, and were very supportive of me. Oliver was 8 months at the time he was transferred to their care. Dorothy

Nannies

If you are lucky enough to have a good source of income, you may be in a position to employ a nanny. Nannies often live in your home and may also help out with other household chores. You will employ the nanny and pay her salary directly to her. Check out *The Nanny Handbook* by Karen House and Louise Sheppard or *The Good Nanny Guide* by Charlotte Breese and Hilaire Walden, both of which are good guides to choosing a nanny.

Occasional Care

A blessing for single stay-at-home mothers, occasional care services are for parents who need short periods of care for children under school age. These include crêches in shopping centre, health centres or fitness clubs. You can use them regularly, booking in your baby for a period each week or just when you need a break, or have to attend appointments etc. Usually, you are allowed no more than four half-day sessions in four weeks. They can be a good way to let your child get used to other children and socialise.

● ● ● ● I felt so selfish leaving Lilly there the first time, but I was desperate to get a hair cut and had no-one to look after her. She didn't seem at all fazed when I left and apparently didn't cry or fuss once. I felt like I'd had my right arm cut off at first though, but once I relaxed, it was bliss. After I had my hair done, I sat in the café and read a paper and had a coffee, the first time since Lilly's birth. I felt normal again and realised how isolated I'd been, just her and me, 24 hours a day. After that, I booked her in once a week for a few hours. It makes such a difference, I feel so much more relaxed and happy after those few precious hours and she seems to enjoy being with other kids too. Jenny

Care by a Family or Friend

If you have a willing relative you trust, this could be the perfect option. Knowing your child is with someone they know, can be a huge relief and lessen the effects of separation anxiety. There is also less chance of your child catching colds or other illnesses from children. Having a child stay with a parent or friend also means flexibility of hours plus less disruption to the child's routine. The downside of having your child cared for by a family member or friend is that if you come into conflict with them over care, it can result in an increase in stress tension.

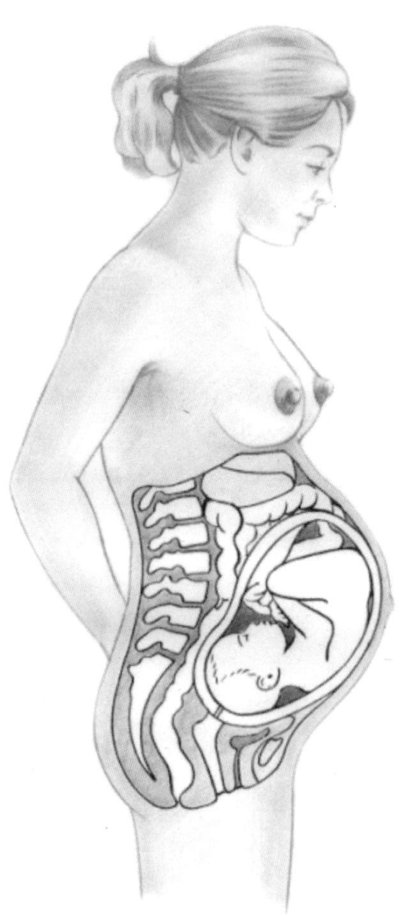

What's Happening? Week 35

You may feel different, as the baby drops lower into your pelvis. This is known as 'lightening', and means you'll be able to breathe better, but like the beginning of the pregnancy, you will probably have to go to the toilet more often. The majority of babies are in a head down position by now, but about 4% will be breech (see next chapter for details). You may have swelling of the feet and ankles.

The baby will weigh approximately 2.3kg and is about 45cm long. The fine downy hair (lanugo) which has covered its body is probably beginning to disappear. Your midwife will palpitate your stomach to get an idea of how big the baby is likely to be (this is just an educated guess though!) The baby's skull bones are soft and flexible for delivery.

This Month's Checklist

- ✔ If you continue working right up until the birth you'll need to give notice now.
- ✔ From week 36, your doctor or midwife may see you weekly, so don't forget to make these appointments.
- ✔ Investigate your child care options and put your name down on any waiting lists.
- ✔ If you've ordered a birthing pool take delivery of it and set it up if possible at the end of this month.

CHAPTER NINE

WEEKS 36–39

Are We There Yet?

How You Might be Feeling

Most women feel that the last few weeks of their pregnancy drag by. You may be feeling a heightened sense of anticipation, or even fear. You may worry that things aren't 'ready' or even that you yourself aren't ready. You may think about the birth and be preoccupied with things going wrong, or whether you will be able to cope with labour. You may feel excited about this new little being you are going to meet. You may feel aroused and feel like having sex. You might feel an incredible sense of contentment. You may be dreaming a lot, as your subconscious prepares you for this huge life change. You may feel sad or angry that you don't have a partner to share this experience with and worry about how your life is going to change and whether you will be able to cope.

I got very depressed during my pregnancy and was put on antidepressants to help me through. I had dreams that my baby was taken away from me and I had given birth to an ugly little alien creature. The stigma of becoming a single mother really bothered me as well. I had always been a super-achiever and now felt that people were looking down on me and judging me because I was going to have a baby and raise it alone. Nadene

Physically, you may find yourself unable to sleep. It can be hard this late in pregnancy to find a comfortable position and your mind may be ticking over with all the things you have to do yet, or worrying about labour. Try to have some gentle exercise every day, have a warm bath before bed and a glass of warm milk or chocolate drink. Try listening to a relaxation tape as you drift off. You may also be experiencing other ailments, including:

- Back pain. Massage can help, but it needs to be gentle and done by a professional. Try some pelvic tilts, cat stretches and a hot wheat pack.
- Leg cramps. Make sure you are getting enough calcium. Again a warm glass of milk before bed might help, as will stretching before retiring.

- Shortness of breath. As the baby grows and compresses your diaphragm you have less room to breathe. Although with some women this eases in these last few weeks, you might still find yourself prone to occasional fits of breathlessness. It may help to sleep or rest in a semi-reclining position propped up by pillows.
- Fatigue. Not much you can do about this except try to have an afternoon nap and make sure you are eating and drinking well.
- Heartburn. This may have eased somewhat as the baby drops, but if not, avoid spicy foods, stay upright after eating and have a glass of milk afterwards.
- Pubic bone pain. As the baby's head engages in these last few weeks, you may start to feel an uncomfortable pressure in your pubic area. Try using a hot wheat pack to relieve the discomfort.
- Balance problems. Big and unable to see your toes, you may find yourself becoming unusually clumsy. Take extra care getting in and out of the bath, cars etc and don't worry too much about the baby; if you do have a fall, it's well cushioned in there.

Pack your Bags

In TV sitcoms, the mother-to-be always has a neat and very small suitcase waiting in the hallway. In reality most of us are more likely to have an empty overnight bag sitting reproachfully at the end of the bed. I personally found the packing of the hospital bag a daunting task, both practically (I'd never been to hospital) and emotionally (oh my God, this is REAL – I am going to have a baby!)

More important than your hospital bag is what you want during labour. (You'll no doubt have visitors who can bring anything you've forgotten for your hospital stay).

Things for You

Following are some suggestions of what you might need for both your labour and hospital stay.

- A couple of front opening nightdresses or pairs of pyjamas (preferably older ones) and a nightdress for giving birth (some hospitals will offer you one of theirs).
- A spray bottle of water (a chemist will make you up a bottle of rosewater which you can decant into a spray bottle).
- Your birth plan if you have one.

- Hair band or elastics if you have long hair.
- Camera.
- Small change/phone card. Mobile phones are often banned in hospitals.
- A pair of warm socks (your feet often get cold during labour).
- Lip balm.
- Cards, a game book, magazines.
- An electric aromatherapy burner and essential oil of choice; if allowed at your hospital.
- Music tapes/CDs (check your hospital has something to play them on in the labour room).
- Slippers.
- Dressing gown.
- Breast pads.
- Two nursing bras.
- Toiletries.
- Two packets of maternity pads.
- Some 'going home' clothes.
- Earplugs. Hospitals can be noisy places and you might find it difficult to sleep.

You might like to take the following things for your pregnancy partner:

- Snacks and drinks.
- A copy of the birth plan.
- A book or pack of cards.
- A telephone list with people you want notified.

Things for your Baby

Usually while you are in hospital, you will need to provide clothes, nappies, creams and lotions. You will also need to take:

- Some 'going home' clothes, such as a 0–3 month babygro
- A couple of nappies with pins and overpants, if using cloth nappies.
- A matinee jacket.
- A warm hat if the weather is cool.
- Shawl or blanket.

If you have chosen to have a home birth, it may be worthwhile preparing your home for your baby's imminent arrival. Meet with your midwife and ask what she thinks may be necessary in addition to what you personally want.

Arrange for delivery of your birthing pool if you're having one and set it up, ready to go. Have music, candles, beanbags and anything else you think you might want close at hand. It is a good idea to pack a hospital bag just in case you need to be transferred to hospital.

Breast or Bottle?

At this stage it is probably a good idea to start thinking about whether you intend to breastfeed or bottle-feed. The message is constant – 'breast is best' – and there are unlikely to be many women who would debate this fact. Breast milk has been proven to be better for newborn babies than formula. Here are some of the advantages of breastfeeding:

- Protects your baby from illness and infection.
- Provides the perfect food for your growing baby.
- Aids the development of your baby's eyesight, speech and intelligence.
- Lowers the risk of cot death.
- Reduces the likelihood of allergy.
- Saves money – there's no need to buy expensive infant formulas and feeding equipment. Also, because breastfed babies are apparently healthier, you'll save on doctor and hospital visits.
- Is environmentally friendly – it saves fuel, energy and resources.
- Provides long-term health benefits for both you and your baby.
- Promotes a special loving bond between mother and baby.

In addition to being best for baby, breastfeeding also helps the mother, as it causes small contractions that help the uterus to go back to shape sooner.

If you do choose to breastfeed and have any problems, there is an enormous amount of help available – from hospital infant feeding advisors to the National Childbirth Trust breastfeeding counsellors, as well as books. See Chapter Ten for more information.

Bottle-feeding

Remember it is your body, your baby and your decision. You may have reasons why you don't want to breastfeed and whatever they are, you shouldn't be condemned for them (or have to explain to anyone else). Unfortunately, you're bound to encounter at least one disapproving look, or comment whether from a midwife, friend or relative

Don't let anyone make you feel guilty for your decision. Take heart, there are many, many children out there who have grown up perfectly healthy and happy on formula. The formulas available today are excellent and while they don't precisely mimic breast milk they do a pretty good job and your baby is unlikely to suffer unduly from being bottle-fed. The main advantage of bottle-feeding is convenience. Bottle feeding means you can leave your baby with someone else if necessary. You know exactly how much your baby is getting, a frequent concern of breastfeeding mothers.

On the down side, bottle-feeding can be expensive with tins of formula costing up to £5. You also have to buy and sterilise all your equipment. You do need to discuss with your midwife about drying up your milk supply as soon as the baby is born if you are not going to breastfeed.

Providing the water used has been thoroughly boiled and all the teats and bottles have been correctly sterilised, there are minimal associated health risks with bottle-feeding. Bottle-fed babies are more prone to stomach upsets, such as diarrhoea and vomiting. Make sure to always use the correct amount of milk powder for your baby's weight as specified in the instructions, and throw out any unused formula.

Kahla had severe sucking problems. She was a 'floppy baby' born with a hole in her heart and not very strong. She would attach but really just play around, not sucking hard enough to get anything. When I asked for help, I was told she was lazy and to just keep trying. Well, I tried for 4 months. I bottle-fed her with expressed milk with a fast flow teat and constantly tried to get her to take the breast, but she just refused. Eventually I had to give up expressing and give her formula because I was so exhausted, especially since going back to work. I was made to feel stupid by the health visitor who said I hadn't tried hard enough. I feel very bitter about it now, the guilt and anguish I went through for those months. God, the nights I sat with my expressing machine crying because I couldn't get more than 80 mls of milk and somehow had to supply four times that by the time I went to work the next day. Elisabeth

How does your Baby Lie?

You may find now that the baby is moving around less, (though you may be kicked just as much). This is because at around week 36 the baby's head engages (lowers into the pelvis). Most babies at this time are lying head down (cephalic) in the uterus either to the right or left of your pubic bone with their back facing your front. This is called the OA (occipito anterior). This is the easiest position to deliver in, best of all is the right occipito anterior, when the baby's back is to your front and its head is tucked into its chest. The other position that the baby takes is called the OP (occipito posterior), when the back of the baby's head is against your spine, usually facing the right. Most OP babies rotate during labour, however, having an OP means you will feel the contractions particularly across your back. If your baby isn't one of the 95% who rotate during labour, a forceps delivery may be necessary.

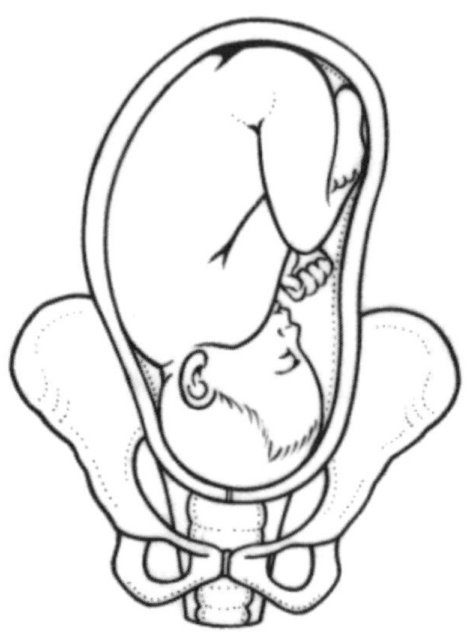

Right occipito anterior

Left occipito anterior

Breech

This is when the baby is not in a head down position, but bottom or feet first. About 3% of babies at 37 or more weeks are breech. There are different types of breech positions, including footling (when the baby is presenting one or both legs below his buttocks), or a frank breech (when the baby is bottom first). If your baby lies across the womb it is called a transverse lie which requires a Caesarean. It is more common to have a breech baby if:

- You've had a baby before.
- You have excessive amounts of amniotic fluid (polyhydramnios).
- Your uterus has growths or anomalies.
- Your baby has anomalies.
- Your placenta is low lying or you have placenta praevia.

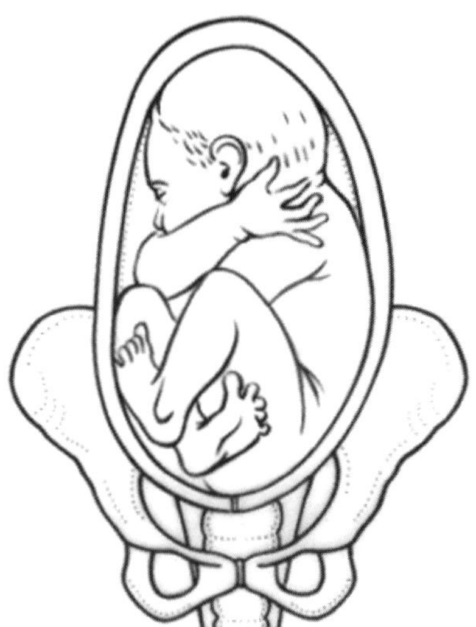

Full breech presentation

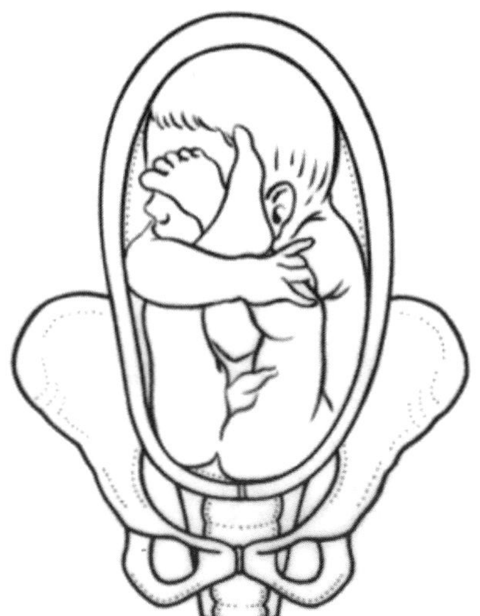

Frank breech presentation

Footling breech

Left occipito posterior

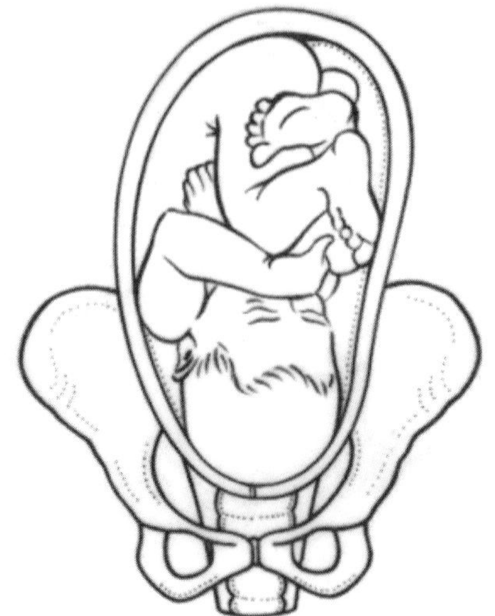

Right occipito posterior

One of the problems with breech presentation is that without the pressure from the baby's head on the cervix helping to 'ripen' it, you may go into labour without the cervix being fully ripe, which might mean a long slow labour.

If at this stage your doctor says you are breech, he or she may try to turn your baby using an external cephalic version, in which the doctor tries to coax it into a better position by gently pressing their hands on your stomach. However, even if this is successful the baby may turn around again. There are several things you can do to try to encourage your baby to turn around.

Acupuncture

Many women report great results after having acupuncture, particularly moxibustion. This involves the burning of herbs to stimulate acupuncture points. A report in the *Journal of the American Medical Association* cites a study which found that there was more fetal activity in a group treated with moxibustion with 75 fetuses changing their position to the correct head down position.

● ● ● ● I don't know if he would have turned anyway, but 5 days before my due date I was starting to think a c-section would put paid to my lovely drug free birth.

However, when my doctor suggested I have acupuncture I agreed. I'm an absolute phobic about needles, so you can imagine how desperate I was. Anyway, I went to see this guy and he was fantastic. I had moxibustion and it didn't hurt at all. In fact I felt so relaxed I went home and had the best sleep I'd had in months. Good thing too, cos I woke up at 2.00 a.m. with my first contraction and gave birth to my daughter Ella at 8.00 a.m. (during the night she had turned herself around). Judith

Tilt Positions

This is probably the most frequently heard DIY method of trying to turn the baby – it involves having your feet lower than your head. This theory suggests that this position will make the baby's head disengage from the pelvis and turn itself around. You can do it the easy way and use an ironing board lying on the couch with your head on the floor, feet up. It's generally recommended you do this 20 minutes a day until the baby turns. Some women report dizziness from being in this position. Always discuss this or any other exercise with your midwife or doctor.

Light and Music

The use of light or music directly at your pubic bone is said to encourage the baby to come towards the light or sound. Many women report success with this. As this has no side effects, it's definitely worth a try! Don't make the sound too loud though, remember it'll be magnified due to all the fluid in your womb.

Water

Some claim that a gentle swim will help turn the baby. There's no medical evidence, but it certainly can't hurt. Some women claim that diving into a pool is a sure way to turn the baby, but check with your doctor about the safety of this.

Homeopathy

Pulsatilla has been used for centuries in turning a breech baby. However, it's important you don't self-treat but speak to a practitioner or qualified homeopath.

External Cephalic Version (ECV)

This is when the baby is manually turned by the doctor using fetal monitoring and ultrasound.

The Nesting Instinct

You may find that at the end of this month you have a rush of energy and start cleaning and organising your baby's room and clothes, or spring cleaning the house from top to bottom. This is called nesting. Just be careful not to overdo it – you'll need all your energy for the days to come! If your finances allow it, hire a cleaner for a couple of hours to come and lend a hand.

Financial Help After Birth

Your finances probably sit like a big black cloud on the edge of your consciousness, and while it's true that single mothers often have more financial worries, there is help available.

Government Assistance

You may be entitled to government assistance following the birth of your baby. it is worth looking at the Maternity Alliance website as they clearly show what you would be entitled to (see Useful Contacts, page 211). You will be entitled to Child Benefit but this can take some time to be processed. You may be able to claim the following:

- Statutory Maternity Pay (SMP).
- New Deal for Lone Parents.
- Working Families Tax Credit.
- Maternity Allowance.
- Sure Start Maternity Grant.

Child Support

The father of your child (if you know who he is) is legally required to pay you child support. To receive this, you may have to first prove he is the father of the baby, which may involve a paternity test, should he dispute it. If you put the father's name on the baby's birth certificate, you are required to show that you have taken steps to locate him and request child support (even if he lives overseas). If you don't do this you may lose some of your benefits. There are several ways of arranging child support:

1. The amount of child support can be a private arrangement between you and the father, with payments collected by you.
2. The amount can be a private arrangement but collected by the Child Support Agency.

3. The Child Support Agency can work out the amount of payment and you can collect it.
4. The Child Support Agency can work out the amount of payment and collect it for you.

What's Happening? Week 39

Your weight should remain stable now. You may have a 'show' when the bloody mucous plug at the mouth of the cervix falls away. This doesn't necessarily mean labour is imminent. You may find it difficult to sleep, both through excitement and trying to find a comfortable position. You may have a rush of energy this month. Your breasts will feel very full and firm. Your cervix (the mouth of your uterus) will begin to soften and possibly dilate.

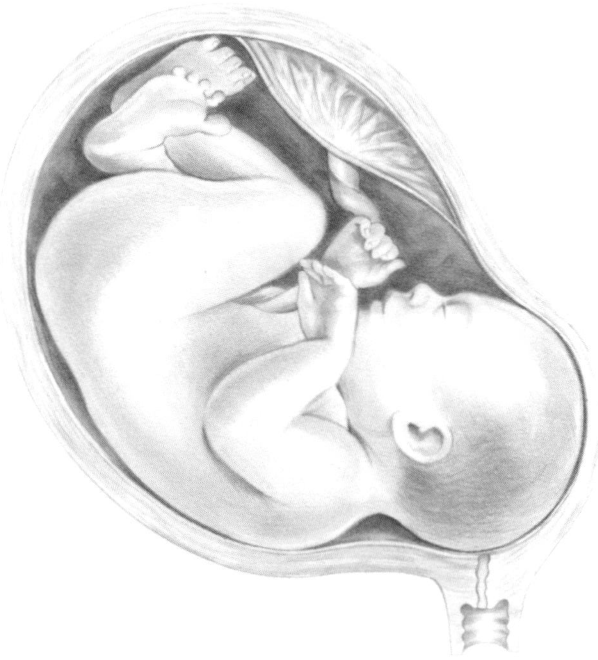

Your baby will weigh approximately 3.5kg and is about 51cm long. It has its eyes open when awake and has moved right down into the pelvis (known as 'engagement' or 'lightening'). The baby's immune system is still undeveloped and it receives antibodies from the placenta. Most of the lanugo (the fine hair covering the baby) has disappeared.

This Month's Checklist

- ✔ Pack your hospital bag.
- ✔ Pre-programme your pregnancy partner's, hospital's or midwife's name into your phone – you may not remember it later!
- ✔ Utilise your nesting instincts and prepare a whole lot of freezable meals.
- ✔ Wash some of your baby's clothes so they are ready to be used.

Happy Birthday!

Despite your impatience, many healthy pregnancies will still be in full gear past 40 weeks' gestation. This is very normal – only about 4% of women will actually give birth on their due date, but only 3% go over the 14-day mark.

Is This It?

Probably the greatest worry on your mind at this time is how to know you are in labour. Many women suffer under the delusion (perpetuated by TV and the movies) that labour begins when the waters break. It's true that breaking of the waters may herald labour, but only if accompanied by contractions. However, labour is different for every woman, but almost certainly one of the following will occur:

- You will have regular contractions which become longer and stronger in intensity and at increasingly shorter intervals.
- You may have lower back pain, and a crampy, menstrual feeling.
- Your cervix will ripen, become progressively thinner and softer and dilate (start to open) up to 10cm.
- You may have a 'show' – a bloody or browny-tinged mucous discharge.

When Should I Call My Midwife?

Don't worry about false alarms – your midwife is used to being called by women who are not sure they are in labour or whether it's time to go to the hospital. If your waters have broken, if you're bleeding, or if you're leaking amniotic fluid, you should do so immediately. You should also go to the hospital if you suspect a decrease in fetal activity. Normally you should call your midwife when your contractions are 5 minutes apart and last about 45 seconds in length. If you have irregular, erratic contractions, it may mean your cervix hasn't dilated yet and you are in false labour. If you're not sure, this can be confirmed with an internal examination.

During the early phase, it's important to drink lots of fluids, to get some rest and to try a warm bath or compress to ease any aches or pains – it should also help relax you. Have your pregnancy partner come over for support and comfort, even if you think going to the hospital is a way off yet.

At the Hospital or Birth Centre

If you've chosen to have your baby at a hospital or birth centre, you and your pregnancy partner should head straight to the admissions section on your arrival. Here you'll sign in and be taken to the delivery suite in the maternity hospital where you will be introduced to the midwife on duty and any other staff. She will do an examination including checking your blood pressure, heart rate temperature and checking the baby's heart rate. You'll be given an internal exam, to see how far your cervix has dilated and how far down the baby's head has come.

Into Position

In our mother's day there was no choice. She spent most of her labour lying flat on her back, usually with her legs in stirrups – the most convenient position for a midwife or obstetrician to function. These days, the idea that there is only one way to give birth has thankfully gone out the window, and today labouring women are positively encouraged to be as active as possible. Unless you have had an epidural, you'll probably find yourself needing to frequently change positions throughout your labour anyway. Staying as upright as possible has also been found to ease pain and even make your labour marginally shorter.

Pregnancy yoga and prenatal classes will give you some ideas as to possible positions for pre-labour and birth. Most delivery suites also have pieces of equipment such as birthing stools, birthing bars and balls. Here are some positions you might like to practise to use during labour. As for your actual position during the birth, simply listen to your body. It'll instinctively try to move into the most comfortable position.

Standing and Leaning

Many women find it helpful to stand and lean on a wall, with arms outstretched and palms flat. Pelvic tilts may also alleviate pain. You may also try leaning over a chair or stool, providing it is a comfortable height, or your bed.

Sitting

Have your birth partner sit on the floor with open legs or kneeling. Lean back and let him or her support your weight.

On All Fours

This can offer tremendous relief from backache. Keep your legs wide apart and your back straight. When a contraction hits, you may want to lean forward onto your hands.

Supported Squat

Good for the pushing stage of labour. Have your pregnancy partner stand behind you and support you under the arms.

Tips for Pregnancy Partners

Being a pregnancy or birth partner is an extremely important and very honoured position! Giving birth can be a painful and often frightening experience, possibly the only time in a woman's life when she has so little control over her body but you can help make the birth process a much more positive experience.

Ask Questions

You may have to be the eyes and ears of the mother, who may be too distracted to notice what's going on around her. While doctors are no longer invested with the demi-god status they once were, they and midwives don't always explain what they're doing, or whether it's mandatory. Ask questions, then confer with your partner and convey her wishes to the medical staff. You are her spokesperson, and as such must have some idea of her desires before labour begins and be able to convey this to staff.

Have Your Bag Packed and Ready to Go

Labour can be a long process, so don't forget to pack some things for yourself – comfortable shoes and perhaps a change of clothes. Something to eat and drink and consider bringing your swimming costume if the hospital offers a birth pool or for the likely event of the mother needing the relief of a shower. Often mobile phones are banned inside hospitals, so bring lots of change for the public phone.

Be Educated

You may never need those breathing patterns you learnt with the mother at antenatal classes but knowing what happens in labour from start to finish, and the terminology involved, will help you both feel in control. So bone up on your reading beforehand!

Be Flexible

Encourage the mother to try different strategies – what works for one woman may not work for another. Remember to keep an open mind and make decisions as they arise. Prepare for the mother to change her mind on issues decided beforehand!

Help Her Find a Compelling Distraction

Talk to her, help her count through her contractions or focus on her breathing. Bring her back to this distraction when she gets frustrated, panicky or emotional.

Be a One-person Support Team

The mother will need support and patience during labour, whether it's feeding her ice-cubes, holding her hands, listening to her curse, helping her suck some water through a straw, giving her sweets, wiping her forehead, or giving her verbal encouragement. Labour can be long and arduous and you may find yourself physically and mentally exhausted, so be prepared. You may need to arrange to take the day off work the following day or to cancel important meetings.

Labour

There is no way to describe labour accurately to a woman who has never experienced it. I personally found myself totally unprepared for the level of pain and felt very resentful at both pregnancy books and other women, who seemed to have so inadequately described it. However, in mid-labour, I became determined to 'spread the word'. I tried to come up with a description, so I could tell other women 'what it was really like' and failed. The pain of labour is not comparable to anything else – the feel of a contraction is unlike anything you will have ever felt. Also, all women experience it differently because of different pain thresholds, mental attitudes, and pain relief methods. What is so important to keep focused on though, is what an incredible miracle nature has created – it's such an amazing thing you're doing as you push your baby out into the world.

The First Stage

Once you've begun labour you enter the first stage. Contractions are greater in intensity and more frequent, usually occurring about every 3 to 4 minutes and lasting up to 60 seconds. This stage can last for up to 6 hours or can take minutes. During this time, you can have a shower or bath, which can be wonderfully soothing, or move around as much as you like. This is the time that your birth partner can help most actively with support and massages. Your cervix will start to dilate, up to about 8cm

Pain relief in the form of pethidine, an epidural, or natural methods, such as breathing exercises or relaxation techniques may be needed sometime during this stage. Some women find this stage very frustrating, when they feel regular and strong contractions for ages then are told during examination that they have dilated very little or not at all. By the end of this stage the baby's head is firmly down into the pelvis.

Transition Stage

During this phase, the cervix dilates from 8cm to 10cm at an average rate of 1cm every 15 minutes. Contractions last an average of 1 to 1½ minutes and occur every 2 to 3 minutes. Once your cervix is fully opened and you have a strong desire to push, you are in the second transition of labour. If your waters haven't broken, they will now. You'll feel a lot of pressure and the contractions will be coming hard and fast. You may feel spaced out (even if you haven't had drugs), nauseous or cold or even sensitive to touch and not wanting anyone to touch you. You might have strong emotional swings. This stage can last between 20 minutes to 2 hours. You'll be monitored by your midwife or doctor.

> I remember being furious at this stage. I felt hatred for men, all men, not just my baby's father. I also knew I was never going to have sex again – after all look what happened! I called my friend over, held her hand and made her swear to me that she would never, ever do this. Of course, a few weeks later, I was trying to set her up with all my male friends, so she could experience the wonder of motherhood herself! Linda

Second Stage

Once you're about 10cm dilated, you'll probably feel the involuntary urge to push as the baby begins to move from the birth canal. If you've had an epidural, this sense will be dulled, and the midwife or doctor will advise you when you need to push. If it's needed, you may have an episiotomy now.

This stage can last anywhere from minutes to more than 3 hours and is characterised by contractions that come every 2 to 5 minutes and last about 60 to 90 seconds. The baby's head will crown, and if you're able, with the use of a mirror, have a look or at least put your hand down and feel your baby's head. You may feel an incredible need to push now, and each time, the baby's head will advance a little further, until you are told to stop to let the contractions push the baby out. This will allow the vagina to stretch gently and minimise tearing. There's usually a great sense of relief when the baby's head is out. The midwife will check that the cord is not wrapped around the baby's neck, wipe any blood or mucus from its eyes and gently suction any liquid from the baby's nose or mouth. The baby is usually born in one go in the next contraction and will be placed on the mother's abdomen, then the umbilical cord is clamped and cut.

Third Stage

This is when the placenta is delivered. After the birth, your body will resume contractions to help expel the placenta (increasingly it is common practice not to cut the cord until it has stopped pulsating). Sometimes, a hormone injection will be given to hurry the expulsion of the placenta.

The midwife will examine it to make sure it's intact, and will continue to check if your uterus is clamping down properly in order to stop the bleeding from the placenta attachment site. This can take anywhere from 5 to 30 minutes, and in the meantime the midwife may repair any tears or episiotomy cuts. You may be hardly aware of what is going on, with all the attention on your baby. You will have had a huge adrenaline rush and may be feeling euphoric, shaky or emotional. However, some mothers do feel the contractions which expel the placenta and the after-pains which shrink the uterus quite strongly for several days.

NOTE

Most women having their first child have a labour and delivery lasting around 14 hours.

Interventions

It may be necessary sometime during your labour for one of the following medical interventions to be applied:

Electronic Fetal Heart Monitoring

There are four types of fetal monitoring used. The midwife may listen to the fetal heart, using a Pinard stethoscope (which looks like a plastic trumpet), a Doppler ultrasound (where a transducer is passed over gel applied to your belly), a cardiotocograph (a belt which picks up uterine contractions and the baby's heartbeat) or an electrode which is clipped to the baby's head while still in the womb (this is known as electronic fetal heart monitoring). Electronic fetal heart monitoring is usually done if there is any evidence of fetal distress, particularly in high risk labours, to ensure the baby is not in any difficulties. While electronic fetal heart monitoring can be reassuring, it means the woman is unable to move around during labour.

Episiotomy

This is when the woman's perineum is cut to facilitate or speed up delivery and is the most common intervention in childbirth. While it was once standard procedure, it is now often argued that women who tear naturally during birth suffer less long-term pain and quicker healing. However, an episiotomy is often used if there are signs the baby is distressed and needs to be delivered quickly or is being delivered by forceps or ventouse delivery (see below). It is performed after an injection of local anaesthetic. After the birth enquire about the experience of the person who will be stitching you up after your episiotomy, as it can affect bowel and bladder function and sexual enjoyment later on.

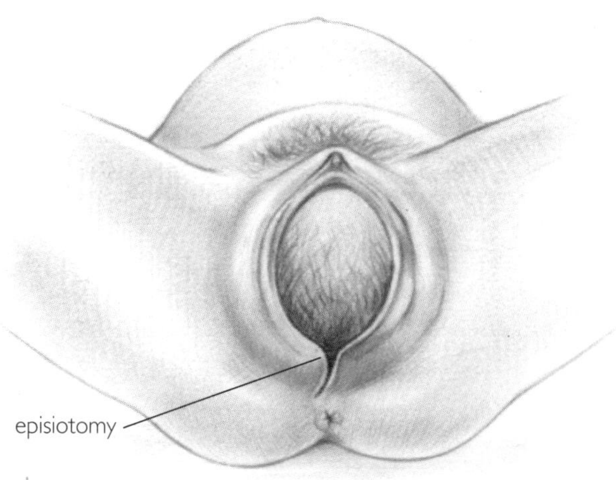

Sometimes called 'the birth cut' an episiotomy may be used when a quick delivery is vital.

Forceps

They may look like a barbeque implement but forceps are often used to help deliver a baby when it's in a posterior or breech position, when the baby's head fails to descend further in the pelvis, when the woman has had an epidural and cannot bear down, or when there is some evidence of distress. They are lightly applied to either side of the baby's head and used to draw the baby down in time with the mother's push.

Ventouse

Ventouse, or vacuum extraction is often used as an alternative to forceps. A small cone-shaped cup is fastened onto a vacuum device and inserted into the vagina and attached to the baby's head, the gentle suction causing the baby's head to descend into the pelvis. This method is less traumatic than forceps and an episiotomy may not always be necessary. A vacuum extraction often results in a large swelling on the top of the baby's head, which will disappear within days.

Induction of Labour

Nearly one-quarter of all births are induced. An induction is simply the artificial starting of labour through hormone gel or pessaries, hormone drugs or breaking of the waters (also known as 'sweeping the membranes'). The reasons for doing this may be due to:

- The pregnancy having passed 'term' and the placenta no longer functions properly.
- The pregnancy has gone over 42 weeks.
- Pregnancy-induced high blood pressure.
- Carrying multiple babies.
- Gestational diabetes.
- Simply for the convenience of the mother.

If induction is being suggested, ask questions. Why is it being suggested? How would it be attempted? What happens if it doesn't work? What happens if you do nothing? Induction shouldn't be used for the convenience of the practitioner! There are several medical methods used to induce labour:

Sweeping the Membranes (Amniotomy)

This is done once the cervix is already ripened and often in conjunction with the use of prostaglandin gel or syntocinon. It's slightly uncomfortable, but not painful and only takes a few seconds. Using a plastic hook inserted through the cervix, the bag of waters is nicked, which will cause the water to begin leaking out. Contractions usually begin within 12 hours.

Prostaglandin E2

This is a gel or pessary which is used when the cervix is not yet ripe and the waters haven't broken. The gel is applied to your cervix (or a pessary is placed in your vagina) and you are asked to lie down for 30 minutes. It helps to ripen or dilate the cervix and most women prefer it to syntocinon (see below), as it doesn't restrict their movements.

Syntocinon

This is an artificial form of the hormone oxytocin that causes the uterus to contract. It's administered via a drip. It can be used simply to establish labour or may be used throughout and left in place for an hour after birth to make sure your uterus doesn't stop contracting. Generally the amount used is increased every 15–30 minutes until a good regular pattern of contractions has been established.

Non-medical Inductions

For as long as women have been having babies, there have been old 'tried and true' natural methods on how to get labour started naturally and you're likely to hear all of them from family and friends should you go over your due date, even by a day! Always check with your practitioner before using any of these methods.

Sexual Intercourse

A slightly more pleasant way to induce labour than having a 'crochet hook' inserted through your uterus! This is believed to work because semen contains prostaglandins; however, you need your partner to remain inside you to give time for the semen to pool around the cervix.

Orgasm (With or Without a Partner!)

An orgasm can cause slight contractions that will sometimes lead to stronger ones.

Nipple Stimulation

This causes mild contractions as oxytocin is released but needs to be done about every 15 minutes for 5 minutes at a time.

Other non-medical methods some women have found to work include:

- Certain foods, such as spicy or hot ones.
- Bumpy car rides.
- Castor oil.
- Certain herbs and homeopathics, but make sure you seek advice from a qualified practitioner, as they may cause miscarriage if taken earlier in your pregnancy.

What Happens When the Baby is Born?

Practitioners do NOT slap babies on the bottom once they're born! Usually the change of environment is enough to trigger that first breath and not all babies cry anyway. The first few moments of a baby's life will be spent being cuddled and breastfed before the baby is weighed and measured. An Agpar test is performed at one and five minutes. This involves assessing how the baby has coped with the birth and whether it is recovering from any initial difficulties. The midwife will note 'appearance' (colour), 'grimace' (crying), 'pulse' (heartbeat), 'activity' (muscle tone) and 'respiration' (breathing). The baby will be given a score of 0, 1 or 2 for each category. They are usually tested at 2 and 5 minutes and for a healthy baby a good score is 7 or 8 at 2 minutes and 9 or 10 at 5 minutes. After the baby has been pronounced healthy, it should be given to you, where you can hold him or her, preferably skin to skin so they can hear that familiar heartbeat. The baby may instinctively want to suckle. In the meantime, the cord may have stopped pulsating and you or your birth partner may be asked if you'd like to cut it. Some hospitals will ask you to donate cord blood, the cells can be used instead of bone marrow in children with leukaemia. Within the first few hours, your baby will be given an injection of vitamin K which will prevent vitamin K deficiency bleeding (VKDB) or haemorrhagic disease.

What your Baby might Look Like

When my own son was born I instantly fell in love with him, but worried at the thought of the teasing he'd have to endure in his life, what with his conical head and squashed nose! Needless to say, his head returned to a normal shape and his little squashed nose popped out. Babies don't come out like the sweet little things we see tucked up in prams. The are usually covered in vernix (the creamy white substance which has protected their skin), and/or blood. His or her face and head may be squashed or

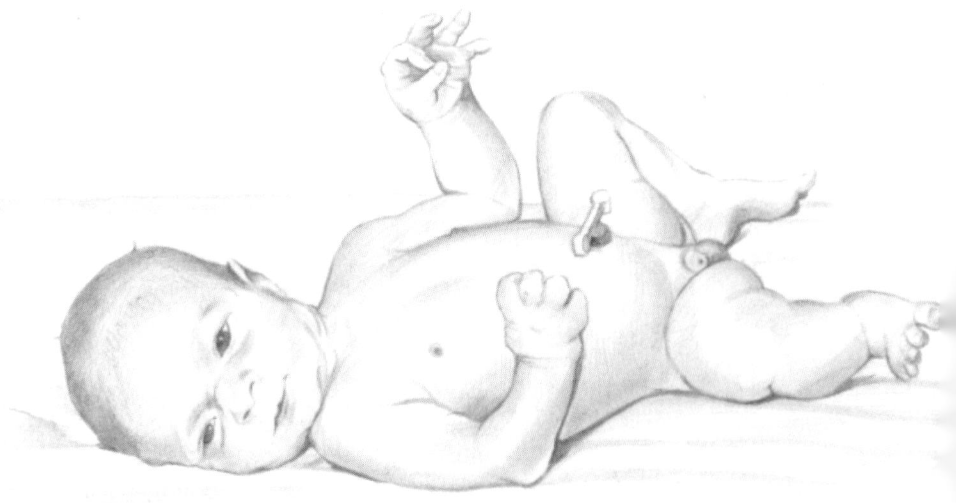

After a few days, any major lumps or bumps from the delivery will disappear from your baby.

oddly shaped and the skin blotchy, pale, flushed or yellow. Nails are long and the genitals may look very prominent (the genitals and breasts may be quite swollen due to hormones crossing the placenta). Some babies may have lots of hair, others none at all. They might have pink splotches, known as 'stork spots' which will disappear after a few days, tiny white spots called 'milia' or strawberry birthmarks which will fade over a year, or port wine or coffee coloured birthmarks which are permanent. Total weight will be around 3–4 kg and length about 50cm.

After a few days any marks from forceps or the birth itself will disappear and your baby will be gorgeous.

Birth Stories

Anita: An Impending Birth

I am in my early 30's and have been married once. After recently leaving a relationship of over 2 years, I discovered (surprise, surprise – what timing) that I was going to have a baby. He was seeing someone else and had been for a little while.

I am now 6 months on and it's been an interesting journey. I have had to decide who I want to be there at the birth to help support me. I have my daughter from my previous marriage but at only 10, I think it's a bit much for her. .

My ex-partner was informed, but as yet has not been at all interested. As he runs his own company he is very busy, so has just forked over some money to help me set up a nursery etc. I have turned to my close friends, among them a male friend who has been lovely. He understands the situation and we keep each other company, but no rubbing of feet etc.

So instead I have enjoyed my pregnancy so far. Doing what? Setting up a 'Single Mother and their Children' branch (apart from my paid part-time employment, and still doing my other most enjoyable volunteer work). I have revelled in the information I have found out, the people I have met, the empowerment over my 'situation' I have claimed. Yes, I have loved it. Helping me and helping other women in the same position.

I have not felt lonely or like I have missed out on what it 'should' be like or what I 'should' be having done for me. I have found the stigma from others a little unnerving but have held my head up high, because I believe this is where life is going, I am just one of the pioneers.

My first husband never helped with anything. He wouldn't even go out to get me my one craving I had in the whole time I was pregnant (right at the end when I was the biggest!) He never changed a nappy and was jealous of the baby etc.

Yes, have I enjoyed this pregnancy more being single, you bet! Really, really. My daughter is great company though. I had honestly not even thought about it too much up until right now. The last 6 months have gone so fast.

I give myself tummy rubs/massages, foot baths/spas, relaxing baths, I bought myself a dishwasher so I didn't have to do the dishes!

I can't wait for the baby to be in our lives.

Ngaire and Jade

It must be really beautiful and warm and comfortable in your womb because this baby wasn't going anywhere in a hurry. I loved having it in there, but I also wanted it out. I wanted to see my baby, hold it in my arms. I also wanted to be able to walk.

Six days after my due date something began to happen. This was it. Today was the day. It all started at around 6.30 a.m., no pains, but I just knew something was happening. About 6 hours later I thought I was experiencing pain and I thought that, like in the movies, that once labour started it went straight into having the baby and then a few 'Aaarghs' and out it came. So we went to the hospital where they checked me and then basically laughed and told me I was only 1cm dilated and to go home. We all went for chocolate milkshakes instead. I had my three best friends, two cousins and their baby and my best friend's mum, my mum's best friend and my mum there for support. It was great to have them all there and made me feel better that 'he' wasn't there.

So, two chocolate milkshakes and a cookie later the contractions were getting closer and more intense so I went for another check – 4cm. I went for a walk to ease the contractions. I walked around for about 1 hour then went back to the ward. They then broke my waters. That made me really scared. I thought it meant that something was wrong and it felt really yuck. The reality was starting to set in and the horrible midwife wasn't helping matters. She offered no comfort and asked me why I was crying. I was scared.

After the 'water' stopped pouring out I went back out to the room where everybody was playing scrabble and watching 'Survivor'. I now knew what a contraction really felt like and laughed at the fact that I thought I was in pain before. Every time one came on I just closed my eyes and breathed and tried to relax my body. The contractions started to get really intense and I was totally unaware of what was happening around me. That's when they put me in the bath. The hot water felt so good.

The contractions were almost unbearable and I was now beginning to have second thoughts. They had given me the gas and air to suck on, but it just spun me out. The whole thing was intense enough without being off my head as well. Aaargh... It was awful, I couldn't stand it anymore and I was feeling the urge to push.

Another midwife came and got me. She was lovely, and walked me to the labour room and checked me again – 4cm and the baby was lying posterior. I didn't know what that meant, but it sounded scary. I think they said something about the baby facing the wrong way and they needed to turn me on my side. One thing I definitely heard was that they thought it would take another 8–10 hours before it was delivered. NO!!! They turned me over and gave me some pethidine to help the baby and I relax and turn around the right way. They then asked me if I wanted someone with me. 'My mum!'

I started to feel an incredible, unbearable urge to push. I thought, 'This is it, I'm going to die right now'. I told mum that I was pushing and the midwife told me to stop. Now, if you've ever been in labour you know that there is no stopping that pushing. I told her that I couldn't stop, not in so many words and maybe not that nicely, but I told her. So she said she'd take another look. Oh, the baby was nearly out. Oh.

The midwives were trying to keep me focused and telling me to look at them when all I wanted to do was kick them. So I did, a couple of times. I couldn't stand them touching me. I didn't want it anymore. I just wanted to go home. I couldn't do this. Labour is beyond words and the words I was using at the time I don't think can be published. I really thought I was dying. Nobody could go through that much pain and not die. 'I can't do it!" I screamed. 'I can't do this, I CAN'T DO IT!' It reminded me that we are still animals, especially all the grunting and groaning I was doing!

The midwives said just one more push, but I knew that with that one push something was going to have to give so one more push turned to one more hour of pushing. Then I'd had enough, this thing just had to come out. Rrrraaa!!! Swoosh, out it came.

They put it straight on my chest. What was it? A girl? Wow, the whole time I had thought a boy, but here she was. All the pain was forgotten, for the moment anyway. I rang her father straight away. He did a good job of concealing his excitement. I didn't care. She was beautiful, perfect, she was mine. I would call her Jade, Jade Caitlin Cohen.

I managed a little bit of a sleep with Jade in my arms and awoke to find her sucking on my arm. The midwife came in to help me feed her. It was amazing, there she was. The little soul I had been carrying inside me, a perfect beautiful princess.

Michelle

My baby's head never engaged and 11 days after my due date I was booked in for an induction, but the morning before that was to happen I went into labour, I waited a few hours, had a bath etc, and made sure I really was in labour. When I was sure, I rang my mum as she had to travel 3 hours to get to my place, then I rang HIM to let him know I was in labour. He was at the girlfriend's house, so his flatmate rang him there, and he arrived about an hour later, only to have a go at me because I hadn't done the dishes and accusing me of exaggerating the pain (apparently the girlfriend had told him all about it – she had a son). I wasn't ready to go to the hospital yet, plus I wanted to wait for my mum, so I went and lay down on my bed, he came in lay down next to me and informed me that he had a big night and promptly went to sleep! When my Mum arrived I was still resisting going to the hospital (I think I was scared of getting sent home again). Finally I let them take me to hospital, after 10 hours of labour, during which my wonderful mum stayed by my side the whole time and he went and got a hot dog, and then feel asleep in the chair (the midwife gave him the dirtiest look I have ever seen). Finally, they decided to do a emergency Caesarean. I then made a choice which I regret to this day. I only could pick one person to come in with me during the Caesarean. And who do you think I chose? My mum the person that supported me during the whole pregnancy and labour? Oh no, I picked HIM, I thought it was the 'right thing to do' after all it was his first child! Ha, what an idiot I was!

It all went well, and I had a beautiful baby boy. Once in my room and settled I told my mum to go back to my place to have a shower and get some rest. He asked if my mum could take him home on her way, and got my mum to drop him off at the girlfriend's house! He made one other brief appearance at the hospital as I had asked him to come to sign the birth certificate. This is another mistake I made. Giving my son his last name, and no offence to his parents, I wish I hadn't, makes him seem more important in the situation than he really was or is. Five years on I am in a wonderful relationship and am getting married soon, and my partner would love to give my son (who he considers to be his own) his name and to adopt him, however, this is made harder because my son has his father's name and he would never agree to it! But at the time I was trying to do what I thought was the 'right thing'.

My mum once again travelled down to pick us up from the hospital and took two weeks off work to stay with us. She was wonderful and really helped us get on track. When the time came for her to leave, I came inside, shut the door, sat down against it with my son asleep in my arms and cried and cried and cried. I have never felt so alone in my life. Until my son woke up, then I realised I would never be alone again and that I needed to get on with things, and make a happy safe place for him to grow up in.

Jane and Ben

Pregnancy was a wonderfully positive and fulfilling experience for me. I felt so energised yet incredibly calm, relaxed, happy and sooo full of love for my baby and myself. In the last few weeks I began to get lower back nerve pain, and I was becoming quite uncomfortable. I was mentally prepared for my baby so I decided I didn't wish to drag the pregnancy on to a possible stage where I was no longer enjoying the experience.

I booked in for an induction at the hospital on my due date. Five days before, I attempted a natural induction by acupuncture. I felt very positive about this but nothing happened (though my back pain was cured). I went to hospital for the induction feeling incredibly excited but as the day wore on not much was happening. I had begun to have very minor contractions and was about to be sent home until I was in established labour when my baby's heartbeat rapidly dropped from 150 bpm to 78 bpm. It scared me so much. My obstetrician was paged and suggested an immediate c-section. I have never been adverse to c-sections for whatever reason, so I agreed. One quick hour later my beautiful baby boy, Ben, was in my arms. It was a truly wonderful and positive experience even though they had some trouble finding my spinal space on my 'tough' spine to put the epidural in.

Ben arrived complication-free and very calmly. The umbilical cord was wrapped twice around his foot and was probably the reason for his heartbeat drop. Six weeks down the track Ben is still incredibly calm and complication free!

Post c-section has been little problem for me. There was pain for a few days, but nothing unbearable. The joy of my baby, in and out of pregnancy, far outweighed any negativity of having a c-section. In fact, I am now a firm advocate of c-sections!

Natasha and Emily

My baby was due to be born on the 7 March 1998 which was a Friday. When I was a few months pregnant, the hospital informed me that its maternity wards were closing on Monday 3 March to be refurbished and maternity patients were being sent to another hospital which they were merging with. The alternative hospital had been my second choice for giving birth and I wanted to avoid the merger confusion, so I was hoping for an early birth (i.e. prior to 3 March) and repeatedly told my baby so!

Being single (thus needing as much money saved as possible) and having had no problems during pregnancy, I had decided to work until 2 weeks before I was due – being Friday 20 February. I had a few Braxton Hicks contractions on Friday 13 February whilst at work, but they weren't painful and only lasted for an hour or so. At home over the weekend, I felt 'different' or 'funny' – I'm not sure what it was in words, I just knew things weren't the same as normal. I kept catching myself thinking I'd have the baby within that week and kept telling myself to stop imagining things, as I wanted to at least finish work first! Other than being tired and wishing I'd finished work a week earlier, I was fine at work on the Monday morning and dismissed the feelings as imagination only.

At lunchtime, I got up from my desk and felt a trickle of liquid down my leg. It was a very small amount with no associated pain or other feelings, so I was a bit surprised. I went to the toilet and everything seemed fine so I went off to lunch as usual. After sitting down for 45 minutes or so for lunch, I stood to return to my desk and felt another, slightly bigger trickle. Was it my waters or had I suddenly become incontinent? I went to the toilets again and the wetness definitely smelt sweet so I rang the hospital. On their advice, I stayed at work for the afternoon wearing a sanitary pad so as to 'record' the amount of liquid I was losing. I rang my support person, Sam, and warned her it may be sooner than expected – she was more thrown by this than I was! I didn't move off my chair until it was nearly time to go home when I stood to go to a private phone to report to the hospital. As soon as I stood, there was a gush of liquid down my leg, which removed any doubts for me about what was happening!

A midwife answered the phone and told me to come straight to hospital without panicking or rushing. Feeling very uncomfortable in wet leggings, the girl I was training to replace me drove me to the hospital (via my house to collect my bag as I live close to work) and my support person, Sam, met us there. The maternity staff was amused, as 'We've never had the support person arrive an hour before the mother before!' As a midwife helped me undress for an examination, she felt how wet my pants were and agreed it was my waters – obviously, they had doubted me somewhat previously. As soon as the midwife touched me for an internal, another big gush of amniotic fluid came out and she too was convinced. As I had still felt no contractions, they put a fetal heart monitor on me for a while and then sent me home for the night, saying to come back if anything developed or at 7.00 a.m. Sam spent the night with me and neither of us slept too well in anticipation, so we were tired when we returned next morning.

A monitor was attached at about 8.00 a.m. and the doctor arrived at 8.30 a.m. or so and came to see me at 8.45 a.m. – I could have had an extra hour's sleep and still been on time! Anyway, as I still hadn't felt anything, they inserted a drip to induce me before the doctor did an internal examination to check dilation – I am still cross that this wasn't done in the reverse order. I was already 5cm dilated and everyone questioned my lack of contractions, as if I was lying about having them. The midwife then laid her hand on my abdomen and told me I was having one then! From then on, I only knew a contraction was happening by feeling my stomach with my hand! I walked around the ward a lot, drip in tow, and made a phone call or two to alleviate the boredom. I felt my first contraction at about 11.00 a.m., and it hurt. This was quickly followed by more contractions that were increasingly painful. At first, the thought of a gas mask over my face made me feel nauseous so I refused to try it. As things began stretching, I found it hard to be comfortable and stay still from the pain of my anus – a pain I'd never thought or been warned about as part of birth. Hot face flannels eased the pain and I started on the gas as I moved onto the bed, leaning over a beanbag. I don't know that the gas actually helped, but concentrating on using the mask properly distracted me and helped me breathe better. Eventually, the midwife admitted that the gas itself had been turned off! By 12.30 p.m., I was ready to push and could see the end in sight – after all, birthing classes said pushing takes up to 1 hour for a first baby on average.

During the next 3 hours, Sam and the medical student who'd been there all day took turns rubbing my back and holding my hand and giving me sips of water – I didn't register I was thirsty, but devoured every bit of water that came near my mouth! At one point, there was excitement because they could see the head, and started calling the baby 'Blondie'. They helped turn me around and placed a mirror so I could look too (something I had always intended to do) but I couldn't see anything resembling a head (at the time I thought it was me, but now I realise it was probably my lack of glasses as I'm shortsighted!) and was in agony in that position. I can remember the midwives saying 'just push through the pain, you're almost there', and mentally replying, 'Fuck, the pain, I'm exhausted and can't push anymore. I want to sleep. You guys finish this off however you like, I'm going to bed.' At that point, I thought, 'Okay, this is my last effort. I'll pull together the last shreds of energy I have for one push. If that doesn't work, too bad 'cos that's it. After that, I don't care if they use forceps, a Caesar, whatever, I'm not doing this anymore.' So, I gave a great big push and out came the head, thankfully. The push for the body is nothing after that and then I got to hold my beautiful little girl and forgot the exhaustion and discomfort. Mind you, it was after a few minutes cuddling that a midwife lifted the cord out of the way so we could see she was a girl – it just wasn't important there and then.

So, Emily was born at 3.40 p.m. on Tuesday 17 February after 4 hours of labour, 16 days early. I am lucky enough to be able to say that birth was an okay experience – not one I'd repeat often for fun, but certainly bearable and worthwhile.

Being single had an impact on the day, apart from the obvious lack of partner, in three ways. Firstly, the midwife asked whether my partner (I think she actually said husband) was coming then spent about 5 minutes complaining about irresponsible men not accepting fatherhood. Secondly, I feel a partner would have been more prepared and more forceful than Sam in terms of 'defending' me and my rights (e.g. the internal examination before induction, introducing medical staff as they entered the room). And, finally, when my grandmother and uncle arrived to visit me I was still in the labour room on the bed where I gave birth. There was no warning – they just walked into the room, so I'm glad I had a sheet over me! When my father rang, he also was told to come to the birthing suite to visit me. Maybe I'm oversensitive, but I suspect the lack of privacy the hospital staff gave me was out of pity that I was alone!

Robyn and Jazz

I woke up on Sunday at midnight lying in a large wet patch on the bed and felt very excited thinking I would soon have a baby to hold. It turned out to be another 3 days before I would hold my baby. I walked a lot and my midwife came and looked at me and told me to keep a close eye on my temperature.

Three days later, on Wednesday evening, I decided to venture from home, as I hadn't wanted to go out previously. I went off to the cinema to see a suspense film called Cliffhanger. And yes it was suspenseful and I sat on the edge of my seat for the whole film, not that you can do much else when you've got a mound for a belly.

However, this film probably helped the process along because that night, at midnight again, a big gush of water came from between my legs and I decided to get up and go for a walk to try and get the show on the road, so to speak. I was just too excited to sleep and lay around pretending to sleep and eventually got up and boiled an egg and cleaned the house. When the sun came up, I decided to try belly-dancing movements to move things along.

At about 8.00 a.m. I rang my midwife and she said to give her a call when things get going. I was having twinges but nothing really strong and at about 11.00 a.m. I phoned my midwife and asked her to come and see me. I wanted to know how things were going and my midwife did an internal examination and said I was 3cm dilated and to call her when I needed her. My father phoned to see how things were going and asked if he would have time to go to the races, and I said I'd be a few more hours and my midwife gave me this look and I knew I was nowhere near as close to giving birth as I hoped. She obviously didn't see things happening for quite a while and this made me pissed off because I wanted to give birth NOW. My impatience was a real nuisance and I longed to be more accepting of nature.

I called my mother, who was coming to the birth and my friend, Tanya, who was going to also attend the birth. I told them both to take their time, but they were both over very quickly and by lunchtime nothing was really happening so we decided to have a picnic. After lunch everyone slept. I slept for 15 minutes, which was really stupid because I had a long night ahead and not a 4- or 5-hour birth as I hoped my young fit body would provide. By about 3.00 p.m. I had to concentrate a little through the contractions and my mother, who is a midwife but hadn't practised midwifery for many moons, tried to time the contractions. About half an hour later I called my midwife and she wanted to listen to me having a contraction, so I put the phone on the floor and had a contraction and moaned a lot and called my midwife a weirdo. She said she would feed the kids and come over soon. I really lost all track of time from then on.

We had hired a hot tub, and my birth helpers had spent the last 2 hours filling it up because of the hot water situation on the property, they had been driving to the next door neighbours with buckets to get more water, they needed something to do anyway. I got into the tub, had one contraction and hated being in the water—Aquarian or not I didn't want to be in that tub and swiftly got out. I walked over to the stereo and put on some music and had a really strong contraction and stayed there until my daughter was born. I seemed to go into a totally insular space and closed my eyes and didn't open them again until Jazz was born. The contractions were really painful and I had to hold on to someone to deal with them and I had a lot of lower back pain, which was relieved by pressure from a hot water bottle.

My midwife arrived about an hour on, I don't really remember, though I do remember her phoning the other midwife and saying, 'Come over and don't stop to chat', and I thought, 'Yipee, this means I must be close, ha ha!' Little did I know!

I really worked my birth helpers, my midwife had another midwife who was working with her and they both stayed with me the whole way. My mother got tired and drank lots of tea, my friend took photos and made lots of tea and toast. My midwife would listen to the baby's heartbeat with a 'Doppler' which amplified the sound, so I could hear it. She mainly sat with me and talked to me and I felt very safe and trusting of her.

Contractions, contractions, contractions, some thoughts that were going through my head were, 'I am not having sex for at least a year', 'I AM going to get through this because I don't want to get in the car and go down the bumpy driveway'. The idea of going to hospital didn't worry me, just having to go down the driveway.

I remember hearing my midwife describing how she wanted her toast and I thought, excuse me but I am trying to have a baby and I could hear everyone talking and laughing and that really pissed me off. I was getting very tired and was sleeping in between contractions. At about 1.00 a.m. my midwife suggested I get up and move around, which I did not want to do, but figured it was worth the effort if it meant giving birth. I did about 20 minutes of rotating my hips, hanging off my partner and my midwife did an internal examination and shifted a lip of skin and said if I wanted to push, I could. I remember pushing and pushing and hearing our dogs outside howling and barking at the door. I found the pushing very painful and was hoping the harder I pushed the sooner the baby would be born, but it didn't seem to matter how hard I pushed, the baby seemed to come out in its own time and that was about 2 hours later. The head was in view and I was getting excited, but the burning sensation felt like someone had turned a blowtorch on my vagina. My midwife said that it was the head and she hated this part too, but the sensation would be over very quickly, which it was and I could hear my midwife giving instructions for the heater to be brought closer and her bag of goodies to be brought to her.

I was squatting and lying back on my other midwife. My midwife and my partner were discussing who was going to catch the baby. I gave a push and the head popped out, everyone gasped, my midwife said to my birth partner get ready to catch her (she knew it was a girl from just looking at the head) and then one more push and out slipped Jazz. My partner caught her and handed her to me and I lay her on my stomach and she was a very beautiful looking baby, very peaceful. Jazz was making noises and started to suckle on my breast and then my midwife reminded me that the placenta had to come out. So I gave a feeble attempt to push it out and my midwife said, 'Oh come on', and I said 'Oh all right' in a jokingly annoyed way, and I pushed the placenta out. The cord had already been cut and I remember thinking now I can relax. My midwife did the routine check of the baby, measured her and weighed her. I had a shower, crawled into bed and stayed there for a week feeding my beautiful baby.

What Next?

After repairs to any tears or episiotomy, you will be taken to your room and providing all is well with the baby, he or she will come with you. A midwife will help you to have a shower and show you how to breastfeed your baby. If you've had a Caesarean you will be stitched up and perhaps taken to a recovery room for a little while.

You will feel exhausted, but exhilarated. You might be on a high and need and want to sleep but be unable to. You might have hundreds of thoughts whizzing through your head and may be feeling very emotional. You'll probably feel very sore and going to the toilet can seem an ordeal. You may have low blood pressure and feel a little giddy when you stand up. If you've had a Caesarean, or pain relieving drugs, you might feel spaced out or groggy.

I couldn't sleep for 2 days. I felt sort of hyperactive – I had so much energy and I found it really frustrating I couldn't do much as I was so sore from the episiotomy. Sara

When the midwives came to get me to have a shower I remembered all too clearly what I had been through the night before, the pain was excruciating. Walking was bad enough, but then they told me to do a wee. Aaaarrrgh! At least my body was alive, unlike my mind. When the midwives spoke their voices seemed foreign and far away. I think I was in shock. I was in so much pain, but numb at the same time. Anthea

Letting the Father Know

It's hard to imagine it now, but sometime down the track you and your baby's father may have to have a civilised relationship. He has a right to know when his child is born (generally!) and involving him from the outset will help father and child to bond should he request access.

If you don't want to tell the father yourself, write a note, or have your support person notify him. Just be aware that the news may not be greeted with jubilation. In fact, the reaction may be downright hostile. Don't get angry; instead look at your beautiful child and have pity that the father is missing out on so much. If the father has shown no interest in you or the baby and you are not going to involve him in any kind of co-parenting, you are probably justified in not letting him know.

The Next Few Days

You'll be assisted with breastfeeding and establishing a routine with your baby. The midwives will note down everything, including bowel movements, feeds and sleeping patterns, the baby's weight and colour (many babies are jaundiced). These days babies usually 'room in', that is, they will remain in the room with you, in a cot. However, you should take advantage of the midwives' offers to take him or her off to the nursery to let you get some rest. The baby's first bowel motions will be a greenish-black, gradually changing to lighter greenish motions in breastfed babies and yellowish ones in bottle-fed babies. You'll probably feel very tired the first few days and well-meaning but constant visitors can be a problem. If you need to sleep, don't feel guilty, just tell the midwives to not allow visitors or calls for a period of time.

As your uterus contracts, and returns to its normal shape you'll have a bloody discharge known as 'lochia'. Similar to a period, it can last from 14 days to 6 weeks and will change in colour from bright red, to rusty brown then finally yellow or white-ish. You need to wear pads, rather than tampons throughout this time.

If you've had an episiotomy or tear that required stitching, you may feel very sore as the area heals. Try having warm salt baths, and get some air to the area to assist healing.

If you have had a Caesarean, you will still experience lochia and changes in the uterus. Your abdominal wound will be painful and may well start to burn and itch as it heals. You may need to ask for suggestions for positions for breastfeeding if it hurts too much. You'll probably be advised to move around as quickly as possible after a Caesarean to stop the possibility of blood clots.

Breastfeeding

For the first few days of your baby's life, it will feed on colostrum – the thicker, yellowish milk, which is more concentrated than normal breast milk. This is particularly important, as it is rich in antibodies, which will help your baby build up resistance to disease. Over about 10 days your milk will gradually change colour becoming bluish-white and thinner in consistency.

How to Breastfeed

A breastfeeding baby is not just sucking on its mother's nipple, but the entire areola. This is called 'latching on' and if it is not done correctly and the baby just sucks on the nipple it can cause painful, cracked and bleeding nipples. To breastfeed correctly, hold you baby in one of the positions described below, whichever feels the most comfortable. I helps your baby to latch on correctly if you hold your breast and position your thumb lightly just above the areola. Put the nipple on the baby's lips and guide the entire areola into its open mouth. If you feel pain after 10 seconds, your baby is not latched on properly and you need to break the suction by inserting your finger gently into the corner of your baby's mouth. Apart from preventing sore nipples, latching on correctly helps your milk flow, thus stimulating production, making sure your baby is satisfied and helping to ensure your breasts do not get engorged (see below).

When breastfeeding try to keep your baby awake until it has finished or it will constantly demand more and more milk and your breasts won't be stimulated to produce more. As a baby normally feeds longer at the first breast, but not necessarily the second, you should take it in turns as to which breast you offer first. Some maternity bras even have a little sliding clip you move to indicate which breast you last fed from! How long your baby breastfeeds varies, ranging from 10 minutes to 30 minutes on each side. If your baby appears to be bright and alert, is settled, is putting on weight and has 6–8 wet nappies a day, then they are getting enough milk. If you have any concerns, speak to your midwife, health visitor or lactation consultant (see Reading Recommendations on page 216).

Let Down

When you are breastfeeding, within the first few minutes you should experience 'let down'. All women feel this differently, some just feel a gentle tingle, others find it slightly painful, while others may find their other breast begins spurting or leaking milk. For the first week or so, you may also feel your uterus contracting as the hormone, oxytoxin, which stimulates milk supply, also causes the muscles of the uterus to contract, shrinking it back to its normal size.

Positions

The most common position used to breastfeed is to sit down and cradle your baby, supporting its head and neck in the crook of your arm, facing it into your body. However, there are some other positions that may feel more comfortable with. You can breastfed lying down on your side with your baby facing you – this can be a real plus if you decide you are going to sleep with your baby, and it can be very relaxing. The 'football' hold is another common position, where the baby's head and neck is cradled close to you but the length of the baby's body is held to your side. Changing positions can be worthwhile if your baby doesn't seem to latch on properly or you have sore nipples.

Sore Nipples

Sore nipples are usually the result of the baby not being latched on properly. Try changing positions and guiding the entire areola into the baby's mouth when it reflexively opens it to begin feeding. If you use any products, such as nipple balms, make sure to wash your nipples before feeding your baby. After a feed, squeeze a drop of milk out of your breast and massage in into the nipple area, and try to expose your nipples to fresh air and sunlight if possible.

Cracked nipples are usually caused by the baby not latching on properly. Do not use plastic backed breast pads, as these do not allow the air to circulate and can aggravate the problem. Try changing positions, and ask your midwife for advice.

Low Milk Supply

Low milk supply can be caused by stress so relax and let your baby feed a little more often. While feeding, gently stroke the breast, using a little pressure downward towards the nipple from all sides. Try to get the baby to feed well on one side before you start on the other, or change sides during feeding, which may help renew the interest in sucking. Try expressing a little milk between feeds (you can freeze this as an 'emergency' supply). Keep yourself well nourished with good healthy food, drink plenty of water and get enough rest, well as much as possible under the circumstances! Some women have found herbal treatments can help, but make sure to see a trained herbalist.

Blocked Duct

A blocked duct can usually be felt as a lump and general soreness, which can be alleviated by applying a cold pack between feeds. When feeding, massage the lump downwards and let the baby feed from the affected breast first. Try changing positions. You may also need to express milk, particularly at night.

Engorgement

Engorgement is when the breasts are swollen and painful and is usually a sign that the milk is not flowing out properly from the breasts. If untreated, engorgement can lead to mastitis. Engorgement can be treated the same as a blocked nipple. My own hospital had cabbage leaves in the freezer which you put on your bra against your breast to provide relief from pain (and a few strange looks from visitors at the crunching sound when I moved!) Draining hot water from the showerhead onto the breasts can help too.

Mastitis

This is when the duct becomes infected and needs to be treated medically, usually with antibiotics. Symptoms are a hot, red area around the breast, a temperature and general feeling of unwellness. You need to keep breastfeeding through mastitis, although it can be uncomfortable. Offer the affected breast first and change sides frequently if the baby seems to favour the other breast. Gently massage the breast with stroking movements towards the nipple. Try to get as much sleep as you can and eat acidophilus yoghurt if possible to counteract the effects of the antibiotics on your gut.

Expressing

Expressing means removing milk from your breasts. You may need to do it if you have one of the above problems, or if you know you will have to leave your newborn with someone else for a few hours. You can store expressed milk at room temperature between 4–6 hours, and it can be refrigerated for a week or frozen for use between 3–6 months. Breastmilk is best stored in a plastic container with a tightly sealed lid clearly labelled with the date of freezing. There are three ways of expressing:

- Hand expressing. Where you simply use your hand to squeeze milk from one breast. This can be more difficult if you have a low milk supply.
- Hand-held manual expressers. These are small devices that use air to create a pumping suction, which draws the milk out. Some products on the market are very good these days, with little pads that massage around the areola as you are pumping.
- Electric breastpumps. You may be given one of these when in hospital to express milk. They are efficient, fast and not particularly dignified! They work on the same system as a manual pump, but instead of you having to work the handle, it works electronically. You can usually hire breast pumps through larger pharmacies.

NOTE

The amount of milk you can express is not necessarily the same as the amount your baby gets. They are much more efficient than any machine as the sucking motion is different!

Looking After Yourself While Breastfeeding

While breastfeeding, you probably need extra calories, as well as vitamins and mineral supplements to replace those taken by the baby. Snack on healthy foods such as milky drinks, cereal and fruit and keep up your calcium by eating dairy foods such as cheese, yoghurt or calcium fortified soymilk. Boost your iron with red meat or chicken, legumes, dried fruit, cereal and leafy green vegetables. You should avoid alcohol and caffeine, which are absorbed into your breast. In addition, some women find that eating chocolate or spicy foods may cause the baby to have an unsettled stomach. While breastfeeding, you may need to get lots of rest and drink plenty of water to keep yourself hydrated.

If you have any breastfeeding concerns or problems, contact your midwife, health visitor or breastfeeding support group.

I remember laughing when I first heard the words 'lactation consultant'. I thought it was so simple, you just put your baby up to your nipple and he sucked. Why on earth would you need a consultant for this easy and natural process? Three days after the birth of my son my nipples were bleeding and I was in excruciating pain. In the end it was discovered my son, despite sucking for ½ an hour per side, wasn't getting any milk and had to be 'comped'. I was so secretly relieved that I was going to be given a reprieve. Then the lactation consultant arrived and eventually hooked up a 'supply line' which was a thin tube connected to a bottle of formula taped to my nipple. This was so that he could have some milk, but still be sucking on my nipples, which helps stimulate milk supply and means he wouldn't get used to the bottle teat and refuse the breast. She showed me how to make sure my son was attached to the nipple properly and voilà! – what a relief. As he was getting the milk, he stopped sucking so hard and as he was attached properly it didn't hurt anymore. I stopped feeling resentful towards him for being such a source of pain and my milk supply increased of its own accord and we had no more problems. Natalie

I felt so lucky being able to breastfeed. I knew I was giving my baby the best start possible and it was so convenient – I didn't have to carry around all that stuff my friends did – getting bottles warmed up in cafés and sterilising everything. It was also the time I felt closest to my daughter and I missed it after I weaned her. Marie

Bottle-feeding

Bottles for feeding come in all shapes and sizes – from strange curvy ones designed to minimise the baby sucking a lot of air which can cause wind and stomach pain, to short stubby ones. The choice is yours, however longer, narrower bottles mean babies can easily get their hands around it when older and so may be able to feed themselves earlier.

However, the most important part of the bottle is the teat. Make sure you buy the correct one, either a slow flow (for newborns) or a 'variflow' which depends on how hard the baby sucks as to how fast or slow the milk comes out. A medium flow teat tends to be for older babies, 6 months plus. Latex rubber teats, which are dark yellow or brown in colour, tend to be softer than the clear silicone ones which are harder wearing and don't squash together, restricting milk flow when the baby sucks hard on them. You may also find orthodontic teats which are supposed to be shaped more like a natural nipple and encourage the baby to take them further into their mouth, like they would a real nipple. Make sure you don't forget to sterilise new teats.

There are also three main types of milk powder to feed babies. 'Infant powder' is suitable for newborn babies up to 6 months. 'Follow on' formula is used after 6 months. 'Soy based' milk powder is also available if there is a history of allergies to cow's milk in your family. In addition, there are special formulas which are thickened for babies who suffer reflux, the regurgitation of stomach acids into the oesophagus.

How Do I Make Up a Bottle?

There are several steps to making up a bottle:

- Always read the advice on the packet.
- Wash and sterilise the bottle by using one of the methods detailed below.
- Boil fresh tap water and let it cool.
- Wash your hands thoroughly and fill the bottle to the required level.
- Measure out the correct amount of milk powder as per the instructions on the tin using the scoop provided.
- Level the powder with a sterilised knife but don't pat it down, and add to the water.
- Place teats and lids on the bottle and shake well to mix powder thoroughly.
- Place the made up bottle in the main part of the fridge (not the fridge door as the temperature here can vary from constant opening and closing) and discard any unused milk after 24 hours.

Sterilising Bottles

There are several ways to sterilise a bottle and whichever method you choose may depend on convenience and cost:

- Cold sterilisation. This simply means using tablets or a liquid, such as 'Milton' with plain water. The equipment is then immersed in the water and left for at least 60 minutes. The advantage of this method is portability.
- Steam. Steam sterilisers are electric and use steam to sterilise the bottle! They take about 10 minutes and the equipment can be left inside with the lid on for up to 3 hours.
- Microwave sterilisers. These are put in the microwave and take about 7 minutes plus a couple of minutes standing time.
- Boiling water. This was the traditional method of sterilisation before chemicals and sterilising units appeared and is probably the most cost-effective method. Simply place the bottle in a pan full of boiling water for about 10 minutes (five for teats, which will disintegrate with too much boiling). Allow the bottle to cool before using for feeding.

Safe Bottle-feeding

There are certain instructions you should follow to ensure you are safely bottle-feeding your baby:

- Be scrupulous about sterilising the bottles.
- Dry sterilised bottles with paper towels rather than a tea towel, which may have bacteria.
- Do not leave a warmed bottle of milk sitting around too long as bacteria can build up.
- Throw away any milk that's been in the fridge for more than 24 hours.
- Never keep or reheat milk left after a feed.
- Use a bottle warmer or jug of hot water to heat your bottles – microwaving can cause 'hotspots' in the milk.
- Always test the temperature of the milk on the inside of your wrist before giving it to your baby.
- If using the boiling water method, ensure that all the parts of the equipment to be sterilised remain under the water. Fill the bottles with water so they don't float.
- Never carry warmed bottles around with you; they are a breeding ground for bacteria. Instead have the required amount of milk powder in a container and add to the bottle of water when needed.

How to Bottle-feed

Try to always feed your baby in a warm and relaxed place. Stroke your baby's cheek gently with your finger as this will encourage the suckling reflex and your baby will turn its head. Touch the teat to your baby's lips and it should open them automatically. Don't expect your baby to finish the entire bottle. If your baby seems finished, let it be. Newborns usually take around 60ml at first. Bottle-fed babies may fall into a pattern of feeding every 4 hours, less often than breast-fed babies, as formula milk takes longer to digest than breastmilk.

The Baby Business

Babies are big money spinners, and unless you have a 'do not disturb' sign on your door, you're likely to be visited by photographers who will take a professional photo of your newborn, 'artists' who will offer to make a bronze sculpture of your newborn's hand and newspaper salespeople who'll urge you to put an announcement in their classifieds. Having mementoes of your newborn can be nice (albeit often expensive) however, make it clear to the midwifery staff if you don't want any of these people disturbing you.

You may also be given your very own post birth 'sample bag' via the midwifery staff. Unfortunately there are no chocolates or salt and vinegar chips inside, only rather boring stuff like nappies, creams and lotions and vouchers for further products provided by baby product manufacturers competing for your custom.

●●●● One thing that drove me mad was the constant stream of staff and other people who visited me for a variety of purposes, from wanting to flog televisions, to photographs, to one unfortunate woman who came in and wanted to speak about contraception. Being a tad oversensitive, I didn't realise that she was speaking to 'everybody', but thought she was just speaking to the hopeless single mothers who obviously didn't know how to handle their contraception. So, I informed her frostily, that I would be practising abstinence, and that, thank you very much, I did know how contraceptives worked. The poor lady looked a little beaten when she left the room. Kathryn

Going Home

In our mothers' day, it was at least a week before they were 'allowed' to go home, seen off by a ward of smiling, proud midwives. Today, women are staying in hospital for anything from a few hours to 3 days after a 'normal' delivery and while it's touted as a good thing by hospitals, some of the more cynical may think it has more to do with hospital finances than simply doing the 'best thing' for the mother.

Recent studies have shown that PND (postnatal depression) is more common in women who have been discharged early from hospital and is more frequent in single rather than partnered women. If you're going home without any support, you need to make sure you sort out any feeding or medical problems before you leave.

Some women loathe hospitals and can't wait to get out and, providing you feel well and rested both emotionally and physically, there's probably no reason not to go home early. No matter how confident you are, it can feel like a momentous occasion, walking out through those hospital doors.

I remember the drive home from the hospital with my baby son in the car. I drove at a funereal pace, my heart beating at a million miles an hour, terrified. Scared of someone hitting us, even more scared of what lay before me; for the first time since falling pregnant, full of serious doubts of what had I done, the irreversible result visible in the rear vision mirror. Nat

The day came to go home. I didn't know whether to be happy I was going home, or scared I was leaving the hospital where help was only a buzz away. When I walked outside everything looked so different, so intense. The car ride home was so scary. I sat in the back of the car while Mum drove. I cried the whole way home. When we finally arrived home everything seemed so different. Surreal, like I was seeing everything for the first time. A place that once felt so comfortable and familiar now seemed so new and strange. Ngaire

If you've given birth at home, of course, you'll have less of those feelings. Just make sure you do rest for the first few days and are not tempted to do housework or anything else until you've had some rest and recovery. Put a note on the door and take the phone off the hook if you want to properly rest and deter callers. Even better would be to have a friend or family member stay for a week or so to offer support and to help with the chores.

Breasts, Bellies and Bladders

It's unlikely that your once flat, firm tummy is going to spring back into its former shape straight away. More likely, you'll have a bit of a loose 'pouch' for a short period of time as a result of the abdominal muscles being stretched. This will eventually shrink back, helped in some part by gentle exercise.

You may find you leak urine when you laugh or sneeze or if you don't get to the toilet quickly enough. Some form of urinary incontinence is extremely common among women who've given birth, so don't feel embarrassed to speak to your doctor if it becomes a problem. Doing pelvic floor exercises will help immeasurably.

It's normal to feel some vaginal slackness, or a slight numbness after giving birth. Again, pelvic floor exercises should help, but if it becomes a concern, see your doctor.

The hormone responsible for the softening of your ligaments during pregnancy is usually excreted from your body during the first week or so, but it takes about 12 weeks for the muscles and ligaments to return to their normal strength, so take it easy with physical exercise. Instead of hitting the gym, work your way up, perhaps with some gentle yoga or a good brisk walk with the pram!

Don't forget to book in for your 6-week appointment check-up with your doctor or midwife.

Why do I Feel like This?

There's a mythical 'average newborn' out there, who apparently sleeps 14–18 hours a day, feeds every 3 hours and is unsettled for between 1½ and 5 hours. Ignore the 'average baby'. Statistics will only succeed in making you depressed, as will that annoying friend who looks fabulous and boasts her baby sleeps from 8.00 p.m. to 8.00 a.m. while you haven't looked in the mirror for 3 days and are shaky with sleep deprivation. On top of this you'll have the helpful granny/aunt/mother who'll be an unending supply of unwanted advice and veiled criticism. Then there are the endless visitors who you just know the second they walk out the door are tut-tutting about the state of your house. Add to that the lack of a partner to take over, just for an hour, while you grab some sleep and you may end up feeling anything from irritation to collapsing in a heap of tears. It's essential that you accept all offers of help. It's not necessary to have to prove to the world that you can cope, so swallow any ridiculous pride you may have about it. ALL new mothers need help, not just single ones and your baby will benefit much more from having a mother who is calm and has had some rest than one on the edge of a nervous breakdown.

Approximately 80% of women suffer from the 'baby blues', which often hit between days 3–10. You might be feeling scared, apprehensive, strangely let down or overwhelmed by the responsibility of caring for this needy being. Some of these feelings are bound to be hormone-fuelled, due to the dramatic drop in oestrogen and progesterone, but we wouldn't be human if we didn't feel some sense of trepidation, or anxiety about what is after all the single most important event in our lives. To get above it all, try some of the following tips to help relieve the stress:

- Take natural remedies.
- Look at your diet and make sure you are getting plenty of fresh fruit, vegetables and enough fluid. Being tired due to a poor diet will only exacerbate any emotional stress.
- Try to get a little gentle exercise, even if it's just a short stroll every day.
- Have a warm bath with a few drops of chamomile or lavender essential oils.
- Don't isolate yourself – even if it's just a chat on the phone, keep in touch with friends and family. Babies are also very portable at this stage, so don't be afraid to go out.

●●●● The first few weeks are a bit blurry. I was somewhere between asleep and awake, between a dream state and reality. I couldn't stop crying. I felt horrible. The day my milk came in was the worst. I looked hideous. My boobs that once needed no bra to stay pert were now down around my navel and my navel was somewhere down around my knees. All I could do was cry. I was so scared and felt so alone. I had people around to support me, but ultimately I was on my own. Clare

●●●● The first 2 weeks were spent in a zombie-like state and my cheeks were never dry. I had a beautiful, healthy baby girl and I felt I should have been ecstatic and over the moon, but I kept crying. I was so tired and sore. It didn't help that her father told me down the phone that he never wanted her so why should he come and see her. I was heartbroken. The thing that really helped me snap out of my sadness was getting out of the house. It was just to go to Mothers' Group but it helped so much. It got me out of the house and amongst other new mothers and it also made me realise how good Jade was. I began to accept the changes in my life. It was about that time that I looked at Jade and thought she was so beautiful, so helpless, innocent and so mine. I had chosen to bring her into the world and I had made a commitment to her. She became number one. I had to realise that I came second now. She was my life. Ngaire

●●●● During those first few months, I was up every few hours either feeding or consoling. I never got much sleep and was always crying. On the outside I was determined to be seen as coping, while on the inside I was a mess. How I got through those months, I will never know. People would call me to see how I was and I always told them that I was doing really well. They were envious that I was coping so well and that I didn't have to deal with anyone else but Alex and myself. Little did they know how close I was to dumping Alex on his father's doorstep... Sophia

Postnatal Depression

While the 'baby blues' rarely last more than a few days, if these feelings don't go away, or if they're accompanied by a sense of disinterest, disconnection, constant weeping, feelings of isolation, or even a lack of love for the baby, it's vital to discuss your feelings with a practitioner, as you may be suffering from postnatal depression. Many women find that once their baby is a little more established in routine, they feel able to cope. Postnatal depression is very common, particularly among single women and can last from 3 months to 1 year, or even longer without treatment. There are many support groups and lots of help available from parenting hotlines (see Useful Contacts on page 215–216). There are some ways you can avoid postnatal depression, including:

- Having some practical help when you bring the baby home, such as a relative, friend or pregnancy partner.
- Sorting out any feeding problems.
- Not isolating yourself from others, but attending mothers' groups and letting friends know you are happy to see them at a pre-arranged time.
- Getting some rest, even if you have to let the house go to rack and ruin!
- Eating properly.
- Accepting the help of others.

●●●● Through my pregnancy and birth, I had a lot of emotional support from my friends and family but after that I was basically left alone as I couldn't leave the house and my family couldn't come to me (they don't drive). Looking back, I realise that I suffered PND but didn't want it to appear that I couldn't cope. I would cry myself to sleep each night only to be woken an hour or so later to deal with a screaming child. I was a wreck inside but on the outside I was coping well (my friends believed I was). It was only in the last 12 months that I admitted that I needed help and spoke to my local GP who put me on anti-depressants. I still have my bad days but now have ways of dealing with them. Michelle

The Birth Certificate

This can be tricky. While still in hospital, the midwife will complete a notification of birth form which is made available to the Registrar of Births and Deaths. You are then required to register your baby within 6 weeks at the local Register Office. There has been many a single mother who sat, pen hovering over the 'father's name' box wondering what to do. If you don't know who the father is, it's irrelevant. If you don't name him and then claim benefits, you may have to prove that you have taken 'reasonable measures' to locate him (to pay you child support).

The father has to also sign the birth certificate acknowledging that he is in fact the father, so you can't just put his name down yourself. If he refuses and you want him named on the certificate, you may need to prove paternity with a paternity test. If you do name him, he will be liable to pay child support.

● ● ● ● I did not put his name on the birth certificate, and I advise other women NOT to put the father's name on the birth certificate as you have to get his signature if you want to get your child a passport etc. Sarah

The Last Word

For me, personally, the journey so far has been an extraordinary one. Motherhood grabbed me by the soles of my feet and shook all the senseless, self-important stuff out of my head. It spring-cleaned my values, replacing them with earthier, more meaningful ones. It gave me the gift of understanding how you can love someone so much you would die for them. It made me see my body, once just a clumsy encumbrance as an astoundingly, perfect creation. Doing it on my own has made me aware of how strong I am, how capable and how I have underestimated myself.

There are, of course moments of self-pity, but they vanish in a second when I picture that cheeky grin, those warm arms, the funny things my beautiful clever child has said or done that day.

My son has made me laugh and has filled my heart with overwhelming love every day of his existence. If the price I have to pay is a few years of financial hardship, and the occasional snide comment on my single state, it's the best bargain I've ever made!

While being a single mum is not always an easy thing, there are some distinct advantages, such as not having to explain decisions you make regarding discipline etc, and you can be proud that when you have a charming, intelligent, happy child that brings joy to everyone they meet, it is all thanks to you and you ALONE! Moya

If a new mother were to ask my advice all I could really say is to stay calm. Accept the changes. Go to a support group and talk babies. Hold your baby and kiss her and tell her you love her. Don't feel guilty if you don't feel instantly at one and in love with your baby. It's a huge, overwhelming and scary experience. Most importantly remember that amidst all the screaming, pooey nappies and sleepless nights there is your beautiful baby who loves you more than anyone could ever and is relying on you to keep it together and love her back. A baby who thinks you are the most wonderful person in the world and who, even with bags under your eyes, a bulging tummy and sick on your shoulder, thinks you are beautiful. Ngaire

My top ten tips for surviving and thriving as a single mother would be:

10. Have a super sense of humour – don't take everything too seriously.
9. Exercise – I personally adored swimming (up to 2 kilometres) daily.
8. Practise yoga both for pregnancy and after – it was simply wonderful and incredibly peace-giving for myself and my baby.
7. Eat well.
6. Meditate – to keep your sanity.
5. Home in on the love and support of family and friends – the positive ones only.
4. Read widely on parenting, but remember to always keep an open mind.
3. Be prepared – materially, emotionally and physically.
2. Seek out other sole parents – once again, only the positive ones.
1. My number one piece of advice is to ENJOY the experience and the incredible unity between yourself and your child, without interference! Jane

The innate desire to have a child is common to most people. I fail to understand how a couple is unselfish if they desire a child, but a single woman, with all the same reasoning, is deemed to be selfish. If anything, the sacrifices that she will have to make throughout parenthood will be greater than if she were in a partnership, so if she is 'selfish' she is in for a big surprise. There are many people in partnered situations who are inappropriate parents. The fact that they are partnered does not make them better parents, just as a single woman is not an inadequate parent. Dorothy

● ● ● ● I do not buy into the pseudo-scientific studies which stipulate that the children of single mothers are more likely to grow up to commit crime etc. Like I'm sure that there are many other factors involved in those findings, such as poverty and marginalisation. I can dig out many more that say that the reason that these children are not turning out well is not because their mothers are single but because of thousands of other reasons. In fact, I can dig out studies that say that the happiest children are those who are loved, listened to, and made to feel secure. Interestingly enough, those conditions can occur across the board in 'normal' marriages, same sex marriages, de-facto marriages, and with a single parent.

My daughter is the most wonderful thing to have ever happened to me – even when she keeps me awake all night! It was a difficult pregnancy, and plenty of things went wrong, but it never occurred to me not to have her. My own family life had left a lot to be desired, and I believe that I can raise her successfully to be a productive member of society, and to be loving and compassionate. She has filled my life with so much, and I couldn't live without her now.

Although it's a struggle at times, financially and emotionally, never a day goes by when I don't think to myself how incredibly lucky I am to have such a beautiful baby. It makes me very religious, let me tell you. Of course the down side is that I'm petrified that I'm going to lose her. Part of me thinks that maybe the Universe, or God, or whoever, is going to decide that I forced things by having her in the manner in which I did, and therefore is going to take her away from me as punishment. Very fatalistic I know, and probably more than a little paranoid!

Do I regret anything? Not at all! Though I could have wished that I was a bit better off financially before I had her, but hey fate stepped in. I just knew that if I didn't take the available opportunity, that it might never happen. Kathryn

● ● ● ● I love my son so much. I never thought I had the capability to love anything so much. He means everything to me. That doesn't mean that it isn't hard at times. And sometimes I wonder what the hell I am doing raising a kid. But the good days make up for that – the toothy grins and sloppy kisses that he gives me. And when he climbs up on my knee to give me a cuddle. Being a parent is an incredible, life changing experience. Single parent or otherwise. Nadene

● ● ● ● Being a single parent is tough but very rewarding. You don't have to share the cuddles and kisses, the 'I love you's' or the special artwork made by your angel. I don't regret anything. My son is a happy and well-adjusted child who is the light of my life. Michelle

Reading Recommendations

Chapter One

Eisenberg, Arlene., Hathaway, Sandee E., Murkoff Heidi, 1989, *What to Eat When You're Expecting*, Harper Collins, London.

Anderson, T., Swinney, B., 2000, *Eating Expectantly: A Practical and Tasty Guide to Prenatal Nutrition*, Meadowbrook Press.

Elliot Rose, 1997, *The Vegetarian Mother and Baby Book*, Panthenon Books.

Chapter Two

Clapp, J., 2002, *Exercising Through Your Pregnancy*, Addicus Books.

Simkin, Penny, 2001, *The Birth Partner: Everything You Need to Know to Help a Woman Through Childbirth*, Harvard Common Press, UK.

Ryan, Adrienne, 2001, *A Silent Love: Personal Stories of Coming to Terms with Miscarriage*, Marlowe & Company.

Balaskas, Janet, 1994, *Preparing for Birth with Yoga*, Element Books, UK.

Katz, J., 1994, *Water Fitness During Your Pregnancy,* Human Kinetics Publishers.

Chapter Three

Kitzinger, Sheila, 1994, *Birth Over Thirty-five*, Allen & Unwin, London.

Chapter Four

Gardner, Joy, 1987, *Healing Yourself during Pregnancy*, The Crossing Press, California.

Nolan, Mary, 1998, *Book of Antenatal Tests*, Harper Collins, London.

Pearlman, Eileen and Ganon, Jill Allison, 2000, *Raising Twins: What Parents want to Know (and What Twins want to Tell Them)*, Harper Resource, London.

Luke, Barbara and Eberlein, Tamara, 1999, *When You're Expecting Twins, Triplets or Quads: A Complete Resource*, Harper Resource, London.

Chapter Five

Campbell, Don, 2003, *The Mozart Effect for Children*, Coronet.

Balaskas, Janet, 1997, *Easy Exercises for Pregnancy*, Frances Lincoln, London.

Chapter Six

Lansky, Bruce, 1997, *15,000+ Baby Names*, Meadowbrook Press.

Davis, K., 2001, *Forever Silent, Forever Changed: The Loss of a Baby in Miscarriage, Stillbirth, Early Infancy*, Booklocker.com.

Wallace, Carol, 1995, *20,000 Names for a Baby*, Quill Press.

Diabetes Foundation America, 2001, *Diabetes and Pregnancy – What to Expect. Your Guide to a Healthy Pregnancy and Happy, Healthy Baby*.

American Diabetic Association, 2001, *Gestational Diabetes: What to Expect*, McGraw-Hill.

Chapter Seven

Davis, Linda, Byrne, Jo-anne, Cullen, Susan, 1992, *Women in Labour – Thirty-two Personal Accounts of Childbirth*, Text Publishing, Melbourne.

Balaskas, Janet, 1992, *Active Birth: The New Approach to Giving Birth Naturally (Revised Edition)*, Harvard Common Press, London.

Balaskas, Janet, 1986, *The Active Birth Partners Handbook*, Sidgwick & Jackson, London.

Leboyer, Frederick, 2002, *Birth without Violence (Revised Edition)*, Healing Art Press.

Leboyer, Frederick, 1985, *The Art of Breathing*, Element Books, UK.

Harper, Barbara & Arms, Suzanne, 1994, *Gentle Birth Choices: A Guide to Making Informed Decisions*, Healing Arts Press, UK.

Gready, Meg, 1995, *Birth Choices*, National Childbirth Trust, London.

Chapter Eight

Morissey, Sian, 2002, *The "Which" Guide to Baby Products*, Which Books, London.

DiGeronimo, Theresa and Manginello, Frank, 1998, *Your Premature Baby: Everything You Need to Know about Childbirth, Treatment and Parenting*, John Wiley & Sons.

Chapter Nine

Deveny, Catherine, 1999, *Babies, Bellies and Blundstones*, Lothian Books, Port Melbourne.

Chapter Ten

Lothrop, Hannah, 2002, *Breastfeeding Naturally*, Fisher Books.

Kitzinger, Sheila, 1994, *The Year after Childbirth – Surviving the First Year of Motherhood*, Oxford University Press, Oxford.

Smale, Mary, 1999, *The National Childbirth Trust Book of Breastfeeding*, Vermilion, London.

Decon, C., 2002, *Breastfeeding for Beginners*, Harper Collins, London.

England, Alison, 1999, *Aromatherapy and Massage for Mother and Baby*, Vermilion, London.

Walker, Peter, 2002, *Baby Massage for Beginners*, Carroll & Brown, London.

Dougherty, Dorothy, 1999, *How to Talk to Your Baby*, Avery Publishing Group.

Useful Contacts

Chapter One

Internet Chat Sites

www.babybabyuk.co.uk

www.thebabycorner.com

www.baby-greenhouse.co.uk

www.babycentre.uk.com

www.mothersover40.com

Pregnancy Support Networks

Association of Radical Midwives
Tel: 01695 572776

The Miscarriage Association
c/o Clayton Hospital
Northgate, Wakefield
West Yorkshire
WF1 3JS
Tel: 01924 200799

Mothers 35 Plus
www.mothers35plus.co.uk

National Childbirth Trust
Alexandra House
Oldham Terrace
Acton, London
W3 6NH
Tel: 0870 444 8707 or 0870 444 8708 (breastfeeding line)

British Pregnancy Advisory Service
Tel: 08457 30 40 30
www.bpas.org

Association of Breastfeeding Mothers
Tel: 020 7813 1481

Association for Improvements in Maternity Services
Tel: 0870 765 1433

Birth Crisis Network
Tel: 01865 300266

Advice on Medicine, Alcohol, Nicotine or Illicit Drugs

For information on drugs and medicines to use in pregnancy contact:
www.nhsdirect.nhs.uk

Give up Smoking
www.givingupsmoking.co.uk

NHS Smoking Helpline
Tel: 0800 169 0169

Chapter Two

Finding an Obstetrician or Gynaecologist

Royal College of Obstetricians and Gynaecologists
27 Sussex Place
London NW1 4RG
Tel: 020 7772 6200

Midwives and Home Births

Royal College of Midwives
15 Mansfield Street
London
W1G 9NH
Tel: 020 7312 3535
www.rcm.org.uk

www.homebirth.org.uk

Association of Radical Midwives
Tel: 01695 572776

Nutrition

British Nutrition Foundation
Tel: 020 7404 6504
www.nutrition.org.uk

Exercise and Yoga

www.babycentre.co.uk/fitness
www.mothersbliss.co.uk/nine/exercise.asp
www.ivillage.co.uk/dietandfitness/getfit/pregfit/
UK Aquanatal Register: www.aquanatal.co.uk/
Yoga: www.zenyoga.co.uk/yoga/pregnancy

Chapter Four

Information on Twins or Multiples

TAMBA
2 The Willows
Gardner Road,
Guildford
Surrey GU1 4PG
Tel: 0870 770 3305
www.tamba.org.uk

Twinline (confidential helpline for parents of twins, triplets or more)
Tel: 01732 868000 (open 7pm-11pm weekdays; 10am-11pm weekends)

Twins and Supertwins
www.twins-supertwins.co.uk

www.twinsclub.co.uk

Maternity Clothes

Mail order maternity clothes are available from:

Maternitywear Exchange: 01628 851187

Mother Nature: 0161 485 7359

www.mothernaturebras.co.uk

NCT Maternity Sales: 0870 112 1120

www.nctms.co.uk

Buying Equipment Online

Mothercare Online Shopping

Tel: 0845 330 4030

www.mothercare.com

www.nctms.co.uk

Predicting the Sex

For a bit of fun, go to http://www.thelaboroflove.com/chart/index.html where you'll find an ancient Chinese gender test!

Chapter Five

Time off for Maternity Leave

Department for Work and Pensions

www.dwp.gov.uk/lifeevent/benefits/time-off.htm

Department of Trade and Industry (for online leaflets)

www.dti.gov.uk/publications

Benefits

Maternity Alliance (deals with benefits and the rights of pregnant women)

45 Beech Street

London EC2P 2LX

Tel: 020 7588 8582

www.maternityalliance.org.uk

Statutory Maternity Pay or Maternity Allowance
www.dwp.gov.uk/lifeevent/benefits

For information of free NHS dental treatment contact:
Benefit Enquiry Line: 0800 882200

Employment Issues

www.dti.gov.uk/er

Travelling when Pregnant

www.nhsdirect.nhs.uk

Chapter Six

When There's Something Wrong

Helping After Neonatal Death: www.handonline.org

SANDS (Stillbirth and Neonatal Death Society) have 7-day, 24-hour telephone counselling service by women who have suffered the same kind of loss. They also offer support groups, booklets and have a library.
Tel: 020 7436 5881
www.uk-sands.org

The Foundation for the Study of Infant Deaths
Tel: 0870 787 0554
www.sids.org.uk

Action on Pre-Eclampsia
Tel: 020 8427 4217
www.apec.org.uk

The Miscarriage Association
www.miscarriageassociation.org.uk

Ability (Alliance of Genetic Support Groups)
www.ability.org.uk/Genetic-Disorders.html

Equip (Genetic Disorders)
www.equip.nhs.uk/topics/genetic.html

Birth Defects Foundation
Tel: 0870 0707020

Ectopic Pregnancy Trust
Tel 01895 238025

The Name Game

Here are some fun baby name Internet sites:
www.namechooser.com/baby.html
www.babyzone.com/babynames
www.popularbabynames.com.

Chapter Seven

Further Information About Antenatal Classes

Contact your local hospital's midwifery service or see advertisement in your local GP surgery.

National Childbirth Trust
Alexandra House
Oldham Terrace
Acton, London
W3 6NH
Tel: 0870 444 8707
www.nctpregnancyandbabycare.com

Aquanatal – contact your local swimming pool for details of courses in your area.

Active Birth Centres: 020 7561 9006

Birth and parenting information

Magazines about birth and parenting include:

Mother and Baby

Practical Parenting

Pregnancy and Birth

Practical Pregnancy

Videos

Ace Graphics have more than 24 pregnancy and birth videos to choose from and deliver nationwide.

Tel: 01959 524 622

www.acegraphics.com

Videos are also available through internet-based companies such as Amazon at www.amazon.co.uk or from childbirth.org. on www.childbirth.org who also have an online bookstore.

Books

Amazon: www.amazon.co.uk

Online Birth Plans

Birth plans for home birth

www.homebirth.org.uk/plan

Baby Centre (for writing a birth plan)

www.babycentre.co.uk

Chapter Eight

Buying Second-hand

www.babybabyuk.co.uk

Maternity Wear Exchange

Tel: 01628 851187

Getting help

National Childbirth Trust Postnatal Support Groups
Tel: 0870 444 8707

Contact your local health visitor or midwife for advice.

The Real Nappy Association
www.realnappy.com

Real Nappy Supplies
www.changeanappy.co.uk

Nappies Direct
www.nappies-direct.co.uk

Nappies UK
www.nappies-uk.co.uk

Child care

You can also obtain information on the location of child care services from:

- *Yellow Pages*
- Local councils
- Social Services
- OFSTED
- Children's Information Service: 0800 096 0296
  www.childcarelink.gov.uk

Premature Babies

BLISS: www.bliss.org.uk
Tel: 0870 770 0337

Chapter Nine

Child support

Child Support Agency (CSA)
www.csa.gov.uk

Chapter Ten

Single parenting

Gingerbread

First Floor

7 Sovereign Close, Sovereign Court

London E1W 3HW

Tel: 0800 018 4318

www.gingerbread.org.uk

National Council for One Parent Families

Tel: 0800 018 5026

www.oneparentfamilies.org.uk

Ivillage Single Parent Support

www.ivillage.co.uk

Meet a Mum Association (MAMA)

Tel: 020 8768 0123

Breastfeeding information

Contact your local midwife, health visitor or infant-feeding advisor.

The Breastfeeding Network Support Line

Tel: 0870 900 8787

www.breastfeeding.co.uk

Food Standards Agency

www.foodstandards.gov.uk

The National Childbirth Trust

Alexandra House

Oldham Terrace

Acton, London

W3 6NH

Tel: 0870 444 8708

www.nct.co.uk

La Leche League

Tel: 020 7242 1278

www.laleche.org.uk

Postnatal depression

Contact your local health visitor by ringing her direct or through your GP surgery.

Meet a Mum Association (MAMA)

Tel: 020 8768 0123

Legal Help

National Association of Citizens Advice Bureaux

www.nacab.org.uk

Legal Services Commission

Tel: 020 7759 0000

www.legalservices.gov.uk

Index